£3

*Romantic
Railways*

Steam over the Lötschberg! A unique scene at Kandersteg station on the Berne-Lötschberg-Simplon railway. To commemorate the centenary of the first Thomas Cook tour of Switzerland, in 1963 the B.L.S. put on a special steam train, which few people knew they had, for the occasion.

ROMANTIC RAILWAYS

KENNETH WESTCOTT JONES

London 🎺 Arlington Books

ROMANTIC RAILWAYS
first published 1971 by
Arlington Books (Publishers) Ltd
38 Bury Street, St James's
London S.W.1
© Kenneth Westcott Jones 1971
Made and printed in England by
The Garden City Press Ltd
London and Letchworth
ISBN 0-85140-192-9

Contents

Illustrations

Indicative of the high standards of passenger convenience, maintained by the railway company, the vistadomes are washed at Livingston.

Breakfast aboard the Northern Pacific.

The scene at Bellingham, Washington State, as the Great Northern International stops just south of the Canadian border.

The Gold Rush to Alaska resulted in this narrow gauge 2–8–0 of the White Pass and Yukon Railway coming to Dawson City, Yukon Territory, in 1899, where it is preserved to this day.

Passengers alighting from the International Limited at Vancouver.

Inside the parlour car en route from Seattle to Vancouver.

A recent photograph of Juneau, capital of Alaska.

Train No. 101 from St. Johns to Port-aux Basques arrives at Gander railway station.

The Trans-Newfoundland express near Gaff-Topsails the highest part of the island province.

[Between pages 96 and 97]

The re-inaugural postwar run of the 'Royal Highlander' which first ran under this title in 1927. Princess Victoria, 46205, is seen heading north near Watford.

North of Crewe at present the 'Royal Highlander' is hauled by two Class 50, 2700-h.p. diesel locomotives.

The 'Royal Highlander' travelling northwards at 100 m.p.h., south of Rugby.

The exterior of Inverness station, terminus of the 'Royal Highlander'.

The 'Flying Scotsman' in 1888 passing the now defunct Holloway station, hauled by a Great Northern Railway Stirling '8 footer' No. 53, built in 1875.

The 'Flying Scotsman' in Edwardian days hauled by an Ivatt 'Atlantic' of the Great Northern Railway.

The northbound 'Flying Scotsman' in her hey day, in 1929 headed by Gresley Pacific No. 4478.

The present day 'Flying Scotsman' approaching Hatfield hauled by Class 60, 3,000-h.p. diesel locomotive.

A typical rake of Southern Pullmans headed by a rebuilt West Country class Bulleid Pacific.

The 'Bournemouth Belle' at speed near Fleet, Hampshire during its last year.

The 'Brighton Belle' in its new livery. British Rail's only electric multiple unit Pullman train.

The Great Northern of Ireland in 1963. A 4–4–0 is leaving Belfast's Great Victoria Street station.

[Between pages 128 and 129]

The author on the footplate of Boyle, *former Great Northern of Ireland 4–4–0 leaving Great Victoria Street in November 1963.*

A former Great Northern of Ireland 4–4–0 heads a Londonderry train out of Belfast in early 1964.

The beautiful paddle steamer Lotschberg *owned by the B.L.S. railway company plies up and down the lake from Interlaken to Brienz.*

An electrically hauled express on the narrow gauge Brurug railway, near Lucerne.

Steam on the oldest line over the Alps. The Vienna-Klagenfurt express coming up through the Semmering Pass before the line was electrified.

The 'Warsaw-Sofia Poloma Express' at Breclav in Czechoslovakia hauled by a 4–8–2 locomotive.

A modern Czech 4–8–2 Type 498.1 at Brno station, Moravia, heading the Balt-Orient express.

Engineer Jan Stefanic, 27-year-old technical graduate opens up his 4–8–2 No. 035, as she pounds up the grade from Ceska Trevova.

A quiet ride for the fireman on class 498.1 No. 035 which is fitted with a mechanical stoker.

A dramatic view of two Czech steam locomotives thundering along in the same direction on parallel tracks necessitated by the accident referred to in the book.

[Between pages 160 and 161]

A Woodburning 4–8–2 of the Benguela Railway (one of six delivered by the North British Locomotive Works in the mid-fifties), heads an eastbound train away from Nova Lisboa, 6,000 feet up in the Angola Highlands.

Firing with eucalyptus logs, on the Benguela railway.

A train from Lobito to the interior passing the vast eucalyptus plantations which provide its fuel.

A typically luxurious restaurant car on the Benguela railway.

The Dawn Chorus: eucalyptus burning garretts of the Benguela railway near Cubal, Angola.

The Little Locomotive, *designated a National Monument in southern Africa. The tiny 0–6–0 stands outside Windhoek station.*
A diesel hauled freight train from the Coast approaches Windhoek station.
A mixed train passing through the savannah grasslands of South-West Africa.
With a change of engine at Bloemfontein, the 'Orange Express' headboards are changed.
The 'Blue Train' headed by an electric locomotive, in the Hex river valley, Cape Province.
The station approach and yards at Johannesburg.
The eastbound trans-Siberian train headed by a Class P36 locomotive of Khabarovsk.
The westbound trans-Siberian Express 'Rossia' stopped at Bira in Eastern Siberia.

[Between pages 192 and 193]
The cab and engineers of a Class P36 locomotive, standing at Chita at the head of a westbound trans-Siberian train.
At the rear of the 'Northern Express' to Chiang Mai is the saloon car of the Sultan of Selangor.
One of the railway bridges on the River Kwai, Kanachana-Buki Province, Thailand.
A General Motors diesel locomotive at the head of the 'Northern Express' in Bangkok Terminus.
Kowloon Terminus station in steam days with a train headed by a British built 4–6–2 tank engine leaving for the Chinese border.
The 10.40 to China stopped at Tai Pi Market station.
The 10.40 to China passing through the New Territories.
The new Australian trans-Continental 'Indian Pacific'—one-third of a mile of stainless steel.
The east and westbound 'Indian Pacific' meet at Gladstone, South Australia, and exchange crews.
While the 'Indian Pacific' stops at Port Augusta, South Australia, passengers admire the tiny Sandfly, an 0–4–0 steam locomotive used by contractors to build the line to Port Augusta at the turn of the century.
The rear view of the 'Indian Pacific' halted at Kalgoorlie in the dawn, 408 miles out from Perth.

Introduction

The aura of romance which many of us attach to railway journeys is a hang-over from the days of childhood when such trips were directly associated with holiday pleasure. That is the accepted summary of why so many men, and not a few women, feel an affection for trains even if they do not particularly enjoy travelling in them. But there is much more to it than that. How can it explain the big queues of ten- and twelve-year-olds of today who line up at Swindon Railway Museum to gaze in awe at the Great Western steam engines housed there so close to the rails they once dominated? Or the similar queues of youngsters at Washington's superb Smithsonian Museum's railway section waiting to see the fine Southern Railway Pacific and hear tape recordings of it in action in its heyday on the tracks beyond Atlanta? Nor does it assess adequately the desire of Japanese children to become *untenshis* (drivers of the high-speed New Tokaido expresses). Most of these children, the Americans particularly, have never been on a holiday journey by train. Their parents pack them into a car or even an aeroplane. The train is associated in their minds with school journeys and perhaps even less happy occasions.

The romance of the rails will survive no matter what the traction. It can be felt on a cold wayside station (where such structures still exist to serve their original purpose) when nothing is happening and all one can see is the shining metals stretching into blackness with perhaps the glow of a few signal lights spotting the darkness. The tingle of romance irradiates the blood when a Chicago station loudspeaker blares 'leaving on Track Nine for Omaha, Cheyenne and points West' or when a rake of blue Wagons-Lits glides into the Gare de Lyon in Paris with white destination boards marked 'Belgrade, Sofia, Istanbul' or other cities with an exciting, perhaps sinister, flavour.

The romance of rail travel itself is manifested, at least for me, by moving through a country rather than high above it, in being part of a scene rather than noting it—if at all—as a sepia blur. How else can one feel the atmosphere of India, with its crowded railway stations and colourful people? One is safely esconced in a compartment, without the need of having to struggle for a place, and one can be an observer in comfort. For comfort is an essential part of the enjoyment of railways. Only rarely will any romance pervade the scene if you are standing crushed in a packed corridor on a hot day. One must feel comfortable and even smug to get the best from a train journey. Surely everyone has enjoyed that superior feeling when you are eating a good meal in a dining car, be it York, Philadelphia, Kimberley, or Dijon, and the train pulls in to a crowded platform where people are dashing about in a harassed way, concerned with getting themselves and their bags aboard. Later on, perhaps, these joining passengers will have the opportunity to turn the tables, watching while they dine smugly as the former passengers disembark into rainswept darkness, coping with luggage.

One thing railways do not pay enough attention to, with some honourable exceptions, is relieving passengers of the worry of their baggage. This is a score point for the world's airlines. Some lessons could surely be learned, from the provision of simple conveyor belts on station platforms with insufficient porters to an elaboration of the North American 'checked baggage' system. Britain and the Continent are the main offenders in this sphere. Scrambles by elderly ladies to climb steep steps into coaches by end doors on Continental trains, hampered by heavy bags, are both disgusting and out-dated. For them, the romance of the journey cannot be too evident.

In this book the reader will find a number of journeys which fulfil its title. Most of them can still be made at the present time, although not always in the manner described. There are some nostalgic glances back into a fairly recent past. But, even so, virtually all of them are in operation and will be for some time; the reader who finds his way to South Africa, to

Thailand, or to the Pacific North-West, will be in a position to enjoy the romance of the journeys.

Some railway administrations at the present time make the mistake of trying to copy aircraft (in all except baggage handling), to seal their passengers in and whisk them to their destination without reference to the places through which they are passing. Once a traveller loses contact with the country or countries and its people, some romance fades. This is true of a ship, even one of the sailing clippers of the past, whose romance was heightened on approaching foreign shores and not while she laboured for weeks on end, a sealed unit, through that dustless absolute desert, the ocean. The train epitomizes the most civilized way of travel, with the best safety record of any mechanical means. Aboard a good train you can eat, sleep, walk about, drink, attend to ablutions (even showering or bathing is possible in many countries these days), read, write (sometimes with difficulty), see the scenery, make contact with the outside world at all times (by telephone on some modern trains or by the time-honoured telegram wrapped round a weight and thrown out as a station flashes past), stop anywhere at any time in an emergency, and meet fresh faces coming aboard at intervals never exceeding a few hours. Apply these conditions to the other means of mechanical transport, plane, car, motor coach, hovercraft or ship, and see how many they can meet. The ship comes closest and is the perfect complement to rail travel.

Perhaps the best tribute to railways came a few years ago from the South African author-historian Mr. Lennox van Onselen: 'Railways represent the hopes and fulfilled dreams of men. Completed they are the pride and joy of a nation.'

These days, some nations appear to forget their pride and joy in spending millions and millions they can ill afford on prestige airlines which in so many cases, especially in those of under-developed countries whose people are heavily taxed to provide them, cannot hope to pay their way. In these same nations, opened up by railways for which so many men gave their lives (how often is it truly stated that under every rail-joint lies a human skull), the lines that brought them contact with the trade of the world and a movement of wealth are totally neglected.

If the passengers desert rail travel, subject to pressures from other forms of transport, then freight should remain on the life-giving lines, a fact clearly demonstrated by the American railway system, but a lesson yet to be learned in the land which was the father of railways and the inventor of the power to make them work.

1

On the Chilean Longitudinal

'Long and lean' is the classic geographical definition of Chile, and it follows that its railway system will be predominantly north-south oriented. Tucked between the cordilleras of the Andes and the Pacific Ocean is a long, rich valley enjoying a Mediterranean climate, and it is along this that the Chilean State Railways' main line runs. They call it the 'Chilean Longitudinal Railway', beginning at Puerto Montt in the wet, cool south and ending at Santiago, capital of the 'heartland'. This is a wide gauge (5 feet 6 inches) system, but in the north, going upwards from Santiago into desert country, narrow (metre) gauge partly privately-owned lines reach to Pesaro. The total distance by rail, south to north, in Chile, is slightly over 1,500 miles.

Travellers who regard Chile as remote and probably a bit behind the times would get a surprise on reaching Santiago's Alameda Station on the broad, dusty Avenida Bernardo O'Higgins (named after a famous Irish-South American general). They would see trains of exceptional comfort and solidarity, hauled by modern, gaily coloured Italian or Swedish electric locomotives of great power. They would find a railway service which is not only fast but frequent to places the world rarely hears of, and then only when an earthquake disrupts them or if some lone yachtsman puts in before or after a Cape Horn passage.

The Chilean State Railways *are* transport in Chile. They own the prime means of movement and the best hotels. They can afford to disregard the national airline which flies a few people about but fails to publish a local time-table. The roads are unpaved for the most part, and where buses run from points on the Longitudinal, the State Railways own them, too, except for a rather splendid French company which operates in strong competition and at low fares on the hundred-mile Santiago-Valparaíso route. Even this is threatened with nationalization under the new Marxist president.

Alameda Station may not impress the visitor because, although it has a fine roof, unlike Santiago's classical Mapocho Station serving the Valparaíso and Andean lines, it has no front and no sides. Nevertheless it is efficient so far as tracks are concerned and the line-up of express trains looks good. There are two *rapidos* for the deep south, going the whole 666 miles to Puerto Montt in the cool, wet, forest lands beyond which few wish to travel and even fewer desire to live. The 'Flecha del Sur' ('Southern Arrow') does the journey in seventeen and a half hours, mainly by daylight, and the 'Flecha Nocturna' is mainly a night-time express. There are slower trains, one taking twenty-four hours, and others which turn off the Longitudinal to serve coastal resorts and ports. Electrification is proceeding apace, and at the time of writing has gone beyond Chillán, 250 miles south of Santiago, but when I made the journey down the Longitudinal in March 1966 the wires were only energized as far as Talca, and trains were changing over from electric to steam or diesel traction (American diesels for the crack named trains) at Panguiteno, short of Talca and some 148 miles from the capital.

March is early autumn in Chile, and on a warm, dry night but with a hint of chill in the breeze coming down from the looming Andean foothills I went along to Alameda Station to board the 'Flecha Nocturna' for the south. This 'Night Arrow' was to take me to a place called Loncoche Junction, where a branch line goes off to Villarrica, and from there it was only a matter of a few miles by road or boat to my destination, the Pucon Hotel nestling below the magnificent volcano of the same name. In the darkness of the station, lit only imperfectly by a few overhead lamps, the express looked large and solid, an impression given by the wide gauge and high, sturdy, semi-streamlined rolling stock (although the older coaches had classic clerestory roofs). The 'Flecha Nocturna' was due to depart at 8.45 p.m., and was due at Lonoche

Junction, 480 miles south of Santiago, at 10.17 next morning.

The long train, headed by a throbbing Italian electric engine painted orange and black, had ordinary sleeping cars of vintage construction with an American nineteen-thirties air about them, followed by 'Pullmans' with deep reclining seats and air-conditioning, and ordinary coaches of fairly modern style with curved steel bodies. I travelled in a 'Pullman' which was a sort of couchette, only one did not stretch full length. It was extremely comfortable, with plentiful leg room and a well-carpeted floor. A table could be fitted for meals at one's seat, and almost immediately after departure a steward came round, serving dinner which proved to be quite good and most modestly priced, with wine to wash it down at nominal cost.

Slipping out of Santiago into the lights of the suburbs the train gathered speed quickly and soon, although the sprawling city runs to nearly three million inhabitants, we had left lights behind and were travelling fast through absolute darkness. Seen in daylight, and I did see it that way a few days later when returning, the scenery is of a rich fruitful valley with glimpses eastwards towards the brooding, hard mountains. The first stop came at Rancagua, fifty-one miles, reached in eighty-four minutes. This is a large agricultural town of some 60,000 inhabitants, its only claim to fame being a battle fought in the streets in 1814 by General O'Higgins and his troops against the Royalists who were trying to cling to the fading ruins of the Spanish Empire.

A blaze of lights seen on leaving came from the Someca tractor factory, evidence of the strong Italian investment and influence in South America. A run of thirty-two miles, covered in fifty-three minutes, took us down to San Fernando, capital of Colchagua Province, a place with about 40,000 people. By now it was after eleven o'clock and the 'Pullman' lights were dimmed, while pillows and blankets, aircraft style, were handed down from the roof-racks. Passengers settled in for the long night and the train thundered off into the darkness with blinds drawn. In fact it passed, unknown to most of its travellers, the town of Curicó and somewhere in the very

2—RR * *

early hours made a long halt at Panguiteno, where the electric engine came off to be replaced by a General Motors diesel.

I woke early, to a rather misty dawn, and the first town I identified was San Rosendo, about 300 miles from Santiago. This was genuine 'Indian Country' in complete contrast to sophisticated, highly European Santiago and Valparaíso. Most inhabitants wore the famous blankets (called *Ponchos* in many parts of South America) and high boots, while women sported stiff trilby-type hats. There were plenty of trees and the land still looked fairly rich. Most towns in Chile with a population of 100,000 or more are situated in the great Central Valley or just off it, or along the coast, but all are reached by means of the Longitudinal Railway and its branches.

Soon after seven o'clock the steward came round and took orders for breakfast, fitting up the tables. Despite the absence of a full-length bed the night had passed fairly well and passengers seemed reasonably comfortable. A hazy sun had begun to penetrate the mist by the time an excellent breakfast of fresh pineapple, melon, rolls, and coffee came on a tray. There was a smart modern dining car if one wanted to go along to it, and I did on the return journey, but letting the steward do it seemed very civilized and comfortable while in this 'Pullman' headed south.

Another hundred miles from San Rosendo brought us to the beginning of the beautiful Chilean Lake District and the city of Temuco with its cathedral. Capital of Cautin Province, this city, with 120,000 people, is one of the most go-ahead centres in the south of Chile, an Indian market town and an exporter of apples and timber. Not only are the lakes beginning around here, but skiing areas have been opened up on the slopes of the Llaima volcano.

A run of about an hour through wooded, hilly country with a glimpse of higher mountains to the west brought our 'nocturnal' Arrow to Loncoche Junction, more or less on time at 10.20 a.m. Alighting on a low platform there was a pleasant and romantic smell of escaping steam and the sound of simmering from several locomotives in and about an engine shed. Across the tracks stood a 4–6–0 tender engine of unmistakably British lineage heading a three-coach train, the cars looking exactly like an American mid-Western train of the turn of the century.

This was the branch train to Villarrica, timed to leave at 10.30 a.m.

Several people from the express crossed over and boarded it with their luggage, joining a sprinkling of people already seated in the gas-lit open coaches. Once the 'Flecha Nocturna' had left, bound south for the end of the line at Puerto Montt, 186 miles away, I thought the branch train would start, but although the engine was blowing off, there was some unaccountable delay and the final whistle did not blow until 10.36 a.m. Through the open windows of the ancient rolling stock drifted some familiar smoke and steam, while the engine made attractive chuffing sounds as it tackled a steep hill on single track.

There were three stops on the twenty-eight-mile branch line, one lasting ten minutes while we crossed a freight and passenger train headed by a vintage Mogul (2–6–0). Cresting the summit of the line, the driver, who seemed to be well aware of interest in the form of a British enthusiast riding in his train, let fly with all he had. The American whistle moaning out its nostalgic notes, for all the world like the sound one used to hear across the Canadian Prairies thirty years ago, we tore downhill, reaching and holding sixty miles an hour, while the elderly carriages rattled and swayed. I estimated a maximum of sixty-five miles an hour, timing with the aid of somewhat faded kilometre posts, and the eight miles from our last stop to the end of the line at Villarrica took ten minutes dead! I congratulated the driver on alighting, and he spoke proudly of his locomotive, which he said was British-built and as good as new, although fifty years old. It was quite clear to me that it had more life in it than the coaches . . .

A Land-Rover was waiting to carry on for fourteen more miles over a track, rutted and dusty in places, to the village of Pucon. The sun had burned through and the view on arrival at the large and lavish HONSA (Chilean State Railways Hotel Department) Hotel Pucon was superb. The mighty Villarrica volcano, rearing 13,000 feet behind the village, was snow-covered half-way down and looked like a traditional Christmas pudding in comic papers with cream over the top. An ominous wisp of steam was rising from its active crater. Spread over many miles in the lava flow was a petrified forest, while in front of the hotel lay Villarrica Lake, a glorious body of water surrounded by stately mountains. The beach was of black volcanic sand but the blue water was vividly clear. A mountain pass with a track curling up to it led through to the Argentine; it crosses the lower slopes of another spectacular volcano, Quetropillan, rounds Lake Quillehue, and goes over the Pass at the relatively low altitude of 3,924 feet, passing Lanin volcano (11,200 feet) before coming to the Argentine village and customs post of Junin de los Andes. The way through is closed by snow in winter.

It was already late in the season, and with blackberries ripe and all the familiar English autumn flowers from Cosmos to Dahlias in bloom in this exact cool temperate reproduction of southern England, the hotel was closing. I was in fact virtually the last person to leave the hotel, the Manager and his wife having gone off laden with baggage to catch an afternoon train, while I took the one departing at 9.30 p.m. to connect with the northbound 'Flecha Nocturna'. Despite the lateness of the season the weather was fine and warm, allowing bathing and boating on the lake. This region in good weather seemed to me to have all the attributes of tourism, containing unrivalled scenery, modest prices, admirable local food, kindly people, and an 'away from it all in the extreme' atmosphere. More than 7,500 miles away from both London and New York, it is hardly likely to be reached by more than a handful of selective holidaymakers.

The same Land-Rover drove me back to Villarrica Station, negotiating the dirt road with some difficulty in the darkness and startling the occasional animal. At the station the train stood waiting, its gas lamps fitful, while two locomotives simmered, their boilers swathed in steam rising in the cold night air. It was one of the most romantic and nostalgic railway scenes I have ever enjoyed, a reminder of what used to be so many years ago all over the world, and now still available in this far-distant part of South Chile. Taking things gently this time, and using more than an hour and a quarter to cover the twenty-eight miles to Loncoche (collecting a few stationmen en route who snuffed out their lamps and closed up for the night), we came into the Junction with a quarter of an hour to spare before the arrival of the Santiago express. This was, in any case, about twenty minutes late.

My northbound 'Pullman' was even more comfortable, with fantastic leg room, than on the way out, and I slept well, awakening to a sunny dawn near Chillán, which showed me the outline to the east of the impressive Chillán volcano, on the slopes of which, at 6,000 feet, there are hot springs and a thermal-cum-ski resort. The train ran well, changing the diesel for an electric at Panguiteno, where we were more or less on time. After an excellent breakfast in the modern chromium-fitted restaurant car (abundant melon and pineapple) I returned to my Pullman to spend the morning reading and relaxing.

But shortly after leaving Rancagua, in fruit-growing country already looking hot and dry in the bright sunshine, we came to a sudden stop. The halt lasted a long time, and on looking out I saw that the track ahead was buckled wildly out of shape for about a mile. There was no reason given, but the delay was considerable before we ran back, crossed over to the 'wrong' line, and proceeded north again, passing the tortured ruin of the other line at walking pace. Then we gathered speed and ran through pleasant Mediterranean-type countryside to the outer suburbs of Santiago, where every open space seemed to be full, on this Sunday noontide, of men and boys playing football. The delay had cost us about ninety minutes and it was nearly two o'clock in the afternoon before the 'Flecha Nocturna' finally came to rest in the Alameda Terminus.

2

Over the High Andes

The spanning of a continent from sea to sea by rail has always had a tremendously romantic appeal, set off by the efforts of Union Pacific in America with its Indian battles and troubles with buffalo herds, and cemented for ever by the story of Canadian Pacific a few years later. Less well known, perhaps, is the conquest of the High Andes shortly before the turn of the century, when it became possible to travel by rail from the Pacific Ocean at Valparaíso to the estuary of the River Plate at Buenos Aires, albeit in a series of trains involving three changes.

The South American continent narrows appreciably towards the south, and from the Chilean coast to the River Plate estuary it is barely 800 miles as the crow flies, assuming a crow could manage the passage over the rearing cordilleras of the Andes. Jet planes do fly, and very frequently at that, from Buenos Aires to Santiago, some 812 air miles, taking about an hour and a half. It is no problem at all for modern jets flying at 35,000 to 40,000 feet, and they clear the highest upthrusts of the Andes by at least 12,000 feet before starting their descent—which must be somewhat gradual and of a spiralling nature to ensure passenger ear-comfort—into the great sprawling city of Santiago which lies so close to the cordilleras. Up to ten years ago, however, flights across the Andes were far from easy with piston-engined aircraft, and the white peaks are liberally dotted with the shattered, burnt-out wrecks of airliners which failed to drag themselves high enough for safe clearance or got caught in violent mountain-top turbulence. During the late nineteen forties, British South American Airways (merged into B.O.A.C. by 1951) lost several converted Lancasters on this route and some of the wrecks were never found.

During December, 1959, B.O.A.C. sent out a Comet 4c jet for some proving flights prior to re-opening the South American service. I was aboard this plane, G-APDR, for two weeks as we made our way down from Lisbon to Recife, Rio de Janeiro, São Paulo, Montevideo and then across to Santiago—having been refused permission to land at Buenos Aires. From Santiago Airport we gave demonstration flights to local dignitaries, airline officials and the Press, showing them the impressive, dramatic take-off tactics for which Comets were justly famed. We roared away and climbed steeply, to clear the Andean cordilleras without any spiralling needed to gain height, and by the time the mighty peak of Aconcagua, 22,834 feet and tallest mountain in the Western Hemisphere, was underneath the wings, we had over 5,000 feet of altitude to play with.

Having done this two or three times, and flown across the Andes about six times altogether, I decided that one day I must really see these mighty mountains from a position where one could respect them. I would take the Trans-Andine Railway all the way across.

It was not until March 1966, when I was touring South America with a photographer colleague, that it became possible to bring this project to fruition. It is never easy to gather much information in Britain about services on the Trans-Andine Railway, and only Cook's offices, in London and the main cities have time-tables with details supplied from their own branches in Chile and Argentina. Letters to South America, particularly to Government information departments or to railway administrations, tend to go unanswered. We flew out to Santiago in a British United Airways VC 10, the trip from Buenos Aires taking under ninety minutes with brief glimpses of snowy peaks through the clouds, and even a few hours after arrival we still had no clear idea about time-tables or even the days of the week that the trains operated.

Cooks-Wagons-Lits offices in Santiago eventually got to work on our request and we learned that there were three trains a week, on Mondays, Wednesdays and Fridays, the Friday effort taking considerably longer for reasons not immediately explained. To buy tickets it was necessary to let the travel agent's representative take our passports to the station, and, even a week before the Monday departure we had agreed on, we only just managed to obtain the last two seats available. This, indeed, confounded the usual denigrators, including some less well-informed and intentioned travel agencies on the spot, who declared 'no one travels by train that way any more'. It seems that demand for seats on the Trans-Andine Railway exceeds supply on Mondays and Wednesdays due to the use of an '*automotore*' diesel unit with space for only 144 passengers. On the Friday, when the service takes longer, there is an ordinary train of carriages allowing a greater amount of accommodation. Presentation of a passport when applying for tickets seems to indicate priority for foreigners, and when we came to make the journey, a rough count showed four Britons, two Canadians, four Italians, six Germans, four Australians, a New Zealander, a French lady on her own, a very elderly Swiss gentleman on his own, and nationals of half a dozen Latin American countries including Chile and Argentina.

The first class single fare was a very modest £7.50 paid in Chilean Escudos which at that time were about thirteen to the pound but have since devalued even more than the pound sterling. An extra £1.25 secured a berth in a two-berth sleeping compartment on the Argentine train making the longest section of the journey, from Mendoza across the wide Pampas to Buenos Aires.

Spanning the South American continent began for us at Santiago's Mapocho Station at 7.45 a.m. on the Monday, a cool autumnal morning in late March. We hoped to arrive in Buenos Aires at 1.30 p.m. on the Tuesday, which was what the schedule indicated. Standing in platform number one of the elegant station with its neat glass-arched roof was an electric-hauled express to Valparaíso, the last two coaches being of a much older type than those nearer the modern Italian-built electric locomotive. These two veterans, looking rather like early American 'Toonerville' stock, were marked 'Trans-Andino Combinación'. We took our places in one of these, on leather seats which had seen better days and were nowhere near the usual Chilean Railways standard. There was no restaurant car on this morning express to the Coast, but men selling coffee and rolls soon walked through the train.

Departure was punctual and the train ran fairly fast through rolling Mediterranean-type country which we had seen before on journeys to and from Valparaíso. The route lay almost due north despite the fact that the Valparaíso train's destination lay to the west. This is because the line clings to the relatively high plain before tackling the coastal range at an easier part well to the north of the Chilean capital. The new road between the port and the capital does, in fact, climb and tunnel on a shorter route, 91 miles as against 116 by rail.

This was the first main line railway to be electrified in South America and one of the first in the world; a start was made with putting up overhead wires in 1909. For the first ten miles the great sprawling city of Santiago gives visible evidence of its expansion on to the central valley and it is not until Colina station is passed, twenty miles out, that the scene is really countrified, and then prosperous farms and fruit production can be seen on either side of the train. Running closer to the coastal range and always with the high cordilleras to the east, the line curves more and more, passes the town of Rungue, and eventually reaches the junction of Llay-Llay. This curious name means 'wind-wind' in the Indian language, and it is no misnomer, for fierce gusts tear down from the high mountains at various times, while at others—mainly in the winter—strong winds rush in from the Pacific and batter against the mountain wall. Pronounced 'yai-yai', Chileans say the name with a hint of reproach in their tone.

At Llay-Llay the two last coaches of the Valparaíso train are detached, and while this is going on the 7.45 from Valparaíso to Santiago arrives at another platform, also dropping off its rear two coaches. When the two expresses have departed the coaches are joined behind a Swedish-built electric locomotive and formed into a four-coach train, which soon sets off in an easterly direction up the valley of the Aconcagua River. While there may be local passengers on board for stations along the line to the end of the broad gauge at Los Andes, most people are bound for the Trans-Andine proper.

Climbing fairly steadily beside the rushing Rio Aconcagua, our train came to a fairly large town which turned out to be San Felipe, capital of the Aconcagua Province with 27,000 inhabitants. We were now seventy-eight miles from Santiago but the kilometre-posts, marked from Valparaíso, showed we were eighty miles from the Pacific terminal. San Felipe is 2,087 feet above sea level and is noted for its pleasant climate.

The next eleven miles were all uphill, though the train managed a reasonable forty miles an hour, while the scenery began to get wilder and the river faster. The next station was Baños de Jahuel, 3,900 feet and a summer health resort. Outside the station were horse-drawn cabs as well as shiny buses and some pleasant parks could be seen. This is a spa with gushing springs, the water being bottled and sold all over Chile. Almost directly ahead we had a glimpse of the Monarch of the Andes wearing a distinctive snow-cap, although the weather was not as good as it might have been, with high cloud.

Unexpectedly, the line began to descend soon after we left Baños de Jahuel and we entered a prosperous-looking agricultural and fruit-farming region. The ten miles to Los Andes took about fifteen minutes, and as we ran into the left-hand side of a large station it was almost exactly 11 a.m. Los Andes is 2,400 feet above sea level, in a sort of well virtually nestling under the Andean wall, and it is noted for its excellent wines, some of which make their way to Europe, and to France in particular these days (apparently to help out supplies of *vin ordinaire*). Several monuments in the big Plaza de Armas outside the station paid tribute to San Martin (he passed this way when crossing the Andes), to Bernardo O'Higgins the famous Chilean-Irish leader, and to the Clark Brothers who built the Trans-Andine Railway. One of their original trains was waiting for us on the extreme right of the station!

This being the end of the Chilean broad gauge, all passengers have to change here, and if going further are required to pass through Chilean Emigration and Customs formalities. This took some time in a large marble hall, but eventually one of the ubiquitous porters seized our cleared bags and took them through to the Trans-Andine platform. Here stood a collection of wooden relics on wheels, rolling stock dating from the 1898 opening of the line, but at the head of quite a long train was a very modern, gleaming metre-gauge Swiss electric Bo-Bo engine built by Brown-Boveri in 1963. The coach we were put into had a broken window, and one which could only be kept open with the aid of string, while the leather seats were exuding horsehair in no mean fashion.

With a jerk one might have expected to break the ancient couplings, the train set off more or less at noon, and therefore on time, with every seat filled. The new power up front dragged the reluctant rolling stock along at a smart pace until, with a bump and a clang, we engaged the rack and started to climb steeply for a while, our speed falling to about fifteen miles an hour on the severe gradient. We passed San Pablo halt and Salto, the scenery became grander and the mountains more and more dominant, while the Acongagua River split in two—we had gone upstream to the confluence of the Rio Blanco and the Rio Juncal. An hour after leaving Los Andes we entered and stopped at our first Trans-Andine station, Rio Blanco, 4,500 feet. Here young salesmen in white coats came aboard and passed through the ancient, creaking rolling stock selling bread rolls and hot pies, the only approach to catering facilities we had seen—or were likely to see—this side of the Andes.

Grinding up the rack, only occasionally coming off it and running faster, we pressed on towards the overpowering mountain wall with frequent glimpses of mighty peaks and glaciers, the looming majesty of Aconcagua to the left and Tupungato to the right. The country was hard and rocky with white water and torrents but with plenty of green vegetation, flowers and small trees showing, for the clouds coming in from the Pacific discharge this side of the Andes during at least six months of the year, from April to November. We ran through the small station of Guardia Vieja at 5,397 feet and then picked up the rack again to climb steeply, sometimes through tunnels and often above precipices, until we came to a stop where sidings developed at a place with a dual name, El Juncal or Hermanos Clark (the Brothers Clark). There was a ten-minute stop while a train of steers coming over from the Argentine was let past. Not much freight traffic traverses the Trans-Andine; it is, oddly enough, more a passenger line.

Leaving this station at its already chilly 7,321 feet we carried on, climbing into what now seemed impassable rock barriers stretching to the sky. But suddenly the vistas opened up in a breathtaking manner and a wide valley appeared, dominated on one side by a vast, bright yellow building. This was Portillo, and as we came into the station with its altitude boards proclaiming that we were over three kilometres above sea level (a breathless 9,406 feet to be exact) we could see the paraphernalia of ski and chair lifts, looking odd in a landscape without snow. The Grand Hotel at Portillo, belonging to the Chilean State Railways hotel division, was the headquarters for the World Ski Championships of 1966, held during August when deep snow covers the Andean Cordilleras down to about the 4,000-foot mark.

It was here that a British team did exceptionally well in strange and unusual terrain, above the altitudes they were used to, which was a factor in their favour, for those from the Alpine regions were, in the main, unused to ski lifts taking them above 10,000 feet. Slopes are precipitous this side of the Andes, but it is well above the tree-line.

Leaving Portillo, the train seemed to gather itself for the final onslaught on the Andes and immediately engaged the rack for a steeper angle of climb than we had known before. It was very evident in the ramshackle coaches to those who were sitting with their backs to the engine, for where the leather was still smooth, one tended to slide off the seat. We were among what is described as the grandest rock scenery in the world, utterly wild and cruel yet spectacular in the extreme. The Official Guide to South America states that 'no word picture can give any conception of the prodigious grandeur of the snow-clad, towering peaks, sharp-pointed in relief against the sky'. The sky in our case was still not blue but a high thin grey, although the 23,000-foot Aconcagua stood out in brittle clarity. There were patches of flowers and greenery beside the tracks, for the clouds from the Pacific discharge against the high Andes and almost never penetrate to the Argentine side, where desert conditions prevail.

Suddenly the angle of climb eased and the track became very winding until a tunnel mouth appeared. We plunged into this, the electric engine's whistle screeching, and were in darkness for the next two miles. This was La Cumbre Tunnel, which we entered from the Chilean side at the tiny outpost of Caracoles (which I must have missed for I saw no habitation). Not only is the tunnel two miles long but it is two miles high, and the lack of oxygen was very noticeable in non-pressurized conditions. Up among the Peruvian Andes, where rails climb to three miles above sea level, and on the famous British-owned Antofogasta Railway from the Chilean Coast to the copper mines and beyond to the Bolivian frontier, which attains 16,000 feet, oxygen cylinders are carried in each coach and most people are given a whiff or two to ward off the unpleasant '*Siroche*' or mountain sickness.

La Cumbre Tunnel took us below the summit of the pass of the same name, where a gigantic statue of Christ dominates the scene. It cannot be observed from the train at any point, but in summer a car or pony can be taken from the next station, Las Cuevas, for a side trip and then the wording at the base of the 220-foot high statue, put up when the organized workers of Argentina erected it, can be read: 'Christ the Redeemer. These mountains will crumble before the people of Argentina and Chile will break the peace sworn at the feet of Christ the Redeemer'.

Although the train has complete right of way through La Cumbre Tunnel, it is used by road traffic for a ridiculously small toll. There are slight prospects of seeing a car coming towards the train if any fault should have occurred to the signalling system. However, with only three passenger trains each way per week, and not more than three cars a day in each direction, the risk is very small.

At all events we burst out of the tunnel into a cavernous, roofed-in station which turned out to be Las Cuevas, already in Argentina. Here it was necessary to change trains, no easy matter with baggage at an altitude of 10,331 feet, only 121 feet lower than the summit of the line attained in the tunnel. There were few porters, and we had to cross the low platform and somehow scramble our bags into the high door of a Czech-built multiple-unit diesel train painted white and blue in the colours of the Argentine San Martín Railway (Trans-Andine section).

The numbered seats from the Chilean train corresponded approximately with those in the diesel, but there was a great difference. They were modern and narrow, the vehicle being in excellent mechanical condition but with high windows and no arm-rests. It was typically modern in that it was austere and lacked even the Chilean antique stock's faded elegance.

Las Cuevas station was built in a vaulted tunnel for protection, the original station in the open having been destroyed with the loss of a train and thirty-five lives late in September 1964, when a Spring avalanche came hurtling down from the steep sides of Tupungato. Although there were Argentine customs and immigration officials there they made no attempt to detain passengers; instead, some of them boarded the train, and as we moved away sharp at 4 p.m., they came round and interviewed every passenger at his or her seat. The lack of space soon became evident as large bags were opened in the narrow aisles, and somehow or other the elderly Swiss gentleman with a huge can of wild Chilean honey was seated beside me. This proved unfortunate for all of us in the seat block, for the high altitude had caused his honey to leak and pools of sticky fluid were on the floor, into which most of us, including the customs and immigration men, unwittingly trod.

Meanwhile the train was moving rapidly downhill, engaging the rack at thirty miles an hour and, when the descent permitted, was running free of the rack at up to forty-five miles an hour. Curves were taken fairly violently but the customs men appeared to be used to it. The scenery had changed completely and, although high snow-capped mountains dominated the more distant landscape, close at hand there was orange-coloured desert mixed with dry, 'mesa'-type country. The sky had turned blue and the sun was shining. In what seemed a very brief but exhilarating run, we had stopped at Puente del Inca, 9,022 feet, where an elderly hotel showed up beside the track. This is an Argentine winter sports resort run by the San Martín Railway and the point of departure for mule trips to the base of Aconcagua. From here the Fitzgerald expedition of 1897 left to climb the 'Monarch of the Andes' and Vines and Zurbriggen became the first men to reach the summit.

Breathing became more comfortable as, with only minor

clicks in the ears, we lost height rapidly on the way down through monumental scenery with high rocks looking like the cathedral buttes of Western America. A tremendous mass of vast pinnacled rocks stood out clearly, and it came as a shock to learn that they were forty miles from the train; they are known as Los Penitentes. We stopped at Punta de Vacas, 7,852 feet, but only for a few seconds; then we were on our way again, dashing rapidly downhill with fewer stretches of rack now. One small station flashed past but there was no habitation.

Still very much in the heart of the enclosing mountains but hemmed in by red and orange canyons, we thundered down, with whistle blowing, to the little station of Rio Blanco (7,000 feet) serving a tiny hamlet apparently called Polvaredas. Again the stop was not long enough to lean out of the window, and then we were on a long run with no stations and no signs of human life, dropping down through a vast area of mountainous rock and desert which can only have one parallel on earth—the Grand Canyon of Arizona. In only one hour we had dropped fully 4,000 feet and covered twenty-five miles of narrow gauge track, some of it fitted with rack rail.

The first service of hot drinks we had seen since leaving Santiago at 7.45 that morning appeared soon after passing Rio Blanco. There was what British Railways would probably call a 'mini-buffet' manned by two men, and one of them brought round coffee and rolls—not substantial but a help during a long foodless journey. On Friday's departure, I am told, the train goes right through from Los Andes to Mendoza, and has a restaurant car attached between Puente del Inca and Mendoza. However, the full-length train takes rather longer for the whole journey, and we were expected to have dinner on the main line express after leaving Mendoza.

Still in Arizona-type mountain desert country, we came to the large station of Upsallata, 5,745 feet above sea level. This is the headquarters of the Argentine section of the Trans-Andine Railway and on various sidings we could see rolling stock, cranes and locomotives. There was a large British-built rack tank engine, a railbus, and a diesel unit. Even here the stop was very brief and then our '*Automotore*' was on its way again, free from any rack restrictions from now on and belting down the line at up to forty-five miles an hour, quite fast for a narrow gauge mountain line.

The descent became more gradual with the mountains and wild desert plain receding as the Mendoza River, tumbling and tossing, kept close to the line. Dashing through short tunnels and crossing the foaming river on lattice-work bridges, the railway was now laid on an old trail which the Spaniards called 'Camino de los Andes'. Cacheuta, a tiny spa town noted for its health baths, was a brief stop, and then we ran on again at up to fifty miles an hour, down now to the 4,000-foot mark. The country close to the line became softer with fruit trees appearing in the valley of the Mendoza River. Once past Blanco Ecalada, at 3,500 feet, we had only ten miles to go to Mendoza and greenery surrounded the station. There was even a hint of 'suburban' or local passenger traffic—not that seats became vacant but a few were taken aboard and allowed to stand in the doorways for the last twenty minutes of our ride through gathering dusk into the big sprawling fruit and wine centre of Mendoza.

Outlined against the glow of the sunset the majestic Andes stood out rigidly, Tupungato and Aconcagua clearly visible. But darkness closed in suddenly and then our train became enveloped in the lights of the streets of the city, and in a minute or so we had junctioned with broad gauge lines and rolled into a terminal platform at the large main station. It was surprisingly hot as the passengers disembarked, a humid overwhelming heat quite unexpected at a resort city famous for its cool airs situated some 2,500 feet above the Argentine Pampa. It was exactly eight o'clock on a late March (autumn) evening and I estimated the temperature to be quite 12° Centigrade (20° Fahrenheit) above normal.

We had an hour to wait before our main line express, 'El Aconcagua', left for Buenos Aires, but the sleeping cars were already drawn up at a nearby siding and access to them was allowed. Depositing our bags in a smart modern two-berth compartment of the streamlined Japanese-built sleeper, we assuaged thirst as best possible and strolled around Mendoza station, noting the reminders of the great days of British ownership of the Buenos Aires Pacific Railway, now the General San Martín Line of the Argentine National System. Dutch diesels,

Chilean Pacific No. 591 (British built in 1913), at Villarica on the Chilean longitudinal Railway.

[Photograph by Tony Hudson]

A mainline express near Llay Llay.

[*Photograph by Tony Hudson*]

Chilean Mogul No. 708 on an east-bound freight waits at Ancahaul station for a passenger train to pass.

[*Photograph by Tony Hudson*]

Right. A trans-Andine train at Hermanos station, 8,000 feet above sea level.

[*Photograph by Tony Hudson*]

Left. From Chile to the Argentine: A trans-Andine train enters La Cumbre tunnel, 10,700 feet above sea level.

[*Photograph by Tony Hudson*]

The 'Del Monte' train backs into Monterey station at 7.45 a.m.

The 'Del Monte' hotel near Monterey which is now occupied by the U.S. Navy.

This is an historic photograph showing the 'Olympian Hiawatha', the first electric train through the Rockies, in 1934.

[*Photograph by courtesy of the Milwaukee Railroad Company*]

Japanese rolling stock, and Czech multiple-units pointed to the complete change of suppliers and a loss of British influence. Until the nationalization of the Argentine Railways in 1946–47, the British-owned railways in that country had represented one of our greatest overseas investments and provided not only splendid export markets for our equipment, but kept our coal export trade going, which in turn paid for our meat and linseed oil supplies from the Argentine. This change-over in South America was the biggest single economic loss Britain suffered in post-war days, crippling not only general trade but shipping to the River Plate.

Promptly at 9 p.m. 'El Aconcagua', now marshalled and composed of air-conditioned reclining-seat 'Pullman cars', sleepers, and a smart new diner, left behind a powerful Dutch diesel. There was a concerted move towards the diner where an excellent four-course meal was served, a mammoth Argentine steak going down very well. The cost was low, since at that time one received more than 600 pesos for the pound and prices had not advanced very much. Inflation continues in that country and, although the devalued pound sterling gets even more pesos, prices are up. Back in 1940 a large steak bought in a Buenos Aires restaurant, accompanied by two eggs, worked out at around one shilling (five new pence). Even on the El Aconcagua, in 1966, the whole meal cost only the equivalent of five shillings (twenty-five new pence).

Before we had finished the meal, a tremendous hail and thunder storm broke and the train roared on through a night constantly lit by flashes, while the noise of the hail crashing on the roof drowned all other sound. Even when we retired to bed, the storm was continuing unabated, and I in the top bunk could hear nothing but the sound of hail striking the ventilator. A glance out of the window showed hailstones nearly as big as duck's eggs bouncing off the train and tending to lie on the fields. Nevertheless, tired by the long journey over the Andes and the changes of altitude, I at least slept right through the night (not noticing that the train was apparently held at a signal for nearly half an hour).

The efficient sleeper attendant, a pleasant man, knocked on the door at 7.30 a.m. and I awoke to a grey day with rain pouring down across the flat landscape. It was typical Pampas country, limitless fields with cattle huddled miserably in groups. We were travelling fast over single track when I went along to breakfast on fruit, rolls, and tea. The whole morning saw the express crossing featureless country at a rapid pace, broken only by a stop at Junin (pronounced 'Hooneen'), the workshop headquarters of the San Martín Railway 159 miles from Buenos Aires. Rain continued without slackening, and only occasional *estancias* surrounded by a few trees broke the monotony of the scene outside the windows. There were vast grain-growing areas and enormous herds of cattle, but nothing exciting in scenery all the way from about sixty miles east of Mendoza to the outskirts of the capital. However, those passengers who had crossed the Andes the day before had had their fill of powerful scenery and were content to let the comfort of the fast train wash over them, for the flat Pampas made for reasonably good riding and high speed.

There was time for an adequate and inexpensive lunch shortly after noon, which came as a surprise for this was the first of two meatless days a week. By 'meatless' Argentinians mean no beef, so the menu offered masses of lamb and pork! The idea is to reduce home consumption so that beef exports can be stepped up. We stopped at the important junction of Mercedes, an old but expanding town of some 40,000 people sixty miles from Buenos Aires, and this left us with seventy-five minutes to reach the capital. The train ran easily and managed an arrival at Retiro by 1.25 p.m., just five minutes early, which astonished friends meeting us who had not made the journey themselves and had been filled with anti-rail propaganda by road and airline organizations.

Retiro, the end of the line, is three big terminals dating back to the days of the British Companies. One is superb (the old Central Argentine terminal), one is modest but pleasing (the Central Cordoba State Terminal) while the one we used remained a leaking tin shed, just as it was when the semi-bankrupt B.A. Pacific owned it. . . .

3

Romance of the 'Del Monte'

A little over a hundred miles down the California coast from San Francisco the land becomes more rugged and forces out into the Pacific to form a substantial peninsula. To many of the people who live on it, this Monterey Peninsula is all that remains of the true United States, and some imagine themselves to be living in a last civilized enclave walled off from the spreading megalopolis and the milling throngs. Certainly many efforts are made to keep it exclusive, and for non-residents of the area who wish to drive around the scenic peninsula at weekends, a charge of two dollars per car is levied.

The attractive town of Carmel is the social hub of the Monterey Peninsula. Neatly laid out on a hill sloping towards the surf of the Pacific Ocean, the air is scented with pine from the forests. There is an 'arty' atmosphere, and boutiques featuring antiques are to be found on all the streets. No brash buildings disturb the symmetry of neat houses, well-laid-out gardens, and sophisticated shops. Instead of hotels there are picturesque inns in what might be called—in England—Mock-Tudor style, well kept and comfortable but with none of the chromium standardization Americans come to expect all over their country.

I think it fair to say that provided one has sufficient means to keep up standards, Carmel is one of the pleasantest towns, and Monterey Peninsula one of the most attractive regions, in the entire world in which to live on a year-round basis. Climatically, it is mid-South California to perfection, never too hot and never cold, the cool ocean always at hand to provide the occasional clean sea fog in case the summer temperatures show signs of becoming excessive. Rain is confined to the winter months but is never very heavy. As the ocean takes so long to warm up, the highest average temperatures occur in October, but even so the daily maximum is only 70° Fahrenheit (21° Centigrade), while the coolest months are February and March, the daily maximum then averaging 59° Fahrenheit (15° Centigrade). Snow is unknown and frost rare. Sunshine is recorded on at least 320 days a year.

They call the Peninsula the 'Golf Capital of the World'. Eight golf courses are to be found spread from Monterey to the Big Sur Country which starts at the southern end of the peninsula. None is cheap to play on and a few are among the world's most expensive.

As one might expect, Carmelites and those belonging to the Monterey Peninsula in general recognize only one city in California (usually only one in the United States, come to that), which is San Francisco, possibly America's most cosmopolitan and sophisticated city. Of Los Angeles, lying about 300 miles to the south, no word is spoken and there is no public communication. The 'Peninsula Paradise' does send one train a day, however, to San Francisco. It is called the 'Del Monte' and it runs to serve the interests of Peninsula dwellers, not those of the city. It was born on the Peninsula and it still works to convey residents to San Francisco for lunch, business appointments, shopping and even a matinee, before returning in the evening.

The only effective railway service between San Francisco and Los Angeles, by the coastal route and the San Joachim Valley line, is maintained by Southern Pacific, a huge company known for countless years as 'Espee'. The outlook of this company towards passenger traffic does not appear to be a happy one, as apparently at every opportunity it axes a train. Espee management has raised the axe against the 'Del Monte' on frequent occasions, but the influential and resourceful citizens of the Peninsula ward it off each time. Why any railway operator should wish to destroy something it originally created to serve people and build a community, and should be engaged in long and profitless dispute with those people, is something railway users the world over would like to know. It does not only happen in America; it is a daily fracas in the United Kingdom. But there is a better chance of fighting in America, because the railway is privately owned and shareholders can be influenced, management threatened. In Britain, Bureaucracy is all-powerful and an Achilles Heel has not been found by all those who protest against the closure of their branch lines.

So the 'Del Monte' continues to wend its leisurely way to San Francisco every morning, leaving Monterey station at 8 a.m. It deposits its clients in Third Street Station at 11.15 a.m., after making nineteen stops during the course of its 121-mile journey. Returning, it leaves the city at 4.50 p.m. or there-abouts (exact times vary with each change of time-table) and gets back at or about eight o'clock, in time for late-dining Carmelites. There is no restaurant car, but a Parlour Car caters to creature comforts with coffee, sandwiches, drinks and other light snacks. In fact it does very well subject to the limitations of its buffet space, and friendly personal service is a hallmark. Coach passengers get nothing.

It all began when Mr. Leland Stanford was President of the Southern Pacific in the spacious days just after the turn of the century. He built one of the largest and most luxurious hotels the world has ever known about two miles from Monterey and the Southern Pacific spur went into the grounds. The hotel was called 'Del Monte'. Ordinary trains stopped at the little station about a mile from the imposing front entrance, but at weekends a special came right in to the hotel's own station yard. This train took its name from the hotel and lay there with steam up throughout the weekend. History has it that Mr. Stanford always came by it and lived in his presidential suite in the hotel, but gave orders that the train must be ready at all times, day or night, to rush him back to San Francisco. Later, when Los Angeles grew in importance, it is said that he ordered a second train to keep steam up throughout the weekend, so that it could take him south, but this story is disputed because the branch line into the Peninsula cannot serve the south and a train would have to come north nearly half-way to San Francisco before reversing to travel to Salinas, Santa Barbara and Los Angeles.

Having featured on the itinerary of the International Set in the days before aircraft, when cars were only town carriages intended to be chauffeur-driven to the station, the 'Del Monte' hotel became too costly a palace to survive economic and transport changes. Its glory had faded even before Wall Street crashed. The United States Navy took it over. Today its structural elegance remains and the internal condition is superb in its new role as an Officers' Training Establishment. But of the attached station there is no sign, and only a broken hut still stands on the line to show where passengers once alighted to be met by coaches if they were going to the 'Del Monte' other than by the weekend special train.

An airport has been built just outside Monterey, and the city boasts a Greyhound bus station opposite the railway terminal. There is even a jet flight to San Francisco, taking fifteen minutes to the International Airport, and forty-five minutes to Santa Barbara. But still the 'Del Monte Express' survives, although you can feel the pressure its owners put on to try and withdraw it. Local government institutions mention the train in their literature and notices, fighting to give it custom. Visitors are encouraged by their friends to use it. But rumours are circulated that it will soon be taken off, wrong departure times are notified, derogatory remarks are passed about its lack of equipment, and local travel agents (susceptible to pressure from top management and from airline salesmen) ignore its existence. I was a visitor, and in company with an official of Carmel I called at a travel agent to buy a ticket in the 'Del Monte' for my return to San Francisco on the Monday morning. He pulled out an airline ticket. I asked again for the train. "There is no train." This was hotly contested both by me and the official from Carmel. "We don't know anything about any train.' So no sale was made, although an air ticket might have been sold to more easily persuaded or less well-informed clients.

A ticket was bought at Monterey Station and a Parlour Car supplement paid, just as the train was backing in on an unexpectedly wet Monday morning. Monterey was a Spanish settlement until 1840 and many of its original adobe houses have been restored. Fishing is the big industry and it was here that 'Cannery Row' existed, made famous by the novelist John Steinbeck. Sardines were once caught by the billion each night and canned in factories stretching along a picturesque street. But one evening in 1940 the sardines disappeared completely, never to return. All the canneries and fish warehouses fell into disuse, their demise obscured by the Second World War. While ordinary fishing prospered, the collapse of the sardine business led to depopulation, most colourful characters leaving for other haunts. Today, Cannery Row is a tourist attraction, the factories and warehouses turned into artists' studios, boutiques and smart restaurants. All this is only a short walk from the station, as is the long pier with its famous 'Fisher-man's Wharf' (more genuine now than the one in San Francisco) liberally peppered with restaurants serving fish meals at very competitive prices.

The 'Del Monte' which slowly drew away from the paradi-sical enclave on America's Pacific Coast consisted of three ordinary coaches and a Parlour Car, all streamlined, air-conditioned and painted in Southern Pacific's colours of black and orange. One diesel unit headed the short train. Having heard so many stories about going hungry and receiving no ser-vice, I was gratified to hear the Parlour Car attendant ask me how many oranges I wanted squeezed for my fresh juice. "How many do you usually do?" I asked. "Some folk make do with four, some like eight, and others a dozen," was his reply. I settled for eight, and this number of juicy California oranges duly filled a tall glass. There were hot rolls and butter, mar-malade and lashings of coffee, even if a cooked course was mis-sing. There were magazines, newspapers, armchairs, writing tables with notepaper. It was a comfortable, possibly luxurious, ride.

There were only twelve of us in the Parlour Car, and six of these got out at San Jose. I heard why coach passengers got no service. It seemed that an elderly Mexican called 'Manny' who had the concession to sell snacks and coffee had died recently. No one had come forward to fill the job, believing it (with a down payment to be made) to be non-profitable. 'Manny' had had no close friends or relatives. His body lay in a morgue for twenty-eight days before anyone came forward to arrange bur-ial. Then, shortly after I arrived in San Francisco, a newspaper story ran to the effect that 'Manny' had left more than a hundred thousand dollars! I expect the concession has been taken up by now and the coach passengers aboard 'Del Monte', if it maintains its struggle for survival, will have something to eat.

The country is flat once the peninsula is left behind, but with hills looming in the distance. The train rolls between fields full of lettuces, fruits and avocados. At Salinas it joins up with the main coastal line of Southern Pacific, the route of the 'Daylight' to Los Angeles. San Jose, fifty miles out from San Francisco, is a big station marking the end of a busy commuter service from the city, where numerous double-decker railway coaches are to be seen. A second diesel unit is put on here, together with a set of commuter stock, so that the 'Del Monte' becomes an outer suburban train. It makes most of the stops and does good business, calling at places like Palo Alto where the Stanford University campus—founded by the great Southern Pacific President—is located. All the way to the outskirts of San Francisco, the train runs on double track down what seems to be the middle of a wide palm-lined avenue, flanked on both sides by buildings. Only in the last two or three miles, when the tracks increase, dive through tunnels, and twist under the new San Francisco Bay Area Rapid Transit rail system, does it look like a busy railway.

I could have wished the travel agent on the peninsula who said there was no train could have been at Third Street Station to see the long line-up of passengers from the 'Del Monte' waiting for taxis, which were in short supply due to the unseasonal rain . . .

During 1970 the United States Department of Transportation got the Railway Passenger Train Act through Congress and past the President. This Act set up a 'Railpax Corporation' designed to help the railway companies to maintain at least one adequate passenger train over main routes, until 1975 or beyond. A subsidy will be available for this purpose, in effect by transferring the losses to Railpax, and it is expected that the 'Del Monte' will continue to operate under this arrangement.

4

A Thousand Miles of Mountains

In 1964 the Northern Pacific Railway celebrated the centenary
of its foundation with a mammoth musical show which was
recorded on a highly successful long-playing disc. The com-
mentary was spoken by the Master of Ceremonies, Raymond
Massey, famous for his screen portrayal of Abraham Lincoln.
Oddly enough, or perhaps not so coincidentally, this President
of the United States had signed the Act of Congress in 1864
which awarded a land grant to the founders of the Northern
Pacific trans-continental project and set the first construction in
motion.

A hit tune from the Northern Pacific's musical was 'A
Thousand Miles of Mountains', the second line of which read
'From St. Paul to the Puget Sound'. It summed up very
vividly—and very melodiously—the features of the great railway route linking the Mississippi River to the Pacific Ocean
across the northern part of the United States.

The distance from St. Paul, Minnesota, on the still wide
Mississippi, to Seattle on the Puget Sound facing west into the
Pacific Ocean is exactly 1,892 miles. Tracks were not pushed
westwards with the force and speed which marked the construction of Union Pacific's trans-Continental further south.
Financial problems arose and the new line lacked the backers
and the full governmental aid attending the prime linkage of
Atlantic and Pacific. There were no real towns along the
proposed route, and even Seattle, the West Coast destination
named after a local Indian Chief, had a population of barely
350 persons in 1864, while Minneapolis had not become a
registered town until 1856 and nearby St. Paul had its first settlers in 1838. In between was wilderness, Indian country,

mountains and forest. The construction of a railway was not an inspiring proposition for investors of the period, most of whom had already put up funds for the Union Pacific which did, at least, aim for the large and established city of San Francisco.

After six years of struggle, in the financial sense rather than physical, Mr. Jay Cooke, a notable financier of the period, came along to the rescue. He may have had too much money, or else was blessed with that rare thing, vision of the fairly distant future, but whatever it was he put up several million dollars which, added to the odd funds already gathered, made possible a start on the line. In June 1870 a contract was fixed for building the Minnesota Division. All that had happened on the Northern Pacific prior to that date was a ground-breaking ceremony a few miles west of what is now Duluth on Lake Superior and the clearing of a few miles of right of way. The first engine on the line arrived in July, a 0–4–0 wood-burner with a four-wheeled tender. It was called 'Minnetonka' and played a big part in the line's tradition and history, appearing in all its publications but without surviving as a physical entity.

In all fairness to the Union Pacific, the first American trans-Continental (excepting the fifty miles of Panama Railroad across the Isthmus), this mid-America line was open and functioning before the Northern Pacific had laid its first mile of main line track. But then in those days no one thought of the vast wild territories, with their Indian wars and bitter winters, lying up close to the Canadian border. There was no population and no one wanted to try and live up there, except for a few trappers. It required enormous strength of purpose and faith in a distant future backers might not live to see in order to push the new line through wilderness and over a thousand miles of mountains.

The whole vast region of the Pacific North-West had only once been explored and partly surveyed, and that was in the years between 1804 and 1806 when the Lewis and Clark expedition started up the Missouri River. Captain Meriwether Lewis and Captain William Clark fought their way, with Indian guides and porters, by canoe and on mule-back, up the Missouri and along the valleys of the Yellowstone and Columbia Rivers, over the Rocky Mountains and through the Cascades, to the Pacific

Ocean. The route finally selected by the locating engineers of the Northern Pacific Railway closely followed that of the Lewis and Clark expedition, and the names of the explorers are commemorated today in special buffet-lounge cars fitted to the several streamlined trains running in the 'North Coast Limited' service.

That famous American military figure, General William T. Sherman, went on record with the statement that 'The Northern Pacific must be built, both as an economic and military necessity. The West can never be settled, nor protected, without the railroad.' He turned out to be correct, and the Indian Wars, which had more or less ceased along the line of the completed Union Pacific from about 1870 onwards, continued to be fought on the Northern Pacific route. Custer's Last Stand took place in 1876, on a hill overlooking the uncompleted line close to the Little Big Horn River. Heavy battles with Indians occurred further west as late as 1879 and raiding skirmishes with considerable loss of life on both sides were recorded even in 1882. The year 1883 saw the main line of the Northern Pacific completed from Lake Superior to tidewater on the Pacific, and history does not show any more troubles with marauding Indians. Instead, the story is one of almost continuous and successful settlement. It is a story too readily overlooked by air and road orientated Americans of today.

Construction gangs built the Northern Pacific in sections, work on the Pacific coast being done largely by imported Chinese labourers who handled materials and equipment brought from the East Coast of America right round Cape Horn in sailing ships. It often took a piece of machinery 150 days to reach the Western workings from its place of manufacture in the East. By 1873, track had been completed from St. Paul to Bismarck, North Dakota, and from Kalama on the Columbia River to Tacoma. But later that year, Jay Cooke collapsed financially and the Northern Pacific went bankrupt. There was a five-year gap during which little or no construction work was done and men were laid off. Further financing was, however, arranged under the presidency of Mr. Frederick Billings who held the senior office in the Company from 1879 to 1881, and construction was resumed with tremendous vigour. Another

15,000 labourers were brought from China, and much steel equipment was brought across the Atlantic from Britain and France.

Rails entered the territory of Montana in 1881 and on up the Yellowstone Valley to Livingston in November 1882, when work had to be stopped for the severe winter. Heavy engineeering through tunnels and overpasses was called for the following spring and by the early autumn of 1883 the Northern Pacific was completed. They held a 'Golden Spike' ceremony at Gold Creek, Montana, the spot where construction crews from east and west had met, and the President of the Company at the time, Mr. Henry Villard, joined with the President of the United States, General Ulysses Grant, and a passenger agent of the line, by name H. C. Davis, in driving home the last spike. It was not a golden one; *this is always legend* and I know of no actual case where such a spike has been used. But this last spike on the Northern Pacific was, in fact, the first spike ever to be driven, thirteen years before. It is thought that the gathering at Gold Creek was the largest and most distinguished to have attended such a completion ceremony, containing as it did the President and senior members of the United States Government and big delegations from Britain, Germany, and the Scandinavian countries (who were sending so many of their people to settle the plains through which the line ran). The British Foreign Secretary was there, none other than Sackville West of Knole, while one of the most famous newspaper editors of all time, Joseph Pulitzer (after whom the famous literary prize is named—much later won by a lady descendant of the British Foreign Secretary) covered the event for his New York papers.

It was now possible to travel by train all the way from Chicago (already a big city and hub of railways) to Seattle and Tacoma. The main line covered a total of 2,319 miles, the first 427 miles of it to St. Paul over the lines of the Chicago, Burlington and Quincy. There were severe gradients in the Rocky and Cascade Mountains, later to be eased and replaced by tunnels, and some rough trackage, but trains could run and the journey was completed inside a week compared to a hundred days (if all went well) by covered wagon and 150 days by ship round Cape Horn. Within seven years of completion, the entire tier of North-West territories had sufficient population to join the Union and achieve statehood. North and South Dakota joined in 1889, as did the States of Montana and Washington. Idaho came in on July 3rd, 1890. One of the by-products of the line was the founding of the Yellowstone National Park from the railhead of Livingston, the first National Park in the world and one which gave the wild-life conservation idea to so many countries.

All did not go well with the Northern Pacific's finances, for it spent more than it received in those first years, building branch lines, improving the track and constructing advanced equipment. In 1893 it was forced into receivership, and stayed there for three years until a new corporation keeping the same name was formed in 1896. This was soundly backed and successfully organized, able to carry out its programmes. From that year, the Company has made money, a happy state of affairs which continues to this day.

An early decision to give passengers the best and latest equipment has never been revoked, and Northern Pacific trains have always been among the most comfortable in the world. In April 1900, the 'North Coast Limited' was born. This name has been carried by its crack daily express train ever since, and to ride in it is an experience which we shall shortly share in this chapter. The first one was the best express in North America, fitted with diners, lounge cars, sleepers, and even a bath-car fitted with a real bath-tub. All trains working this service were electrically lit in an age when oil lamps or hissing gas brackets (with attendant danger of fire) were standard equipment on so many of the world's railways. Passengers from Chicago were taken to the Pacific Coast in a startling four and a half days at a time when some lines required six, or even seven, to connect the mid-West with the Pacific seaboard.

By now, the Northern Pacific had two competitors going to Seattle, the Great Northern and the Milwaukee. In 1901 the Great Northern and the Northern Pacific jointly purchased nearly all of the common stock of the Chicago, Burlington and Quincy, thus securing irrevocable running rights to Chicago from what had become the big 'Twin Cities' of St. Paul and

Minneapolis. The two companies with their trans-Continental main lines, jointly built the Spokane, Portland and Seattle between 1905 and 1909. Today the Burlington, Great Northern, and Northern Pacific are merged as Burlington Northern for stock market trading but operate under separate names and managements. Their sole competitor, the Milwaukee, was shattered in 1961 so far as its passenger service to Seattle was concerned, despite the fact that it had spent a fortune on electrification, providing the longest overhead electrified line in North America. At present its freight service between the Twin Cities and the Pacific Coast does not have too healthy a glow, either.

The romance of steam traction lasted eighty-five years on Northern Pacific metals. The first and second 'North Coast Limiteds' were steam-hauled, but a new and spectacular train introduced for this service in 1954 was headed by diesel units streamlined and blended to match the stainless steel rolling stock. The whole train was sealed and air-conditioned and fitted with no less than four 'bubble top' vista domes. It must be admitted that where above-train-level vista domes are carried, steam traction with its emission of white smoke and other vapours can obscure the view. Complete dieselization, with its attendant changes including the virtual elimination of railway towns like East Auburn, Washington (where hundreds of men servicing steam engines became redundant) took place in 1958.

Northern Pacific's finances received a tremendous shot in the arm in July 1951 with the discovery of oil in the Williston Basin, Montana, on land it had received under the incentive grants provided by Abraham Lincoln's Act of Congress in 1864. The whole Basin proved to be oil-yielding, right across into North Dakota, and an oil development department was set up at Billings, Montana, a city named after the former railway president who had done so much between 1879 and 1881 to bring the planned trans-Continental line to fruition. Rolling in money, Northern Pacific has spent much of it on still more improvements, such as more than a thousand miles of track laid with long, continuous welded metals, push-button freight classification yards, and radio train control, even on passenger trains.

Out of Chicago every day, Northern Pacific has two trains, one of them the 'Mainstreeter' and the other the 'North Coast Limited'. Working on Central Standard Time, which may not be the local time in the city of Chicago if Daylight Savings are in force, the vista-dome equipped 'North Coast Limited' leaves the Union Station daily at 1 p.m. and the 'Mainstreeter' at 10.45 p.m. The former takes forty-six hours to Seattle, the latter fifty-two hours, so most through passengers naturally try for the 'North Coast Limited' while the 'Mainstreeter' is left to serve many intermediate points. This is the situation in 1971 but the future of the 'Mainstreeter' as a daily service is in doubt.

At the beginning of October 1966, I arrived at Union Station, Chicago, at noon to board this famous express for the run right through to Seattle. I know that the comfortable conditions and equipment remain the same at the time of writing, and do not doubt that they will either remain the same or improve still further as the immediate future comes to pass. I counted sixteen shining silver-grey cars, outlined in Northern Pacific colours and lettering, four of the vehicles with glass vista domes bulging from their roofs. A triple diesel set in the colours of the Burlington Railroad stood at the head of the train. My accommodation was a pleasant single-berth compartment in a Pullman, a 'space' peculiar to Northern Pacific and something better than a roomette, slightly smaller than a typical American two-berth bedroom. The train also had 'Slumbercoaches' for one or two persons amid its coach-class accommodation, an economical way to make the long journey to the Pacific North-West. The coach section had ordinary day coaches with reclining seats as well as Slumber-coaches, a vista dome car, a buffet-lounge named after Lewis and Clark, and access to the main diner. A particularly delightful feature of the 'North Coast Limited' is the attractive stewardess assigned to the train for the whole trip. She wears a green uniform and is a fully qualified nurse as well as a guide. The selection and care Northern Pacific put into employing their stewardesses would put many an airline to shame.

With the time-tables of 1966 and 1967 departure from Union Station was at 12.20 p.m. Once clear of the Chicago suburbs, and with the service of lunch in the diner almost over, the line meets the wide Mississippi River and runs alongside it for 300 miles. The scenery is most attractive, with bluffs and hills rising above the river, barge traffic romantically chugging in the broad stream, and wide vistas of Illinois and Wisconsin to enjoy from the high domes. The Burlington is double track all the way, and many trains pass in the other direction, both freight and passenger. There is a particularly fast run between East Dubuque, Illinois, 184 miles from Chicago, and Prairie du Chien, Wisconsin, 239 miles out, the fifty-five miles being timed in forty-five minutes, pass to pass, at an average of just over seventy-three miles an hour. However, in pre-war days this was done by steam locomotives hauling lighter trains in forty minutes, one of the fastest stretches of track in the world at the time.

At five minutes past seven in the evening, with darkness gathering, the streamliner rolled into St. Paul's Union Station, 427 miles from Chicago, completed in six hours, thirty-five minutes, at an average speed of sixty-five miles an hour. There is a twenty-five minute stop here while the locomotive power is changed for the Northern Pacific's own diesels, now about to travel over their own tracks. St. Paul has a population of 315,000 and is Minnesota's State Capital. It is at the junction of the Minnesota and Mississippi Rivers. Minnesota is an Indian word meaning 'land of the sky-blue waters'.

There are only nine miles between the 'Twin Cities' and the streamliner, having left St. Paul at 7.30 p.m., pulls into Minneapolis twenty-five minutes later. Here the population is 465,000, but there is so much built-up area between the cities you cannot easily tell from the train where one leaves off and the other begins. During this short ride, the Mississippi is crossed twice. Not in sight of the train are the famous Minnehaha Falls. At five past eight in the evening (now 9 p.m. on 1971 timings) the 'North Coast Limited' was really on its way, pushing westwards in earnest now across fertile farmlands to the Red River Valley, the same river that flows north into Canada at Winnipeg. In the darkness one may or may not notice the stop at Staples, Minnesota where passengers who have come by bus (until recently it used to be by train) from Duluth on Lake

Superior transfer to the trans-Continental line. But those who have not retired to their various beds or berths before midnight will gain a quickening of interest at 11.55 p.m. when the train stops at the North Dakota town of Fargo, with 50,000 people. Earlier settlers called it Centralia, but it was changed in 1871 to Fargo in honour of William G. Fargo, co-founder of Wells-Fargo Express (once partner of American Express) and a director of the Northern Pacific Railway. The Red River is crossed here, in a region where the soil is considered the richest in America.

The night is dark on the prairies and few lights disturb the blackness, as the train moves smoothly along the welded track, stopping only at Jamestown, North Dakota, before reaching Bismarck at 3.20 a.m. This is the capital of North Dakota with a population of 31,800. It was named by early German settlers after the German Chancellor, and stands at an altitude of 1,670 feet, 873 miles from Chicago. In winter it records some of the lowest temperatures in the United States, often forty degrees below zero (and at this point Fahrenheit and Centigrade read the same). There is a short run here, involving a crossing of the Missouri River, before another stop is made at Mandan, five miles beyond. Here clocks and watches are turned back one hour to Mountain Standard Time (although they do not come along and wake you to make the alteration). Lewis and Clark spent the winter of 1804-05 here, and one wonders if the 'North Coast Limited' is stopping in honour of them, since passengers are unlikely to want to get on or off at this hour of the morning. When the train does leave, it is for a run of a hundred miles to Dickinson, where North Dakota's Badlands begin. The stop is from 4.28 to 4.34 a.m., new time. Dawn will come between here and the next call, at Glendive, Montana, heart of the Williston Basin oilfields, reached at 6.22 a.m. American trains, even the luxury ones like the 'North Coast Limited', have not yet got around to the accepted British and African (and indeed Commonwealth) idea of calling passengers with a cup of tea or coffee, but if they ever do no doubt it will come at Glendive going west on this train, with the sun coming up over spectacular rocks and cathedrals of sepia-coloured stone which are natural bluffs.

4—RR * *

Now we pick up the Yellowstone River and run in sight of it for 342 miles, climbing alongside it imperceptibly, yet at Miles City, the next stop, we are 2,363 feet above sea level, just 1,163 miles from Chicago. It is, or used to be, 7.50 a.m., and the dining car is busy serving breakfast. Both in quantity and quality, Northern Pacific food is extremely good, never less than three eggs being used when ordering 'scrambled', and the famous baked Idaho potato in its jacket being served at dinner on a huge side plate of its own, for it never weighs less than two pounds! As for steaks, they occupy most of the plate and unlike so much American meat they really taste and a fork can cut them easily.

The train is now amid its 'thousand miles of mountains' and we are never out of sight of them all the way to the Pacific coast. Ranches can be seen from the windows, and Fort Keogh, a United States Range Livestock experimental station, is across the river from the train. Signal Bluff, a very high knob, can be seen to the south; from here the U.S. troops from Fort Keogh used to heliograph all the way to the Black Hills of Dakota, 175 miles distant. We are really in Indian country now, and General Custer passed this way with his Seventh Cavalry, based at Mandan. In fact, General and Mrs. Custer travelled by Northern Pacific train to Bismarck, the then limit of the line, not long before his death on the Little Big Horn in 1876.

After breakfast passengers make their way to the vista domes or to the observation lounge at the rear of the train, where refreshments are served and the view of the receding scenery is fascinating. The stewardess-nurse will be much in evidence, giving historical notes about the places of interest being passed. There is a brief stop at Forsyth, then at about 9.15 a.m. the train rolls through Big Horn station where General Custer fought a successful battle in 1873 against Sioux Indians who were attacking Northern Pacific surveyors. He was not a losing General all the time . . . The next station is, in fact, named after him; it serves a community of 350 people 2,737 feet above sea level and is famous as the place from whence Calamity Jane (whose real name was Martha Canary) rode pony express to Deadwood, South Dakota.

There is a tremendous rock near the line beyond Custer

called 'Pompey's Pillar', which William Clark climbed in 1806. This has been dedicated as a national historic landmark. Huntley, Montana, is the next station but the train does not stop, although a very early Northern Pacific work train had to when it was attacked by Chief Black Moon and a thousand braves. Billings, Montana, population 58,000, is the next call and here ten minutes are spent, long enough to get out and stretch one's legs while observing some of the maps, pictures, and relics in the station buildings. Leaving this busy city at 10.44 a.m., westward travellers get their first glimpse of the Rocky Mountains. Climbing begins and in the next 116 miles to Livingston the train ascends to the 4,500 foot mark, passing through Laurel, Columbus (with a view of Granite Peak, 12,850 feet) and Big Timber (with dude ranches all around and glimpses of the saw-toothed Crazy Mountains rearing to 11,000 feet).

Livingston is a large and elegant station, the gateway to Yellowstone National Park where buses pick up passengers who are going on vacation to this 'controlled' wilderness. It is only a short ride by bus to the Park's Gardiner Gateway. The time was 12.42 p.m., and ten minutes are spent here while the train is serviced for water and the vista domes hosed and cleaned. On the new timings this Livingston stop is from 1.32 to 1.42 p.m. Americans never use the twenty-four hour clock. Directly ahead of the throbbing diesels appears a solid wall of mountains, the north front of the Absarokas. In fact there are mountains all around Livingston and the traveller can count dozens of peaks exceeding 10,000 feet.

For fifteen miles after leaving Livingston the train climbs towards the impenetrable wall, through which it bursts by way of the Bozeman Tunnel, only 3,000 feet long but at an altitude of 5,592 feet. Before the tunnel was built in 1884 (and rebuilt in 1945) the Northern Pacific got over this section by a dangerous yet successfully operated switch-back system. It is named after Captain John Bozeman, who implemented a wagon trail across the mountains, and was later killed by Blackfeet Indians in 1867. All the valuable elevation is lost after the tunnel exit and the train rolls down to Bozeman station, 1,450 miles from Chicago and 4,761 feet above sea level. Here it stopped at 1.37 p.m. for a couple of minutes. The town houses Montana State University, and has a population of 16,500.

Another twenty-four miles downhill brings the train to Logan, situated at an altitude of 4,104 feet, the junction for the line to Helena, Montana's State Capital. The 'North Coast Limited' takes the left-hand junction to go through Butte, copper mining centre, while the 'Mainstreeter' runs on the right fork to serve Helena. As the train rolls on through Three Forks, where the Jefferson, Madison, and Gallatin rivers merge to form the Missouri, passengers may wonder what has happened to the much-vaunted Rockies. Surely Bozeman Tunnel, in its bare half-mile, had not conquered them? But the question is soon answered, for at Whitehall, a few miles further along, the line begins to climb again and soon a mighty, awesome view opens out ahead.

We see the eastern wall of the main Rocky Mountain barrier, quite obviously insurmountable. But the train, with three heavy diesels roaring loudly, tackles a steepening grade and works its way up, at between twenty and thirty miles an hour, twisting and turning towards the Continental Divide. The summit is Homestake Pass, little known by comparison with other great passes of the Rockies but one of the most spectacular nevertheless. At 3.56 p.m. the train had topped the high point of the Northern Pacific, at 6,328 feet above sea level. Homestake Pass has a tiny railway community of sixty persons, who suffer some dreadful winter weather as they strive to keep the line open. The stewardess-nurse passes throughout the train to check if any passengers are in trouble from the altitude, typical of the care Northern Pacific take with their travellers. She carries portable oxygen in case of need.

Once over the Homestake the view opens out on the western side into the Silver Bow Valley as the train slides down 843 feet in ten and a half miles. The brakes go hard on as a big town is approached, with mine dumps starkly surrounding it. This is Butte, Montana, population 26,500, sometimes called the 'greatest mining camp on earth'. Mining started here in 1864 and has produced billions of dollars worth of copper, zinc, manganese, lead, silver and gold. This is the headquarters of the famous Anaconda Company which has interests in other mineral producing parts of the world, notably Chile. Electric overhead wires mark the lines of mining trains, and a branch of the Union Pacific goes north out of Butte directly over the mountains. The yellow coaches of the U.P. train can be seen waiting in the station.

The Butte stop lasted from 4.4 to 4.11 p.m., then the 'North Coast Limited' was on its way again, still downhill, passing massive outcrops of industry rather than nature, although the Rockies are all around, with the Highland Mountains to the south, the Anaconda and Flint Creek Ranges to the west, and Deer Lodge to the east, with the Continental Divide and Homestake still visible behind the train. The giant electric furnace plant of Stauffer Chemicals is passed at about seven miles out, in a great canyon formed by the Silver Bow Creek. At Stuart, nineteen miles west of Butte, the huge stack of Anaconda Copper comes into view. At Warm Springs all signs of industry are gone, the train has come down to 4,821 feet from Butte's 5,485, and some institutional buildings for hospitals and curative patients are seen. Deer Lodge is next, under Mount Powell (10,300 feet) but the vista dome express does not stop until Garrison is reached, 1,597 miles from Chicago and 4,332 feet above sea level. It is 5.10 p.m. as the train pulls away, and then follows a fine run of sixty-eight miles through western Montana, downhill most of the way through mountains and valleys, passing at 5.25 p.m. (now 6.10 p.m.) the spot at Gold Creek where the last spike ceremony was held to complete the Northern Pacific. For over fifty miles of this run, another railway line is to be seen following the canyon and valley, equipped with overhead wires, but no trains are usually seen. This is the Milwaukee, St. Paul & Pacific, currently reduced to a limited freight train service to the Pacific Coast, but once proud of its 488 miles of electrified line through the Rockies.

Missoula is the next stop, on my trip at 6.19 p.m., where ten minutes are spent, long enough to venture outside the station to view a Northern Pacific steam locomotive mounted in a place of honour in the square outside. It dates from 1906 and is a standard, handsome 4–6–0 known as a 'ten wheeler' in American railway circles. The University of Montana has its main campus here in Missoula. There are 27,600 people living in the small city excluding students and the members of the United States Forest Reserve service. Along the Bitter Root Valley beyond the city the United States Army runs a mule-breeding station, which has produced some remarkable animals. There is a demand for some of its best products in Vietnam for service where the going is too difficult for mechanical vehicles.

Lewis and Clark went from here in 1805-06 up the Hell Gate Canyon into the Great Falls region, but the Northern Pacific swings away to the right and follows the fertile Bitter Root Valley, after entering the Canyon for a brief while. The running continues to be downhill as darkness gathers, and by the time the train stops at Paradise, Montana, most passengers will be dining sumptuously. Here the clocks and watches are set back another hour to Pacific Standard Time, so although the arrival was at 8.8 p.m. the departure was at 7.11 p.m. We are now 1,736 miles from Chicago and only 2,487 feet above sea level. According to 1971 timings the 'North Coast Limited' will be pulling out of Paradise at 7.56 p.m.

Before dinner is over, the express enters the Idaho 'Panhandle' and the service of alcoholic liquor stops abruptly. Not all States in the Union repealed the Prohibition laws; about four of them are still 'dry' and Idaho is one of them so far as free sale is concerned. This state of affairs lasts for approximately two hours while the train is in Idaho but passengers can consume what may have been purchased earlier. The only stop in Idaho is at Hope, population ninety six, the station for Lake Pend Oreille, where the mountains seem to hang above the hamlet and the fifty-five-mile long lake is one of the finest and quietest resort areas in America. The train later crosses an arm of the lake at Sandpoint on a mile-long viaduct.

The border into the State of Washington is crossed soon after ten o'clock Pacific Time, but many passengers will have retired for the night. Not many stay up to see the arrival, at 10.32 p.m., at Spokane, known as 'Queen City of the Inland Empire'. With a population of 184,000, at an elevation of 1,922 feet, it is one of the main cities on the line, a railway base and a financial centre. This is a jumping off point for side trips to the Grand Coulee Dam on the Upper Columbia River, one of the largest dams in the world, ranking with the Aswan, the Kariba, and the new ones on the Lower Zambesi and Orange River in Southern Africa. It has forced the river waters to form a lake 150 miles long and irrigates semi-arid country set between the coastal mountains and the Rockies.

After a thirteen-minute stop the 'North Coast Limited' rolls away for Pasco, Washington, which is only 380 feet above sea level. Here, at 1.36 a.m., the through sleeper and coach for Portland, Oregon, are detached and worked forward along the banks of the Columbia River by the Spokane, Portland and Seattle Railway, a subsidiary of the Great Northern and Northern Pacific. It is interesting to note that all across the Pacific North-West, the term 'railway' is used, rather than the Eastern U.S.A. expression 'railroad'. This applies in Canada, too, with Canadian Pacific and Canadian National and Pacific Great Eastern. Pasco is a town of 16,000 people on the Columbia; Northern Pacific trains crossed the river by ferry between 1883 and 1888 until a bridge was completed. We are back on the route of Lewis and Clark, who camped here in what is now a town park on their way westwards under the guidance of an Indian girl, Sacajawea.

For four miles after leaving Pasco, although westbound travellers by the 'North Coast Limited' will not be awake to see it, the train passes N.P.'s vast push-button marshalling yard and freight classification centre. There is no further stop until 3.56 a.m., a run of 91 miles achieved in 115 minutes, when Yakima is reached. There has been a perceptible climb, to over 1,000 feet, and the train is back among mountains. This is the centre of a very rich fruit region, and apples are regularly exported to Britain from the 417,000-acre Yakima Valley. The name is Indian, meaning 'Black Bear'. Now comes some more climbing, the train going up another 500 feet to arrive at Ellensburg in the Kittitas Valley. Rodeos are held here and there is a definite 'Western' atmosphere.

Wise passengers arrange for an early call, preferably soon after dawn. In any case they have gained an hour with the clocks going back, and the 1971 later timings help to some extent. We see the conquest of the second pass of the journey as the train climbs through the Cascades, mountains clothed in fir forests, snow-capped and a marked contrast to the arid, harsher Rockies although the summits are not much lower. In this region, the Northern Pacific owns 'tree farms' stretching over 700,000 acres, part of the Land Grant of 1864. About 6.30 a.m. the train will be winding up towards the Stampede Pass and Tunnel, the latter two miles in length and the longest on the Northern Pacific. It was not opened until 1888, trains prior to that taking a switch-back route. The Pass is 2,852 feet above sea level, a negligible height compared to the earlier elevations at Homestake, but because of the changed climate and scenery, this seems more impressive. Going down the western slope of the Cascades, with views of greenery to the blue Pacific beyond and the white-capped mass of Mount Rainier (14,410 feet) to the south and Mount Baker (10,750 feet) to the north, the train crosses the Green River eleven times.

During breakfast, a stop is made at East Auburn, once a busy railway town with huge steam sheds and now reduced to a small diesel depot. Passengers bound for Tacoma alight here and are taken by Northern Pacific bus for the twenty-mile journey. Meanwhile, the 'North Coast Limited' runs through the growing outskirts of Seattle, past the massive private airfield and works of the Boeing Aircraft Factory where 30,000 people are employed (it has its own station and sidings operated by Northern Pacific), and finally meets Pacific tidewater before rolling into King Street Station at 8.45 a.m. (it used to be 8.15 a.m. in 1966). Seattle is 2,319 miles from Chicago and the largest city in the Pacific North-West, with a population of 565,000. The port-city is named after Chief Sealth, a benevolent Indian who helped early settlers in the mid-nineteenth century.

King Street Station is a terminus used by Northern Pacific and Great Northern trains. Adjoining it is Union Station, once shared by Milwaukee and Union Pacific trains, but only the latter operate into it nowadays. King Street is in the Downtown area of Seattle and was rebuilt with a smart concourse and passenger escalators late in 1966. This kind of modernization has been a comparative rarity in the United States in recent years, and points to the wealth of the Northern Pacific-Great Northern combine and its determination to maintain what are among the very best passenger long-distance trains in the world. Frequency of service is not the keynote here, and European passengers are somewhat amused by the great flashing neon signs all over Seattle advertising 'Great Northern Railway—five trains a day', and 'Northern Pacific—three trains a day'. But the emphasis should be on a 'cruise on wheels scenic holiday' through one thousand miles of mountains and the historic terrain of the North-West, when a fair comparison can be made with cruise liner departures.

5

Internationals on the Pacific Shoreline

So much glamour and importance has been attached over the years to the word 'international' that when it is applied to an express train one expects to see a long line of the best rolling stock, smart passengers, and perhaps the odd few suspected spies. It comes as rather a flattening experience, therefore, when boarding a train in Seattle which the advertisements and time-tables have emblazoned with the word 'International Express' to find it is four or five Great Northern Railway coaches, one of them a Parlour Car, no dining car, one or two diesel units at its head, about to embark on a 130-mile journey to Vancouver.

There were two of these trains in each direction daily until 1969, the only double passenger rail service between two big cities on the Pacific shoreline, Seattle with its 565,000 people and Vancouver—growing faster than any city in North America—with 400,000. Now there is only one in each direction! If normal transport conditions applied, there would be a dozen or more trains. And this frontier is considered to be the friendliest and easiest to cross in the world (it is, for Canadians and Americans). But so many people drive their own cars that on the good roads linking these two cities more than ninety-five per cent of the passenger traffic rolls. Those who do not wish to drive use the Greyhound buses, which provide a better than hourly service with 'expresses' doing the run in three hours flat, including border formalities at the 'Peace Arch'. Others go by pleasure boats via Victoria. The Great Northern International trains manage to spend three and three-quarter hours on the way, although the border crossing formalities are carried out in the coaches. There are six intermediate stops.

The 49th parallel is a very remarkable thing. It stretches for over 2,000 miles as the world's longest unguarded, unfortified frontier. If you are a Canadian or an American you can do almost anything on it and beyond it except cross it by train. Along all that vast territory there is only one line going from the United States into Canada, where it comes from Minneapolis and finds its way to Winnipeg to join the Canadian Pacific. The next, and only other, physical steel link is right on the Pacific shore, where the Great Northern tracks go across at Blaine on the way to Vancouver, and here the border has bent a little due to the Puget Sound and the Straits of Juan de Fuca, making the Canadian city of Victoria slightly below the parallel, even if the rail crossing on the mainland between the State of Washington and British Columbia is almost exactly on Latitude 49° North.

There were frontier squabbles which led to skirmishes between British and American troops right through the 1840s and early 1850s. Britain tried to claim the Washington coast-line right down to the 45th parallel, while outraged and belligerent American patriots rushed to the colours to champion their slogan "Fifty four fifty or fight". This was finally settled after minor battles, one of which led to the death of two cows and one soldier, and pots of tea being made for a few American prisoners before they were handed back to their camp. The compromise was a continuation of the 49th parallel except for physical indentations on the Pacific shoreline.

Seattle, named after a kindly Indian chief who befriended the twenty-two first settlers who arrived from New York all the way round Cape Horn by schooner in 1839, and helped the hamlet grow into the beginnings of a city before he died in the Sixties, was the seat of an unofficial World's Fair in 1962. This left a fascinating residue of construction, including a Space Needle rearing 600 feet above the city with an expensive restaurant at its summit, a fair ground, good concert halls and conference facilities, and a monorail which rushes over a mile of concrete track laid above the main street from a mid-town point to the original Fair grounds. If this monorail had been extended downtown to the two railway stations it would have served as a valuable transport medium.

King Street station is the departure point for the 'International's', the only train in 1971 leaving at 3.30 p.m. and its opposite number from Vancouver arriving at 4.35 p.m. When there were two, the first left at 7.45 a.m. and the second at 4.50 p.m., and each did one round trip. When I boarded the early train, armed with a Parlour Car ticket, in October 1966, there was quite a crowd of passengers. The vast majority of them regarded it as just another trip, but all had some concern over the Customs. Border formalities they scarcely knew nor bothered about, but if they were Canadians returning home they needed to worry about 'exemptions' and allowances and were busy making lists of purchases. For Americans the Customs problem would be faced later, on their return home.

Going north for the holder of a British passport was simple. Even less bother and fewer questions than for Americans, who merely had to show a driver's licence or some such evidence of identity but were required to make verbal answers to various questions. But in any case nothing happens on the International for the first two hours. During this time it runs north with good views of Puget Sound, yachts, blue waters, green fields and forests, and the superb bulk of Mount Baker, 10,750 feet rearing up on the inland side of the train. As far as Everett, thirty-three miles (which emits incredible glue factory stenches) we are running on the Great Northern Railway's main line, followed by its trans-continental streamliners, 'Empire Builder' (equipped with bubble domes) and 'Western Star' on their way to Chicago. After the Everett stop, the main line branches off to the right while the International keeps to the coast, often right on the shoreline with pleasant views of the offshore islands. There is a stop at attractive, wooded Mount Vernon, and soon afterwards the big town of Bellingham is reached.

When a large three-funnelled steamer, once a regular excursion vessel in the coastal trade between Seattle, Victoria and Vancouver, comes into view passengers know they are approaching Blaine and start to search for notes, bags, and documents. The ship, by the way, is moored as a floating restaurant. To the right of the train the two-lane dual carriageway highway is in sight, and not far from Blaine station is the Peace Arch where road vehicles must stop for border formalities. The train is luxury by comparison, for Canadian immigration and customs officials come aboard and start to conduct their business from Bellingham while the train moves on to reach the border stop at Blaine.

Of American officials there was no sign. They do not care a jot about people leaving the country. This is the same anywhere, boarding ocean liners in New York, or planes from any United States airport with international flights. But they care, very much, about people coming in, and travel in the reverse direction comes up sharply against red tape. This attitude to the departed is a hangover from the immigration department's somewhat outdated views that everyone wants to come to the United States but that no one wants to leave, except for those being deported, and the officials are glad to be rid of them anyway. I was sipping coffee brought round by the Parlour Car porter when the Canadian officials came in. They looked at my passport, stamped it, and bothered no more, with no customs questions. Other passengers had their bags examined and their lists of purchases inspected if they were returning Canadians. But all the time the train was moving forward, and no time was lost, nor was there any discomfort.

After ten minutes' stop at Blaine, the officials alighted with some friendly waves and smiles. Then the track became single and the going much slower, with a long wait on the southern side of New Westminster for a freight train to pass. We linked up with the Canadian National main line and ran around the spreading city of Vancouver, through a rocky tunnel, and into the Canadian National terminal which G.N.R. trains share. It is about two miles from the Canadian Pacific station. The time was 11.50 and we were twenty minutes late on an already slow timing. In the afternoon, the former second International left Seattle at 4.50 p.m. and was intended to reach Vancouver at 8.30 p.m., which I suppose it more or less did but without real facilities. Snack service arrives aboard in the form of a man with sandwiches and coffee, although Parlour Car passengers are served at their seats by the attendant.

The reverse direction is equally slow and with the same sparse service, but border comfort is maintained, this time with the Americans coming aboard for a close examination of passengers' documents. They do not appear to enjoy finding foreigners (meaning people who are neither Canadians nor Americans) for then they must issue forms, search passports for visas, ask many questions, and get out rubber stamps. But they do manage to complete their business on the train between the border stations, leaving at Bellingham when satisfied. All baggage has to be opened, usually for a merely nominal search. On one trip, I noticed that a young German was taken off the train by the officials at Bellingham and did not rejoin by the time we had left for Seattle.

That is the story of what must be among the world's most mundane 'International' expresses. Apparently there have never been more than three a day in each direction, even when cars and buses were in their infancy. In those days, intensive sea services were more popular and almost as quick. But it is worth mentioning the benefit to foreigners of travelling at least southwards by the Pacific shoreline 'international' compared with the bus. Needing to be in Seattle by 11.30 a.m. on one occasion, I did travel by the 8 a.m. Greyhound express service out of Vancouver, due to make the 128 road miles in three hours. We came to the Peace Arch at Blaine on the border, and American officials climbed aboard, looking at documents. My passport was taken, a slip of paper inserted, and then the officials left. The paper said: 'Report to the Administration building'. I was the only 'foreigner' aboard and everyone looked daggers as I left the bus, the driver muttering about his 'skedool'. I had to fill in the immigration forms, show my visa, be checked through in the black list book, and be subjected to sundry questioning before rejoining the bus twelve minutes later. The bus did wait without grace and made it to Seattle only five minutes late, but the driver commented: 'We'd have been on time without foreigners aboard'. That would not have happened by train!

6

The Gold Rush Trail: Rails in Alaska

The United States of America was formed largely by purchases of territory, like Florida from the Spanish and Louisiana (including all the Mississippi-Missouri lands to the north-west) from the French. But by far the best bargain they drove was in 1868 when they bought Alaska from Imperial Russia for five million dollars. Thirty years afterwards, the cold remote Territory had yielded a hundred times that sum in gold from one of the biggest strikes in history.

The 'Ninety-Eight', as men called the great Gold Rush, brought the first railway to Alaska. It still survives, carrying more tourists today than it ever did miners and prospectors, most of whom had made their grim way over the Chinook Pass long before there were trains ready to carry them. It is called the 'White Pass and Yukon Railway' and its time-tables say 'Welcome to the Gold Rush Trail of '98'.

Another railway serves Alaska, this one built and owned by the Government. It is the 'Alaska Railroad', started in 1915 and completed over the 470 miles of its route in 1923, when President Harding came and drove in the 'golden spike'. This line never carried much gold but it did act, and still does act, as a lifeline for vital stores and it also carries tourists who know it as the 'Mount McKinley Park Route', passing close as it does to North America's highest mountain.

Alaska became the forty-ninth State of the Union in post-war years, which has given it a population boost and brought more prosperity to a cold and somewhat inhospitable land stretching into the Arctic Circle. The wartime Alaskan Highway built across Canada took away its utter dependence upon Seattle and the Pacific North-West, while air transportation, especially by Alaska's own jet airlines, has linked it to many parts of the States. Anchorage is now an international jet stop on Polar routes flown by Scandinavian Airlines System, Air France, B.O.A.C., Lufthansa, and particularly Japan Air Lines on the busy Europe-Tokyo service. New, too, are the vehicle ferries which sail up from Canada to the Alaskan Coast, and some of the non-car passengers on these ships are new business for the railways as they make a tourist trip inland.

Most romantic of the rails in northern latitudes is undoubtedly the White Pass and Yukon with its strong turn-of-the-century Gold Rush associations. Its narrow gauge rails may have opened too late for the 100,000 prospectors who set out for the Yukon, but it certainly brought back the 4,000 who struck it rich. Of these, by the way, it is estimated that only a hundred retained and passed on permanent wealth from the gold strikes. Most of the others were relieved of their money on their way back to Seattle or soon afterwards.

Yukon is a Territory of Canada, not yet elevated to the status of a Province. Its present population is about 14,700, including 2,300 Indians and a tiny scattering of Eskimos, but the area is 207,000 square miles, about the size of Texas. Whitehorse is the capital, and Dawson City (once one of the largest boom towns in North America) is the only other place with a reasonable population. To reach Whitehorse, the White Pass and Yukon Railway starts from Skagway on the ice-free coast and crosses the Alaska Panhandle before nipping into a corner of British Columbia. It then winds its way through the Yukon Territory for fifty-eight miles. The total distance of the main line is only 110, but they are hard and scenic miles, some of the most difficult ever built in the world. As the official history of the line says, it was a thousand miles from the closest base of supplies, and there was no heavy construction equipment. With nothing but horses, shovels, black powder, and men, the right of way was hacked through barriers of solid rock in temperatures which stayed below freezing point for eight months of the year and often sank to 40° below zero (at which point Fahrenheit and Centigrade are the same) for weeks on end.

Above. The view from one of the four vistadomes fitted to the Northern Pacific's 'North Coast Limited' as it nears Custer, Montana.

Below. Another view from a vistadome on the 'North Coast Limited'.

Above. With the Rockies in the distance, the 'North Coast Limited' halts at Livingston, Montana, Gateway to the Yellowstone Park.

Below. Indicative of the high standards of passenger convenience, maintained by the railway company, the vistadomes are washed at Livingston.

Above. Breakfast aboard the Northern Pacific's 'North Coast Limited'.

Below. The scene at Bellingham, Washington State, as the 'Great Northern International' stops just south of the Canadian Border.

The Gold Rush to Alaska resulted in this narrow gauge 2. 8. 0. of the
where it is preserved to this day.

d Yukon Railway coming to Dawson City, Yukon Territory, in 1899,

Above. Passengers alighting from the 'International Limited' at Vancouver.

Below. Inside the parlour car en route from Seattle to Vancouver.

A recent photograph of Juneau, capital of Alaska.

Above. Train No. 101 from St. Johns to Port-aux-Basques arrives at Gander railway station.

Below. The Trans-Newfoundland express near Gaff-Topsails the highest part of the island province.

The first train actually ran on July 21st, 1898, but only for a length of four miles out of Skagway. The 'golden spike' was driven on July 29th, 1900, and a train service over the complete length began the following day. Three years later the Gold Rush was a nearly forgotten event and traffic was minimal but the line survived and today it carries a great deal of produce over a new 'container route' on an integrated system, the products of the Yukon being brought by road to Whitehorse, then railed to Skagway, and then put aboard a 4,000-ton container ship for the coastal passage to Vancouver or to Juneau, coastal capital of Alaska. Tourists bring better summer traffic than the miners of old, and a fleet of heavy duty diesel locomotives and good rolling stock handles both freight and passenger trains.

Waiting by the wharf in Skagway, now a sleepy little port with only 750 inhabitants, will be a train of about six passenger cars with good-sized observation windows, hauled by a diesel unit and booster, the whole lot painted dark green and gold. To many Americans, the train seems miniscule due to the three-foot gauge, but in fact it is as large as British trains running on the standard (4 feet 8½ inches) gauge which are limited by a tight 'loading' gauge. There is a service all year round, the winter train leaving at 9 a.m. on Mondays to Fridays and the summer one every day at 11 a.m. For cruise ships there is a special train operated as far as Bennett, about halfway to Whitehorse, where lunch is served before returning to the coast.

Starting away, the train almost immediately begins to climb, for it has to top the summit of White Pass, 2,885 feet above sea level, in the first twenty-one miles, with an average gradient of 1 in 38 but with the steepest sections 1 in 25. All along the track are 'Points of Interest' markers which should be spotted by passengers and identified by numbers on the Information Map given on board the train. There are twenty-two of these markers, two of which are of outstanding interest. No. 8, marked Milepost 19, is Dead Horse Gulch, a view of the old trail at a point where 3,000 pack animals perished during the Gold Rush. No. 19, marked Milepost 106, is Miles Canyon where Jack London earned his living piloting canoe outfits through the rushing waters.

5—RR

The normal daily passenger train for tourists takes about five hours of running to reach Whitehorse, but in fact this is extended to five hours, forty minutes overall because both north- and south-bound trains stop for lunch at Lake Bennett, forty-one miles from Skagway. It is served in what the railway calls 'family style' at a place where some 10,000 prospectors once stopped to build rafts and boats to carry them through the chain of lakes to the Yukon River. Trains in winter are allowed an hour longer on the whole journey due to snow conditions.

Stations on the line are few, and most are only wayside halts with switches or loops. Glacier is the first one, near the only tunnel on the line, a 250-foot bore through perpendicular rock a thousand feet above the floor of the gulch. Men had to be suspended on ropes from the top of the cliff to drill and blast away the rock. Then comes White Pass, which is the summit of the line and the border crossing between Alaska (U.S.A.) and Canada. Non-North American passengers will have to fill up a form and show a passport here, and, returning from the Yukon, must be sure to have a valid U.S. visa. White Pass is just over twenty miles from Skagway. Log Cabin, a fair description of the 'station', is thirty-three miles out, and Bennett forty-one, then comes Pennington, marking more or less the British Columbia-Yukon border (one without formalities) at fifty-two miles. Carcross is the main station on the line, a definite Yukon town where the Canadian Customs and Immigration are based, sixty-seven miles from Skagway. Cowley comes up at ninety miles out, then at the 104th mile post the line crosses the Alaska Highway, but without a station of any kind although a dwelling or two in the vicinity makes up a hamlet called Macrea. Finally, the wooden terminus at Whitehorse is reached at 110 miles. Apart from the scenery and the romantic history, game in the form of moose and caribou and even on occasions bear are the things to watch for.

The Alaska Railroad is a much larger and grander proposition, built to standard gauge under an Act of the United States Congress. The main line, extending from Seward to Fairbanks, is 470 miles long, and other lines such as the Alaska Northern to Kern Creek, seventy-one miles, and the Tanana Valley from Fairbanks to Chatanika, thirty-nine miles, were purchased by the Government, converted or modernized, and brought into the system in 1923. There are river boats and diesel tugs belonging to the railroad which operate on waterways during the open season.

During the Second World War further lines were built, including one with two tunnels, two and a half miles and one mile long. A complete rehabilitation programme was put into effect in 1947, replacing 70-lb. rails with 115-lb. ones, erecting steel bridges, smoothing curves, and easing gradients. The terminus at Fairbanks was demolished and a new modern structure erected in 1950, the plan being for it to accommodate a railway running all the way to the United States, but this project is not likely in the present railway atmosphere, to reach fruition. Diesel traction was introduced progressively during the 1950s but three 2–8–0 steam locomotives were retained for working specials until 1962, when two were preserved.

Scenery during the ride up from Anchorage to Fairbanks, the 356 miles of line over which a streamlined passenger train operates, is outstanding. The emphasis is on Mount McKinley National Park and the great 20,000-foot mountain after which it is named. As this mountain stands out of a relatively low plain and rears up 17,000 feet, it is one of the most spectacular in the world. Views of it are obtained over many miles during the course of the journey, although the nearest point to which the railroad comes is forty-six miles, at milepost 279.

Although it starts at Seward, the 114 miles from this ice-free fjord port to Anchorage carries only freight traffic with a mixed train for passengers not connecting the same day with the Aurora Express from Anchorage to Fairbanks. Another mixed train runs from the port of Whittier to Anchorage, sixty-two and a half miles. Marine train services called, variously, 'Aqua Train', 'Alaska Train-Ship' and 'Hydro Train' come into Seward and Whittier, from which ports there are good roads to Anchorage for buses, trucks and private cars (the latter can be conveyed by coastal sea ferries up from Vancouver). Both highway and railroad from Seward take the route through Moose Pass, 486 feet, when coming inland, but there are no outstanding climbs or engineering features on this section to compare with the Skagway-White Pass line further south. A view at

Potter, 100 miles from Seward, can in fine weather extend to Mount Iliamna, 145 miles away to the south-west.

Anchorage is a city of 49,700 people, badly damaged recently by earthquakes but now almost rebuilt with pre-stressed buildings rising to twelve storeys. It is only thirty-eight feet above sea level, with fjord-type surroundings and hard-looking mountains apparently always snow-covered. My first sight of it was landing in what was locally early morning after a flight directly across the North Pole from Hamburg in a DC8 jet of Japan Air Lines. It was mid-June but the snow-line was very low and the breakfast time temperature was not much above freezing point. In fact, Anchorage does get midday sum-mer temperatures in the low to middle seventies (Fahrenheit), while January ones have been down as far below zero as minus forty. Modern though some of the new buildings are, there is a rugged atmosphere, and this is aided by a gigantic stuffed Kodiak bear at the airport entrance. Kodiak bears come from the island of that name, and are considerably larger and more dangerous than the famous grizzly.

The city lies on a peninsula created by the Turnagain Arm and the Knik Arm, both fjords off the Cook Inlet. At the modern railroad station the 'Aurora' lives up to its name by being ready to depart at what is dawn for many months of the year, nine o'clock in the morning. Midnight blue and orange is the colour motif for the General Motors diesel and its booster, also the coaches, the broad orange being sandwiched between the blues. This is a day-train operation and therefore carries only coaches plus baggage and mail cars and a snack-bar diner. The coaches are marked in big letters 'Alaska Railroad', and in smaller letters 'U.S. Department of the Interior'. This is the only railway, and I think the only transportation system for public use in any of the fifty States, *built* and operated by the Federal Government's Department of Transportation.

The 'Aurora' takes exactly twelve hours, if it runs to schedule, to cover the 356 miles, which requires an average of almost thirty miles an hour. This includes ten compulsory stops at stations and allowance for slowing down in readiness for thirty-eight flag stops at unmanned wayside huts. The line climbs to a height of 2,337 feet at the summit of Broad Pass, where the Continental Divide is crossed 312 miles from Seward (198 miles from Anchorage) at about 3.40 p.m. As with all especially scenic rail trips, it requires clear weather, not necessarily sunny but a day without fog or rain, to get the best from the line. Winter is clearer, with sharper views in brisk cold, in Alaska, but there is an even chance of good sunny weather in June, July and August. In winter, with only the rare, hardy tourist about, the train runs twice a week, on Tuesdays and Saturdays from Anchorage, returning the following day.

A station stop at milepost 347.9 from Seward (233.6 from Anchorage) is called Mount McKinley Park, the gateway to the Park itself and with road access by bus to the new hotel (200 beds) which is the headquarters of the Park. This covers a vast area, embracing wilderness, mighty mountains including 17,000-foot Mt. Foraker, 14,960-foot Mt. Hunter, and 11,500-foot Mt. Russell as well as the peak after which it is named, and within its borders live some 112 kinds of birds and 35 species of mammal. Caribou herds and giant Alaska moose are the most often seen. Bighorn sheep and Toklat grizzly bears are the most sought after by wild-life photographers.

Where gold was the *raison d'être* and life blood of the White Pass and Yukon, the Government-owned Alaska Railroad is a service enterprise for transport of coal from the Suntana and Matanuska mines (both on branch lines), provision of essential passenger and goods service over 300 roadless miles, and the promotion of tourism. Fairbanks, thanks to the railway, is a growing city and has within its boundary the northernmost university in North America. There are times in winter when only the train can move from Fairbanks, so low are the temperatures. On January 20th, 1971, the morning reading was minus 79° Fahrenheit . . .

7

The 'Newfie Bullet'
through the Wilderness

Thanks to John Cabot, some forty days out of Bristol in the very late part of the fifteenth century, Newfoundland became one of the first settlements on the North American continent. A century before the Pilgrim Fathers set out for New England, men of Devon and Dorset were living and fishing and boating around the rugged shores of the big island in the Labrador Current. There was little change over the centuries and Britain's oldest colony failed either to prosper or expand. A brief period of independence in the nineteen-twenties resulted in bankruptcy followed by the restoration of colonial status.

The Second World War brought some wealth to Newfoundland with its ports in heavy use, its iron ore in constant demand, and its fisheries working to capacity. Reluctant to see the brighter situation fade, Newfoundlanders voted in 1948 to join the Dominion of Canada, and by April 1st, 1949, they had become a fully-fledged Canadian Province, which is a very satisfactory solution. But they had one dowry from Mother England. A railway crossed the island from the Atlantic-facing capital of St. John's for 548 miles to Port aux Basques where the ferries started for the hundred-mile sea link to Nova Scotia.

The Newfoundland Government Railway was built to a narrow, three foot six inch, gauge through utter wilderness, forest and mountain and river, during the great, proud years of British railway construction abroad. It held the poor, undeveloped and sparsely inhabited Colony together and gave it a lifeline to nearby Canada which the ships from England, once quite frequent, could not do all year round due to ice problems at St. John's in the winter. The actual promoter and operator of the railway in its early years from 1893 to 1923 was Sir Robert Reid of Montreal, a Scottish-Canadian.

Trains were not fast, and the going was rough as they climbed to windy heights on the central plateau, fighting great snowdrifts in winter. But they did the sort of job, with fish and passenger traffic, that was called for by such a small population up to the end of 1939. Then the war's impact was felt in Newfoundland in some unexpected ways. It was the aeroplane that made most demands upon the railway and brought it important revenue which continues to this day. Other requirements were the movement of large numbers of military and naval personnel, of iron ore to safer ports, and of newsprint from outports to major collection areas.

It must be remembered that in 1939, Newfoundland, like most of Canada, was a roadless semi-wilderness. Where roads and tracks did exist, they were dirt and quagmire. When Imperial Airways, forerunners of B.O.A.C. decided to open a trans-Atlantic air service with flying boats between Foynes in Ireland and Botwood in Newfoundland, they had to look to the railway to bring building materials and personnel to the site. Had a passenger schedule begun with the 'C' class flying boats of those days, people would have been moved by rail to Port Aux Basques for access to the Canadian Maritimes, and to St. John's. But the outbreak of war stopped proving flights and for a while, trans-Atlantic flying on a commercial basis was solely in the hands of Pan American's Clippers between New York, the Azores and Lisbon.

The year 1940 however saw a number of senior Royal Air Force and Royal Canadian Air Force officers and surveyors examining the line of rail across Newfoundland. They came to the shores of a big lake in fairly flat country near a halt called by some people Fisherman's Crossing and by the Government Railway officials 'Gander Lake crossing loop'. There they started work and before long the whole area was a seething mass of workmen and equipment engaged in tree-felling and earth-levelling operations. Gander Airport was being born and its birth throes kept the Newfoundland Government Railway very busy. The site chosen was 213 miles from St. John's and

335 miles from Port Aux Basques, so the hauls by freight and passenger train were long. There were no towns in the accepted sense of the term nearer than Grand Falls, sixty-four miles away, and that was only a village by most standards. Local resources could not match the demands of hungry, thirsty men, starved of entertainment, for once the builders had gone vast numbers of Canadian servicemen moved in to undertake the defence of Gander. By June 1940, Canadian troops were looking after the entire defence of Newfoundland, including Gander, and the Botwood seaplane base.

It was about this time that servicemen riding the slow trains twisting and turning across the hilly empty land facetiously christened the daily 'express' they were forced to use between St. John's and Port Aux Basques, the 'Newfie Bullet'. Despite its shortcomings, and the grit that swept into the wooden coaches from two hard-working steam engines during summer, they developed quite an affection for the train, especially when westbound on leave, and many rowdy parties are reported by railwaymen who worked on the line at that period. Somehow, the single narrow line stood up to the heavy usage and played a vital part in the war effort, feeding and supplying Gander with the fuel for long range aircraft, moving the ore shipped in from Belle Isle, and getting newsprint from Botwood and Cornerbrook to ships lying in main harbours. One night in 1943, the train lost almost all its through passengers from Canada when the Government Railway ferry from Sydney, Cape Breton, was torpedoed and sunk on its way to Port Aux Basques.

Gander Airport was in constant use by Hudsons and later Liberators being flown directly across the Atlantic, or to Iceland. Soon a town grew up around the airport, and it is now, with a population of 10,000, the most important place and station on the trans-island line between St. John's and Cornerbrook (405 miles from the capital, where Bowaters have their paper plant).

Gander's great days as a commercial airport are over, ended by the big jets with long range, but in the years between 1946 and 1958, Gander was the World's Coffee Stop. All civilian flights landed there, or at Goose Bay in Labrador, developed as an alternate airport soon after Gander was built. They refuelled before, or after, the Atlantic crossing, and passengers went into the vast huts for a cup of coffee. Trains hauled millions of gallons of aviation octane to Gander station, just a few yards away from the main buildings, and base personnel travelled by the passenger train (which they still called the 'Newfie Bullet').

Too late, the Canadian Government constructed a magnificent new airport building about two miles away from the original interlinked clusters of huts. It was the first of a pattern of modern airports now spread across Canada, and the Queen opened it in 1959. But by then the prime traffic was overflying Gander and it became more and more a transit stop for lesser, propeller-driven charter flights to and from Europe. The scheduled service is by Air Canada, formerly known as Trans-Canada Airlines, but even in summer this is only twice weekly from London, falling to once a week in winter. Local flights go to St. John's once or twice daily, and to Nova Scotia by Maritime Central Airways not more than once a day. There are no longer enough services to pay landing fees sufficient to make Gander a viable economic proposition, but it remains a safeguard against emergencies of all kinds and has military support in consequence.

Great changes have come to the railway, too. Shortly after Newfoundland became part of Canada, the Government of Canada's Canadian National Railways system absorbed the local line and the shipping services around the coasts, including the ferries to Nova Scotia. Canadian National soon began to spend a great deal of money on straightening out the curves, smoothing some of the worst gradients, and up-dating rolling stock. In 1959 they brought narrow gauge diesel locomotives into use, and the whole atmosphere of the 'Newfie Bullet' changed. By 1960 the daily express had become a modern train with dining and sleeping cars and even air-conditioning, speeded up to travel the 548 miles across the Island Province in twenty-two hours.

In 1965 under the energetic insistence of Mr. J. R. Smallwood, Premier of Newfoundland, the Trans-Canada Highway was completed across the island, and paved for most of the way. It takes a more northerly route than the railway and loses out on some of the best scenery, but follows it to Gander. As a result, the railway lost most of even the small amount of aviation spirit haulage it had retained, and passenger traffic fell off. However, hard work by Canadian National and new low fares with inclusive meal arrangements for sleeping car passengers kept some sound business for the train, and the 'Caribou', as the daily in summer and thrice-weekly in winter train was called, was far from empty. A new type of business began to appear in summer, with people from Europe landing at Gander after the Air Canada flight (the shortest and cheapest trans-Atlantic crossing) and taking the train onwards for an eventual all-Canada tour. The 'Canrailpass' costing $99 for thirty days, available on all Canadian National trains, meant that a passenger could go from Newfoundland to Vancouver and back by a varied route without additional rail fare.

Nemesis has now overtaken the 'Caribou', as was, I suppose, inevitable once air-conditioned buses were put on the Highway by Canadian National. They are much faster than the narrow gauge and can do the run from St. John's to Port aux Basques in a day, from 8.15 a.m. to 10 p.m. in the case of a daily 'Expedo' vehicle with a comfort-room (as North Americans refer to toilets) and box meals picked up at stops. The railway continues as a freight line and a passenger train is kept in reserve for emergencies, such as total winter blockages by snow of the Newfoundland Highway. The train, with a couple of 'buffet-sleepers' and coaches, has rolled a few times along its hard road but in the main it has not been running since the end of summer in 1969.

One hot day late in July 1966, I landed at Gander from an Air Canada DC8 which had brought me from Glasgow in just over four hours. Spending the night at the Gander Hotel, one of several which had sprung up in the widening township in recent years (mainly to take care of delayed flight passengers), I left by taxi for Gander station early the next morning.

It was a brilliant summer's morning with the sun rising warmly in a cloudless sky, as only an Atlantic seaboard day in July can be, and Newfoundland, for all its winter winds and Grand Bank fogs, has a very fair share of such days between June and the end of August. Train Number 101, the 'Caribou' came slowly from the east out of the rising sun, hauled by twin 900 class 'hood' diesel units, and stopped at 6.24 a.m., exactly on time. Its long line of smart, well-kept coaches, diners and Pullmans had left St. John's the night before at 9.30 p.m., and as I boarded and found my way to the Pullman section indicated on my ticket, passengers were stirring behind their heavy curtains and some were dressing for breakfast. The only extra fare I had to pay for riding in a 'day Pullman' was five dollars, and this included breakfast, lunch and dinner.

Some children bound for a summer camp had joined the coaches at Gander, and one or two Pullman passengers had alighted, but it was clear that after its eighteen years of air activity and bustle, Gander—both from the railway and the civil aviation points of view—was fast receding into its previous wayside status. But just as we left the station, with locomotive bells clanging in true North American railroading style, a DC4 in the markings of a Scandinavian charter company swooped low over us on its way in from Europe, a customer for Gander's fuel and facilities still in the propeller age.

The track very soon became single and as we gained speed the spruce woods crowded in, the large airport terminal buildings disappearing behind thickening forest. At thirty-five miles an hour, which was about the fastest sustained running speed, the rolling stock did, indeed, roll. However, a permitted maximum of fifty miles an hour started at milepost 245 from St. Johns, and the going was smoother at this faster pace, evidence of the work done by Canadian National on the original light roadbed. We stopped briefly at a hut called Glenwood at 7 a.m., and I went along to the diner for breakfast. This proved to be a substantial Canadian one, excellently prepared in very pleasant surroundings, and by the time I had finished the train was pulling in to quite a large station called Bishop's Falls. Here we remained for twenty-five minutes while the train was serviced with fresh water, the windows cleaned, and the locomotive crew changed. In steam days, this had been a locomotive changing point (Clarenville, 131 miles out of St. John's, was the first, Bishops Falls, at 267 miles, was second, and Corner Brook, 405 miles, was third) but now the twin diesels were expected to go all the way across Newfoundland.

Before I left the diner to go for a short walk along the train, the courteous head waiter asked me if I would like fresh Arctic

Char for lunch. He agreed to have this caught and put aboard at a way stop later in the morning, when it would be broiled in the train's kitchen.

We pulled out at 8.45 a.m. and passed over a trestle bridge with fine views of rushing water. By ten past nine we had stopped at the township of Grand Falls, the cascade of whose waters could be heard in the distance. Close by is the town of Windsor, served by bus and a freight branch. It was always possible to flagstop the 'Caribou' at most wayside huts with names, but this did not happen as we passed Badger, Collishaws, and Jerrett. The country was becoming more open, with fewer trees and only sparse vegetation as we climbed on to moorland not unlike Dartmoor with jagged 'tors' showing up in the distance. Millertown Junction was a compulsory stop at 10.25 a.m., and a number of men from a work train off the privately owned ore branch joined us. Both diesels were roaring and the speed had fallen to about twenty miles an hour as we wound into the hilly country beyond, passing West Brook and then Clarke to touch the 2,000-foot mark. In winter the snow drifts deeply on this exposed section of line, and is cleared by rotary ploughs which pile it into banks on either side, so high that the width of loads is reduced in winter by six inches, and the clearance from either side of a loaded freight car is cut from two feet to one foot one-and-a-half inches.

Really hard railroading is the order of the day throughout the long winter all the way across this high wilderness. Very rarely is a train seriously delayed, but later on there is another hazard in the form of fierce winds which have been known to blow complete trains off the tracks. As it was, summer conditions were pleasant and cool, with wide views across an area which has been declared 'natural wilderness' without the designation 'National Park'. One can see moose from the train, but those towards the rear of it do not get a chance of a photograph since the animals tend to run away as soon as the roaring diesels get near them. Herds of caribou keep away from the track-side but can usually be seen in clusters on the skyline. Caribou are, of course, a type of Canadian reindeer, but the moose is not the same as the European elk, being the largest and heaviest buck in existence.

Summit is reached at milepost 328.3 from St. John's, when the train is 2,206 feet above sea level. The curious mountains jutting high out of the moorland are the Topsails, and the train passes close to Gaff Topsail which is on the left going westwards. A small station of the same name serves the area and is a request stop at 11.10 a.m. For the first two miles downhill the speed is allowed to rise to fifty miles an hour, but rocking is considerable and brake snatch shows up violently towards the rear of the train. After Gaff Topsail the speed limit is thirty to thirty-five miles an hour, but motion is not particularly smooth.

Tiny stations are passed going downhill and twisting towards the treeline, names such as Pond Crossing and Kitty's Brook going past without the likelihood of a passenger wanting to get on or off. But at Howley there is a compulsory stop at two minutes past noon, and a few shacks indicate the presence of a small railway community in the wilderness with a school and church (both wooden). Then there are more little wayside huts set in spruce forests, with glimpses of rushing rivers, the oddly named Northern and then Humber Canal sliding by.

When the 'Caribou' stopped at Deer Lake at 12.35 p.m., the children who had boarded at Gander, together with a fair number of others who had been on since St. John's, alighted and formed up under one or two leaders. This was the site of their summer camp. I took advantage of the stop and the smoother conditions to walk through the Pullman cars (these were special narrow gauge stock with longitudinal make-up berths and a drawing room at each end with let-down beds) to the diner, where my Arctic Char was cooking.

An excellent lunch of appetizer, hot soup, Arctic Char and mashed potatoes (Arctic Char turned out to be a firm pink fish very like sea trout), apple pie and ice cream and coffee, was enjoyed while the train wandered through the Bowater Park at Pasadena, past South Brook and Steady Brook, with big trees and general forest interspersed with clearings. In one of these, with a picnic site around it, stood a steam locomotive of the former Newfoundland Government Railway, mounted on a sturdy plinth.

We pulled in to the big town and important division point of

Corner Brook at 1.45 p.m., exactly on time. The second city of Newfoundland, Corner Brook is a maze of sidings and piers, with the enormous paper mills of Bowaters spreading along the waterfront. The 'Caribou' stayed thirty minutes here, time for a walk round, and to see the eastbound passenger train come in. Two private coaches for chief inspectors were lying in the sidings, and one of these was attached to the eastbound 'Caribou'. There was another crew change on the leading diesel and the conductors switched over. I appreciated a unique touch here, whereby a train news bulletin, giving world, local and train running information, was circulated to all passengers by the Corner Brook station staff.

Leaving at 2.15 p.m., we climbed slowly out of the station and up a single track which wound round and above the harbour, giving a fine view of the shipping and the huge plant. The Trans-Canada Highway comes in here, and more or less follows the route of the railway from Corner Brook down to Port Aux Basques. Today's bus passengers will have missed the grandeur of the wilderness and the Topsails. We were soon into the limitless spruce forests again, that valuable source of paper pulp exported by Newfoundland's British paper-makers at Corner Brook and Botwood. Little wayside huts with names were passed at speeds ranging from thirty to fifty miles an hour, Curling, Cooke, and Beaver, until we stopped briefly at Spruce Brook at 3.10 p.m. Then came the fastest run of the whole trip, travelling beside a picturesque river at forty-five to fifty miles an hour for about twenty-three miles to the relatively important stop at Stephenville Crossing. Here was a small community sleeping in what I was told was an unusually hot sun, and lightly clad boys and girls were playing beside the river. One could see the sea and beyond the deep inlet there was a view to Newfoundland's uninhabited north-west peninsula with its high mountains.

Leaving Stephenville Crossing, 452½ miles from St. John's and 230 miles from Gander (we had covered this in nine hours forty minutes at an average of just under twenty-five miles an hour including stops, which was not bad for a heavy train over narrow gauge with severe curves), we ran through Western, St. Georges, Joyce, Flat Bay, and St. Teresa to a stop at Fischell at 4.48 p.m. These are only names on huts, and very rarely is there any sign of life; they exist for self-help in case a trapper, logger, or fisherman wants to stop the train with the signal arm fitted at the side of the named hut, but of course enginemen know where the flag-halts are and keep a careful lookout for passengers, ready to ease down immediately. When this does happen, the brakes are felt violently all along the train.

After Fischell we passed Robinson's, which I gather was a fisherman's camp, and then made a compulsory stop at Cartyville. We were getting towards the sea-girt area where winter gales are magnified and sometimes reach 125 miles an hour. There is a wind-measuring anemometer at Cape Ray further along the line, and when the force exceeds ninety miles an hour all trains are halted. At all times speed restrictions are imposed, with a top limit at thirty-five, but this is more for track weakness resulting from great gales than for the wind itself. However, on the sunny, quiet July day when I was travelling no adverse signals or information about heavy winds came to hand so we proceeded normally.

At 6 p.m. there was a call to dinner, a meal normally taken early throughout Canada, but even earlier in the Maritimes and rural areas, for most families have a huge breakfast, a light lunch (sandwich and milk or hamburger) then a big dinner early in the evening followed by a substantial supper before going to bed. Having had a large and adequate lunch at 1 p.m., though, I was not ready to do justice to another full and well-prepared Canadian National meal in this hospitable diner, and chose the lightest items from the menu.

Meanwhile we had run slowly along the shoreline, with fjord-type scenery and a great deal of rock. The train eased through Codroy Pond and Wesley, then was flagged to a stop at South Branch with a jerk which upset a good many glasses of water and cups of coffee in the diner. At Riverview, ten minutes later, we made another stop. Less than thirty miles remained to the terminus at Port Aux Basques, and this was travelled in fractionally over an hour with halts at Cape Ray—a desolate outpost even on a fine day with broad sea views—and Dennis. We came round sharp bends in the rocky hills and soon saw the port and its buildings ahead. Port Aux Basques was revealed as a sort of Fishguard and Kyle of Lochalsh rolled into one, obviously a packet port carved with difficulty out of living rock.

A large new hotel appeared by the lineside, opened soon after the introduction of car ferries on the Sydney (Cape Breton) to Newfoundland service. I was told that until the coming of this hotel, any serious delay to a ferry meant that passengers stayed the night aboard the train. Despite formidable railway operating problems in winter, it was very rare for the train to miss the ferry, although the ferry in bad weather often missed the train or simply did not sail. There are now three ships on this run, two built in Quebec, the other obtained second-hand from a German company and converted rather crudely. It was with this latter ship, now named *William Carlson*, that I was to travel, and looking out of the window of my Pullman as we turned on the 'Y' so that the engines faced back up the line towards St. John's, there was no trace of her.

I left the train at about 7.35 p.m. (we had been on time) and went into the terminal waiting room. We were supposed to embark at 8 p.m. and sail at 9 p.m., but it was 8.30 p.m. before the ship docked and 9.45 p.m. before they began to let people aboard. There were line-ups for cabins and more line-ups for stewards to take bags down the steep companion-ways to lower deck cabins. The stewards turned out to be students doing vacation jobs and service was at a minimum, in complete contrast to the courtesy and efficiency of the train. Cabins were bare of mats, narrow and sparse, while the lounge and the open deck had slippery, cheap-looking composition flooring. We sailed at 11 p.m. but in good weather arrived at North Sydney shortly before 7 a.m., less than an hour late. Breakfast was a matter of cafeteria service with limited choice.

Sydney was to be my destination on this occasion, and soon after 8 a.m. I was met and escorted to a car, but most passengers from the St. John's train had to take a taxi (for them an unexpected chore and expense) to North Sydney main station where the rail-liners for Halifax and Truro waited. Through trains coming to the ferry's side were reinstated for Expo '67 year and a through run continues now all the way to Montreal, a welcome convenience and improvement.

There is a new ferry link from Sydney now going direct to Argentia near St. John's, cutting out both the trans-Newfoundland highway and the virtually defunct passenger train, but it is a hard sea trip much of the time and already one ship has been lost.

8

Still the Premier Line: the 'Royal Highlander'

From the earliest days of railways, the line that struck north-westwards from London's Euston Station to the Midlands and the Cumberland border was known as the Premier Line. Euston was, of course, the first real railway terminus to be built in the world, and there was no expense spared in creating the splendid square at its approaches and the noble Doric arch, while the enormous carved and painted roof of the Great Hall, designed by Hawkshaw, had no equal in the world until its total destruction by the iconoclasts of Britain's nationalized railway system in the early 1960s. As the London and Birmingham Railway, the line was a going concern and open for 105 miles *before* Queen Victoria came to the throne of England in 1837. Ten years later it had become the London and North-Western Railway, with a main line 299 miles long from Euston to Carlisle.

It called itself the Premier Line and it encouraged this expression in contemporary newspapers and journals, although there were plenty of contenders for the title, such as the Great Northern and the Great Western, to say nothing of the Midland, whose permanent way was considered the best laid in the entire world. Later events, including the grouping of 1923 when the London and North-Western became a major constituent of the London Midland and Scottish Railway, tended to put the title Premier Line into the background, recalled only occasionally by railway historians. However, in recent years a mammoth spending effort resulted in the rebuilding of the main line from London to Crewe and the branches to Liverpool and Manchester, when it was equipped with overhead electrification on the 25 kv. A.C. system so successfully adopted in France.

Despite vested interests, particularly from road operators and lobbying in Government departments, the work was carried through to completion in eight years, and in 1966 the first electric passenger trains began to run from Euston through to Crewe, Liverpool and Manchester. Suddenly, the title Premier Line was revived in a blaze of glory triggered off by the success of inaugural trains which ran the 158 miles to Crewe in 111 minutes, despite an April blizzard. For over a year this high-speed success continued to become marred and blunted by single manning disputes, clumsily handled by both the British Railways Board and the railway unions.

A journey over this Premier Line, still regarded as the 'Great Highway' to the north, may have lost some of the romance of earlier days, but let us take a look even now at the route of the 'Royal Highlander' as it covers the 568 miles from Euston to Inverness on an overnight run. The 'Royal Highlander' may come to the end of its own journey once it reaches the handsome terminal station of Inverness, but there, pointed northwards, is another train waiting to take passengers to Wick and Thurso, the furthest north in Britain.

The 'Royal Highlander' has, since its inception well before the turn of the century (although its name has differed through the various decades), always been one of the two dinner, bed and breakfast trains to operate in Britain. The idea is to have dinner after leaving Euston and to be called for breakfast somewhere between Perth and Inverness, so that one can enjoy one's kippers or bacon and eggs as the Scottish Highlands unfurl past the window.

Today electrification has so speeded the southern part of the journey that departure has been set back to 8.20 p.m. instead of 7.15 p.m. and the arrival in Inverness is now 8.20 a.m. instead of 9 o'clock. The principle remains, however, of dinner, bed and breakfast en route, even if the call the following morning is rather earlier than it used to be. Today's 'Royal Highlander' has a long rake of sleeping cars, plus some ordinary first and second class carriages and two restaurant cars. At its head will be one of the new 3,200 b.h.p. electric locomotives humming powerfully without any emission of fumes or evil smells. As it gathers speed on departure from Euston, the steep ascent to Camden bank is accomplished with no apparent effort, the days of banking engines rousing the echoes of the inner suburban houses having faded into history, just as the hideous roaring of overworked diesels clambering up the bank has also become part of a brief and somewhat sordid immediate past. Within three minutes of departure and at the top of a gradient of 1 in 60, the train is probably doing thirty miles an hour, and on the right can be seen the famous Camden Town Roundhouse, the first classically designed engine shed in the world, which is now used by an artistic group for theatrical and other purposes.

Fast running through the Primrose Hill tunnel and past the ruins of Willesden Junction brings the express into the "Middlesex" suburbs and speed mounts rapidly towards ninety miles an hour. This pace is maintained over long welded track through Harrow and Bushey to Watford Junction, eighteen miles out and passed these days in less than eighteen minutes from departure, a feat known in railway parlance as 'even time'. First dinner is being served in the restaurant cars during this section of the journey, while first class passengers usually enjoy just one sitting, enabling them to take their time and perhaps end the meal with a liqueur which will prompt sleep.

Quite likely the first hundred-miles-an-hour burst will be attained somewhere on the four-track line near Hemel Hempstead, and in these days the long climb to Tring Summit, where the London and North-Western Railway breasted the Chiltern Hills, no longer has any effect upon the powerful electric locomotives. It may well be that, tearing down the other side of the Chilterns past Cheddington and the site of the famous £2,000,000 train robbery of 1963, speed may creep up beyond the loosely permitted maximum of one hundred, but will be held in check around the 105 m.p.h. mark. Leighton Buzzard flashes past, and then it is the turn of Bletchley, forty-six miles out and passed in forty minutes. From here onwards the Premier Line becomes double track and soon the Northampton branch goes off to the right, then the train thunders through Roade Cutting, scene of one of the magnificent primitive engineering feats of Robert Stephenson whose men had to dig out this deep cutting with picks and shovels and push their wheelbarrows up the incredibly steep sides. Many a labourer lost his footing and fell back to be crushed beneath the weight of his barrow and its debris.

A few miles further on the train hurtles through Kilsby tunnel, one of the first long railway tunnels ever built, which claimed some twenty-six lives before it was opened at the very beginning of Queen Victoria's reign. Passengers get frequent glimpses of the M1 motorway paralleling the tracks to the right of the train near Kilsby tunnel. These days, with the motorway speed limit held to seventy miles an hour, even the fastest cars are quickly left behind. The 'Royal Highlander' flashes through Rugby Station, eighty-two and a half miles from Euston, in about sixty-three minutes from the start, and then follows the long undulating passage across the Midland Plain and through the valley of the Trent.

Nuneaton and then Lichfield are cleared at high speed, and later there is a slight slowing for Stafford, with its huge electrical factories. Less than two hours out from Euston the brakes are applied just after passing over the top of Whitmore Summit for the descent into the first stop at Crewe. It was on this descent that the 'Coronation Scot' in 1937 was urged up to a speed of 114 miles an hour in order to beat the existing world's speed record with steam achieved on the London and North-Eastern Railway earlier in the same year. On that famous occasion the Coronation Scot was unable to pull up in the brief time available before the maze of points marking Crewe Station came into sight, and the big crossovers were taken with the train still doing fifty-eight miles an hour. An enormous amount of damage was done inside the dining car, and most people were thrown about with some violence although the coaches stayed on the line, and somehow the driver managed to bring his locomotive to a halt right at the end of Crewe platform.

That was in fact the major steam achievement of the Premier Line, but today's electric expresses reach Crewe on average in a minute less from Euston, not once a day but up to twelve times a day, and their descent of Whitmore is cautious and restrained, since the power of electric traction will have enabled them to climb the bank without any notable effort. With the 'Royal Highlander' coming to a stand in Crewe Station there is a bustle of activity as the dining cars are smartly whipped away. The electric engine is uncoupled and is replaced by a diesel, usually an English Electric Class 42. The fastest six hour day-time expresses to Glasgow are given two diesels at Crewe these days but forthcoming electrification will soon dispense with this waste.

There is no point, of course, in hauling a dining car through the night and at this juncture most people are already retiring to their sleeping berths. There are 141 miles separating Crewe from Carlisle, and it is quite a tribute to the great workmanship that went into the locomotives of Crewe when one reflects that the performance over these 141 miles, inclusive of the stiff climb up Mount Shap, which was set up in August 1895 by a London and North-Western engine, was not beaten until 1935 on a special test run. Even the Royal Highlander of today, diesel hauled, will not achieve so good a time as the stout-hearted 2–4–0 L.N.W.R. steamer 'Hardwicke' of seventy-five years ago.

After Crewe the Royal Highlander quickly traverses the lovely Cheshire countryside before crossing the Manchester Ship Canal, to enter industrial Lancashire, passing Warrington, and Wigan, then stopping at Preston at 11.47 p.m. The country opens out after the Preston stop, but the land tends to be slightly undulating and pastoral through Lancaster and beyond the shores of Morecambe Bay until the outline of the Westmorland Fells comes into sight, or would come into sight if the train were not a night express. Travellers of the past who took the much lamented '2 p.m. Corridor' from Euston to Carlisle and Glasgow spoke eloquently of the joys of having dinner in the plush clerestoried diner with its six-wheel oak studded bogies just as the sun was setting and the slopes of the Westmorland Fells were turning mauve in the evening light.

The steep climb up Mount Shap, culminating in four miles at 1 in 75, offers some resistance to the diesel locomotives which can be heard snarling away as they struggle to hold the train speed at thirty to forty miles an hour, often equalled by 'Coronation' class Pacifics in the best years of steam traction.

Once the line to Scotland is fully electrified, however, the horrors of Shap will be no more and the 3,200 b.h.p. electric locomotives make light work of the stiff climb. The summit of Shap is 960 feet above sea level and in daylight commands a fine view of the fells and mountains of the Lake District.

It is downhill for thirty miles to Carlisle, passing Penrith station where the branch to Keswick, situated in the heart of the Lake District, swings off to the left. Carlisle is passed at 2.03 a.m. when the Citadel Station is still a hive of activity. Once a great railway centre served by the colourful trains of seven railway companies, Citadel is a mundane place these days, dealing only with diesel-hauled trains and multiple units.

Just five miles out of Carlisle the Scottish border is crossed, a moment or so after passing the demolished station of Floriston. To the left, over the marshes of the River Eden, goes the former Glasgow and South-Western main line to Glasgow by way of Dumfries and Kilmarnock, gateways to Galloway and the Burns country.

The first station across the border on that line is Gretna Green, famous for the nearby blacksmith's shop at whose anvil eloping couples from England can marry according to an ancient Scottish law. On the Caledonian main line, which is the route taken by most express trains to Scotland, including the 'Royal Scot' (by day to Glasgow) and the 'Royal Highlander', the station of Gretna is passed seven miles out of Carlisle.

On into the night the 'Royal Highlander' covers the Caledonian miles, rising gently all the way up to Lockerbie and Beattock, but then comes the second (Shap was the first) of three heavy climbs that have to be undertaken by trains going from England to beyond the main chain of Grampian Mountains in the Highlands. This one is the Beattock Bank, surmounting the Southern Uplands, and it starts in earnest just beyond Beattock Station (once the junction for the spa town of Moffat). There are ten miles at 1 in 80, with one mile as steep as 1 in 69. Speed will fall to thirty miles an hour as the diesels roar away, but no banking assistance will normally be taken. Express trains, both steam and diesel hauled, were still getting steam banking help as recently as the summer of 1966.

Down into the valley of the Clyde running is fast, the only station of note being Carstairs, passed at about a quarter past three in the morning. Some eighteen miles nearer to Glasgow the 'Royal Highlander' stops briefly for crew purposes at the big steel town of Motherwell, where the direct line to Perth and the Highlands goes off, avoiding Glasgow. This we take, through cuttings and over high grassy embankments, always in sight of industry and housing estates for nearly thirty miles, slowing through Coatbridge, but eventually joining up with the Glasgow (Queen Street) to Perth main line at Larbert, south of Stirling. Between here and Stirling the train passes Bannockburn, a great name to all true Scotsmen for here the English were defeated by the Bruce 600 years ago on a battlefield less than a mile from the lineside. With its dramatic castle, inspiring Wallace monument and proud history, Stirling marks the beginning of the Scotland of the Clans and the story books.

There is a long climb through rich scenery past Bridge of Allan and Dunblane towards Gleneagles Summit. Gleneagles is the site of the best hotel in the British Transport chain, a seasonal paradise for golfers who have a choice of several first class courses there. This is the only railway station still open on the line from Stirling to Perth, apart from Dunblane (where a branch to Oban used to start from), but there used to be some wayside halts with attractive names like Greenloaning and Forteviot and Auchterarder amid the pinewoods of Perthshire. Into Perth General shortly after half past four in the morning, the 'Royal Highlander' comes to rest in a big station which has known much busier days. During the Golden Age of railways in Britain, widely regarded as 1880 to 1914, rolling stock from every part of the country was marshalled at Perth, to be worked forward to Highland destinations ranging from Inverness, capital of the Highlands, to small private platforms serving shooting lodges. Grouse shooting traditionally begins on August 12th (the 'Glorious Twelfth') and on August 11th, 1912, a record was established at Perth General with 800 coaches passed between lines from England and southern Scotland to the Highlands. The 'Royal Highlander' itself ran in four sections that night, only it was not called by that name in those days. But now, the only marshalling will be the fitting of a restaurant car on the front of the rake of sleepers and ordinary coaches.

Away into what every traveller must hope is a bright and golden dawn, the train leaves Perth at 04.56 and heads north towards the Grampians. It passes Dunkeld, scene of Shakespeare's Macbeth, fifteen miles out, then stops briefly at Pitlochry, twenty-eight miles from Perth, before winding through the enchanting forested Pass of Killiecrankie, famous for 'Bonnie Dundee's' exploits. At Blair Atholl, thirty-seven miles out, there is a stop of longer duration, as if to get breath for the climb to Drumochter Summit. It is six o'clock in the morning and for six months of the year it will be light outside. Early morning tea is already coming round to the sleeping car passengers who have ordered an early call to watch the scenery.

Drumochter Bank is the worst in the British Isles, seventeen miles averaging 1 in 80, with an eight-mile stretch at 1 in 70 and three miles at 1 in 85. In steam days the ascent, either with two engines or one at the head and a banker at the rear, provided railway enthusiasts with a keen thrill. Today there is not much of operational interest since the power units are calculated according to train weight and merely perform their job on pushing a lever—unless a diesel breaks down, which happens not infrequently, and then it is merely a nuisance and an inconvenience waiting for rescue from Blair Atholl or Aviemore. Going up to the Pass reveals magnificent scenery, bleak moors, shapely mountains, forests, rushing burns, gorse and heather. For ten months of the year some summits will have at least a little snow on them.

Struan station, or the ruins of it, are passed four miles out of Blair Atholl, then there are ten wild, steep miles to Dalnaspidal, and three miles beyond that, in an exposed location protected by snow fences, is a big sign saying 'Drumochter Summit—1,484 feet—highest point reached by main line railway in Britain'. A descent follows through Dalwhinnie, and then the line runs through more or less level country with extremely pleasant views to the Cairngorm Mountains until Aviemore is attained at 7.17 a.m.

In the past ten years Aviemore has become world famous as a

Highland tourist centre both in summer and winter. There is a large new hotel and resort complex just outside the town catering for skiing, climbing, pony trekking and all kinds of outdoor activities. The town is the main gateway to Speyside and the Badenoch country in the Cairngorms, with plenty of hotels scattered around. It is also the 'capital' of the Speyside whisky distilleries, whose products are railed to Aviemore before going to Perth and Glasgow for blending.

It is 533¼ miles from London and only thirty-five miles remain to go before reaching Inverness as the 'Royal Highlander' pulls away from Aviemore at 7.21 a.m. The restaurant car is busy with breakfast on this last stretch, with an hour left in which to provide bacon and eggs or Scots kippers, scones and other trimmings of the first Scottish meal taken amid some of the finest scenery in the Highlands. There is one more climb to make, the steepest of all but comparatively short as the direct line to Inverness (there was another way over Dava via Forres and Nairn) is lifted over Slochd Summit. For three miles the gradient is 1 in 60, and speed falls to under twenty-five miles an hour. Once over the top the view opens out to the glorious 'Laigh O'Moray' country beside the sparkling Firth lying several hundred feet below the train. In between lies Culloden Moor which the train crosses, running through Culloden station five miles before Inverness. Close by are the graves of the Highlanders who were killed here in 1746, in the last major battle to be fought on British soil.

Mere minutes later the grey dignified buildings of the Highland capital are closing in on the line and the high hills beside the River Ness make a pleasing setting. The train stops and reverses into the small terminal station, coming to rest 568 miles from London alongside a shorter train which stands ready to leave for Wick and Thurso with some of the mail and passengers brought by the 'Royal Highlander'.

9

Story of the 'Flying Scotsman'

The oldest named train in the world and surely the most famous, the 'Flying Scotsman' still leaves London's King's Cross Station for Edinburgh every day at ten o'clock in the morning. It has done so ever since June 22nd, 1862, when the schedule called for completion of the $393\frac{3}{4}$ miles in ten and a half hours. As this timing included stops at Grantham, York, Newcastle-upon-Tyne and Berwick-on-Tweed, with an allowance for a meal in the York station restaurants, the actual running speed was well in excess of forty miles an hour.

The railways of mid-Victorian Britain were far in advance of any other country in the matter of speed and long-distance running. Since 1848 broad gauge trains of the Great Western Railway from London to Exeter were doing the 193 miles of those days (via Bristol) in four and a half hours. It was nearly forty years before any other railway system in the world came close to challenging such speeds, although the Great Northern and North-Eastern Railways, working the 'Flying Scotsman' and other expresses, were never far behind. But the world impact of such a train as the 'Flying Scotsman' running in the eighteen-sixties can hardly be described today except perhaps in terms of a South American country admiring the United States space flights by astronauts. Anywhere else in the world where about 400 miles of main line track existed at that time one might have found timings of twenty-four to twenty-six hours by the best trains.

Small wonder, then, that the 'Flying Scotsman' achieved universal fame and aided the already high prestige of Britain's railway system. It helped trade, too, because the world sought to buy British engines and equipment and more especially to employ British companies and engineers to build entire railway systems. In these present days of struggle to obtain export orders, and costly investment in projects which stand a chance of being sold abroad, we are accustomed to comparatively small returns provided that those returns come in from foreign sources. But I doubt if in the whole course of Britain's industrial history, so much has been returned from so small an outlay as the exporting influence of that first 'Flying Scotsman'.

Down through the years, well past the train's centenary celebrations in 1962, the name has remained unchanged by the various owning railway companies and now the nationalized system. But people change it in their speech, and newspapers constantly make mistakes when referring to it in their columns and headlines. The usual error is to talk of the 'Flying Scot'; in print the commonest mistake is 'Flying Scotchman'; I have also seen 'Scottish Flyer' and 'Flying Scotch Express'. However, timetables through eleven decades have always printed it correctly, and every day of every year, in war and peace, the name has appeared after the 10 a.m. departure from both London and Edinburgh (King's Cross and Waverley Stations respectively). Very occasionally it has failed to run due to strikes. Once it was derailed. It has often been diverted due to floods or accidents on the line, but the journey has been completed, and a very rough calculation made at the end of 1968 shows that the two daily trains making up the 'Flying Scotsman', one from each end, had completed 438,059 journeys. Some thirty-two have failed most because of strike action (known well in advance), once because of an entry which notes 'coaches damaged by enemy bombs at York Station'.

Such were the high standards and development of Britain's main line railways up to 1862 that even now the time taken by the express is more than half the original timing. The 1971 schedule calls for five hours, forty eight minutes, with one stop—at Newcastle. This is fast, and no one would want to try to reduce it by more than another twenty minutes with existing tracks and equipment, but compare it with, say, the 316 miles from Paris (Gare de Lyon) and Lyons, which took fourteen hours by the best train in 1862 and is now done in a quarter of

that time by the 'Mistral' at over eighty miles an hour average!
In the field of aviation during a much shorter period there have
been some outstanding speed developments; take the London-
New York flight, which in 1947 was performed by
Constellation airliners in seventeen and a half hours and now
(nonstop) by Boeing or VC10 jets in seven hours. The trouble
lies with diesel traction on the 'Flying Scotsman', introduced in
1960. This was not a sound substitute for steam, as electrified
railway lines elsewhere have proved.

But the most dramatic speed-up in the 'Flying Scotsman's'
long history came twenty-six years after the train's inaugur-
ation. This was the occasion of the first 'Railway Race' to
Scotland when the West Coast route from Euston to
Edinburgh (Princes Street) set out to beat the East Coast
(King's Cross) lines. Each week throughout the summer of
1888, the directors of the London and North-Western and
Caledonian Railways operating the West Coast, and the Great
Northern and North-Eastern Railways representing the East
Coast, slashed the schedule of their best train. The 'Flying
Scotsman' suddenly found itself threatened by an express run-
ning over a slightly longer journey in a quicker time.

Fortunately, Mr. Patrick Stirling, Locomotive Super-
intendent of the Great Northern Railway, had brought out
a series of single-driver express engines with a rare turn of
speed. It was not surprising that they could travel fast, because
their single driving wheels were no less than eight feet in
diameter, but they suffered if the load was too heavy or when
hauling uphill in wet weather. The summer of 1888 must have
been mainly dry because the 'Stirling Singles' produced some
of their best work, one of them taking the 'Flying Scotsman' for
106 miles to Grantham, another hauling it on to York (eighty-
two miles further on) where North-Eastern 4–4–0 engines took
over in two stages, one for eighty miles to Newcastle, the second
for 125 miles to Edinburgh. These engine changes were a matter of convenience for the East Coast route rather than marking
the exact borders of the company lines. In fact the Great
Northern only went three miles beyond Doncaster, so its
second engine ran over North-Eastern metals for twenty-nine
miles to York, and the North-Eastern expired at Berwick on

Tweed but its locomotive running powers were extended over North British tracks for more than sixty miles to Edinburgh.

By the end of July 1888, the schedule for the 'Flying Scotsman' was down to eight hours flat. Passengers found lunch hampers dumped aboard and lost their waiting time for meals at stations. The rake of six-wheeled carriages grew shorter and they were more crowded in consequence. I doubt if the running was all that smooth despite the perfectly maintained track of those labour-rich days. And by the beginning of August, when competition for expanding Anglo-Scottish traffic was at its height, the 'Flying Scotsman' was down to seven hours, forty-five minutes, and actually made the run in a record seven hours, thirty-seven minutes. This meant an average speed of fifty-one and a half miles an hour for nearly four hundred miles inclusive of stops at a time when the best expresses in the world outside Britain were just beginning to touch forty miles an hour on runs under half as long. The world's Press as well as Britain's gave great prominence to the races to Edinburgh and huge crowds gathered at the terminals and by the lineside to watch the 'Flying Scotsman', crowds whose size was not destined to be exceeded on the rails until eighty years later when the same named train attracted them for nostalgic and romantic reasons.

After the winter timetables of 1888 were introduced, both West Coast and East Coast routes settled down to slower runs, the 'Flying Scotsman' being fixed at eight and a half hours, a timing it was to hold for at least another forty years. But greater comfort came to the passengers in the form of corridor coaches and a dining car, although it was the turn of the century before first and third class passengers could enjoy meals on the train during the journey. Heavier trains required heavier engines, and the famous 'Stirling Singles' gave way after nearly a quarter of a century of handling the 'Flying Scotsman' to four-coupled locomotives, at first from the same designer and then from Ivatt, who built a series of splendid 'Atlantic' 4–4–2 engines, introduced in 1898 and improved in 1902. These in turn gave way to big, powerful 'Pacific' 4–6–2 engines in 1923-24, after having also shared the work for a quarter of a century. The 'Pacifics', however, held on to their task for thirty-five years and more before being displaced by diesels, at first a 2,500 horse power type and now the 'Deltics' of English Electric, which put out well over 3,000 horse power. No one expects them to last a quarter of a century ... When introduced coincident with the Centenary celebrations in June 1962, the 'Deltics' were given a schedule of six hours, now reduced to five hours forty eight minutes.

The 'Flying Scotsman' did not fade into the background after its efforts during the 1888 races, although it became a comfortable, reliable express of great weight rather than a speedster. The 1895 series of Railway Races did not affect it, for these concerned the Aberdeen traffic and night expresses. Again big crowds turned out to see the racing trains of the East and West Coast rivals, and the former achieved a time to Edinburgh of under six and a half hours with three six-wheeled coaches, inclusive of three engine changes. But by 1906 very high speeds had gone out of fashion, one or two accidents having occurred, directly attributable to excessive speed through stations.

When Sir Nigel Gresley, famous designer for the Great Northern, and its successor the London and North-Eastern Railway, introduced his magnificent stud of 'Pacifics', one of them, No. 4472, was named *Flying Scotsman*. It was rostered to haul the train of the same name whenever possible and on all important occasions. This led, and still leads, to some confusion in the minds of public and press. However, the engine still survives and has achieved tremendous fame of her own under the private ownership of Mr. Alan Pegler, who runs her under a contract with British Railways valid until 1972.

A new train of Gresley bow-ended coaches in the then new L.N.E.R. varnished teak was put on for the 'Flying Scotsman' trains. The early sets included articulated dining cars, a barber's shop, a cinema coach, and a train telephone. This latter facility has never caught on in Britain, and no trains are fitted with it any more, although it has some uses on T.E.E. trains and in Germany. The barber and the cinema slowly faded from the scene, too. But in 1928 the 'Flying Scotsman' again secured world headlines by being given a non-stop run all the way to Edinburgh, by far the longest non-stop run in the world. It was achieved by constructing corridor tenders for the Pacific engines rostered for the duty, so that the driver and fireman could change over, the relief crew occupying the first compartment in the train. On May 1st, 1928, *Flying Scotsman*, hauling the 'Flying Scotsman' train, pulled away from King's Cross on its new, non-stop, eight and a quarter hour schedule to Waverley. This became its normal summer activity, but each winter it reverted to stopping at Grantham, York and Newcastle, an extra fifteen minutes being allowed.

No. 4472 went on to achieve famous things in her own right, being the first engine to attain a hundred miles an hour while hauling an official dynamometer car to record performance, and to haul an express from London to Leeds in a time that has not yet been beaten. The handsome apple-green Class A.3 engine become the symbol of railways for boys in Britain in the twenties and thirties. Her portrait graced the covers of hundreds of railway books and magazines. The first talking picture was made about her, this time hauling the train bearing her own name, and in this the actor Ray Milland made his debut, playing the part of the fireman. This film, *Flying Scotsman*, is now a classic and is often shown at the National Film Theatre. The first half is silent, the second part using speech, for it took so long to make and 'talkies' had not been practical when production started.

One of the millions of boys who grew up with No. 4472 and loved her, as they all did, wanting to ride on her footplate, achieved his dream in January 1963. He was Alan Pegler, fortunately by then a rich businessman. When British Railways retired the famous engine (and her last duty was hauling a Leeds express, not the 'Flying Scotsman' which was by then under 'Deltic' charge) he bought her for £3,000. Since then Mr. Pegler has spent five times as much on restoring her to original L.N.E.R. condition and colour, fitting a second tender to overcome water shortages brought about by removal of water troughs (track pans) no longer required by diesels, and running her in service. He has brought *Flying Scotsman* back to the pinnacle of railway fame, and the world is grateful to him, while the people of Britain who still admire a fine engine turn out in strength not even matched at major sports events to see the locomotive pass

The re-inaugural postwar run of the 'Royal Highlander' which first ran under this title in 1927. *Princess Victoria*, 46205, is seen heading north near Watford.

[*Photograph by courtesy of British Rail, Midland region*]

North of Crewe at present the 'Royal Highlander' is hauled by two class 50 2700-h.p. diesel locomotives.

[Photograph by courtesy of British Rail, Midland region]

Above. The 'Royal Highlander' travelling northwards at 100 mph, south of Rugby.

Below. The exterior of Inverness station, terminus of the 'Royal Highlander'

[*Photograph by courtesy of British Rail, Midland & Scottish regions*]

Above. The 'Flying Scotsman' in 1888 passing the now defunct Holloway station, hauled by a Great Northern Railway Stirling '8 footer' no. 53, built in 1875.

Below. The 'Flying Scotsman' in Edwardian days hauled by an Ivatt 'Atlantic' of the Great Northern Railway.

[*Photographs by courtesy of British Rail, Eastern region*]

Above. The northbound 'Flying Scotsman' in her heyday, in 1929 headed by Gresley Pacific No. 4478. *Hermit.*

Below. The present day 'Flying Scotsman' approaching Hatfield hauled by class 60 3000 h.p. diesel locomotive.

[*Photographs by courtesy of British Rail, Eastern region*]

Above. A typical rake of Southern Pullmans headed by a rebuilt West Country class *Bulleid Pacific*.

[*Photograph by courtesy of British Rail, Southern region*]

Below. The 'Bournemouth Belle' at speed near Fleet, Hampshire during its last year.

[*Photograph by Tony Hudson*]

The 'Brighton Belle' in its new livery. British Rail's only electric multiple unit Pullman train.

The Great Northern of Ireland in 1963. A Local is leaving Belfast's Great
Victoria Street station hauled by *907 Boyne*.

[Photograph by Brian Haresnape]

by. The engine has spent two years in the United States and Canada hauling exhibition trains.

On May 1st, 1968, exactly forty years after *Flying Scotsman* left King's Cross on her first non-stop run to Edinburgh, the scene was repeated. Simultaneously, from adjoining platforms at King's Cross, the Deltic-hauled 'Flying Scotsman' on its then five hours, fifty minutes timing, and the steam-hauled 'Flying Scotsman' with No. 4472 at its head (and Mr. Pegler on the footplate) left for Edinburgh. Despite her forty-five years of age, and the coal of today, the steam train had a schedule half an hour quicker than she did back in 1928. The story of this achievement and the difficulties encountered was told at the time by every newspaper in the land and by television films and newsreels. She did it non-stop in the time allowed, and an estimated quarter of a million people lined the trackside and stations to see for themselves this romantic, nostalgic sight. Steam may return one day to the 'Flying Scotsman' in the form of nuclear power, and the schedule may be cut to timings competitive with the aircraft of today. On the other hand the East Coast route may be abandoned beyond Newcastle if an electrification project for the West Coast line from Crewe to Carstairs and Edinburgh is carried out, in which case the 'Flying Scotsman' might cease to exist. No one can foresee the future clearly enough to prophesy, but one thing is certain—the 'Flying Scotsman' train and the *Flying Scotsman* engine have turned a good many pages of history and made for themselves an ineradicable mark in the affections and repect of men and women of several generations.

10

Fading of the Southern 'Belles'

Someone had an inspiration on the old London, Brighton and South Coast Railway during the Edwardian era when elegant Pullman cars were delivered to the Company. He decided that a train of these Pullmans, equipped to serve meals at every table in an atmosphere of lincrusta, brass, inlaid walnut, and moquette, should run to Brighton from Victoria in an hour and would be called the 'Southern Belle'. The daily journey of fractionally under fifty-two miles became an immediate success, despite the supplementary fare and the near-obligation to order something to eat or drink.

As a steam-hauled express, the 'Southern Belle' ran from 1907 to 1932, with the exception of two of the war years. From 1921 and for about eight years afterwards, a special class of big Baltic (4–6–4) tank engines hauled it, the one usually rostered being *Remembrance*, named as the London and Brighton Railway's war memorial engine. The Company, of course, passed into the Southern Railway combination under the grouping of 1923, but the new concern actively supported the 'Belle' idea and sought to expand it. Their policy was electrification for the outer suburban and coastal lines. The third rail live line reached Brighton at the end of 1932, and there appeared, on January 1st 1933, a new express, the first set of electric motor Pullmans ever built, called 'Brighton Belle'.

Those electric Pullmans are still going strong, all fifteen of them, though some of the trailing cars have been replaced or rebuilt from time to time. Made up either as one train of five, or one of ten, with a spare set, the 'Brighton Belle' travels backwards and forwards between Victoria and Brighton four times each way every day except Sunday, when it does the run three times. It is immensely popular with passengers, although it appears to be an embarrassment to the plebeian 'standardization-minded' officials who run Britain's nationalized railways today. They do not seem to have plans for replacement, although the sturdy, gallant units have clocked up something like nineteen million miles over the past three decades. The 'Belle' had a sort of rest during five of the six Second World War years, but even so the weekly milage of each motor Pullman exceeds two thousand. The schedule still calls for nearly an hour (fifty-six minutes to be exact), not because the stock could not do the 51.87 miles any quicker, but simply to allow adequate time to serve a meal and to avoid too much harsh running. Passengers like it that way; no motorist could drive the distance through all the suburban, outer-suburban, and coastal traffic in under twice the time.

Following the early success of the 'Southern Belle' the London, Brighton, and South Coast Railway decided to put on another all-Pullman train, this time to Eastbourne. The L.B.S.C.R. included a Pullman, sometimes two, in almost all their express trains, but 'all Pullman' meant going for a definite market and cutting out excursion traffic. The Eastbourne train was arranged for Sundays only, to leave Victoria at 11.15 a.m. and take ninety minutes for the sixty-five and three-quarter miles via Lewes. It left Eastbourne at 5.15 p.m. and reached Victoria at 6.45 p.m., at a day return price of 12s 6d. It worked well, capturing the people who wanted to stroll in their best attire along Eastbourne's famous promenade (as late as 1925 it was still obligatory for gentlemen to wear silk or bowler hats), to lunch at the Grand, and to listen to the Palm Court Orchestra. They took coffee outwards on the Pullman, enjoying a huge Edwardian Sunday tea on the trip home. The Eastbourne Pullman ceased in 1915 after five successful years but was restored as a Charing Cross departure from 1932 to 1937, steam-hauled even after electrification of the line in 1935.

The progressive Southern Railway management of the nineteen-thirties decided to add another 'Belle', this time to Bournemouth. The Pullman Car Company owned the cars in those days, the railway merely hauling them or, in the case of the electric Pullmans, merely providing the driver and the scheduled path. A beautiful set of Pullmans was built for the 'Bournemouth Belle' in 1935, keeping to the Company's standard practice of naming the first class cars after girls and numbering the second class (until 1956 third class) ones. The train, made up of twelve Pullmans, was steam-hauled throughout its thirty-two years of existence, except for a brief period at the end, and a farcical try with diesels in 1949. As with the Brighton luxury train, there was no service during most of the Second World War.

It is 108 miles from London's Waterloo Station to Bournemouth Central. The 'Belle' was scheduled to take two hours, inclusive of a stop at Southampton. For locomotive and servicing purposes, it used to be taken on another five miles to the now closed Bournemouth West terminus. Several famous classes of engine handled the train in turn; 'King Arthurs' at first, interspersed with 'Lord Nelsons' and occasionally 4–4–0s of the exceptionally powerful 'Schools' class. But for its last twenty years it was invariably in charge of O. V. Bulleid's splendid Pacific locomotives of the 'Merchant Navy', 'West Country', and 'Battle of Britain' types.

Leaving Waterloo every day including Sunday at 12.30 p.m. the 'Bournemouth Belle' was a romantic train, much sought after as the best moving restaurant in England. Lunch, served in coupés which could be reserved for special gourmet parties, or at tables lit by brass lamps shining on the gleaming napery, was a delight. The food was far better than in any normal train, even if it did cost more, and the wine list was the equal of that in the 'Brighton Belle', which still has a reputation for the best cellar on rails. The heavy Pullmans rolled smoothly, and on every trip the locomotive could be counted on to touch and possibly exceed ninety miles an hour, coming down from Basingstoke to Winchester, or on the up run from Basingstoke to Woking. Many people just rode the train to Southampton to impress their friends with the lunch. Americans often travelled by it and enjoyed it as a sort of 'Savoy on wheels' reminding them of something that had once existed—with wisps of steam drifting past the richly curtained windows—in their own country.

But the 'Bournemouth Belle' was too good to last, with the coming of electrification to the lines of the South-West in 1967. Standardization was the order of the day and unimaginative officials issued its death notice. With all the engineering work on the lines between 1965 and early 1967, the schedule was slowed to two hours, twenty minutes and delays were forced upon the train, its former priority having been cunningly removed. Then, at the beginning of 1967, the officials of the nationalized complex borrowed a diesel to take over from the still-fit steam engines. This broke down on numerous occasions, the train having to be rescued, often an hour late, by steam survivors. But the 'policy' had its effect, and by the time the 'Belle' made its last run early in July 1967, its good days were becoming a memory.

Many people loved the 'Bournemouth Belle' and one who lived close to its route through the New Forest in Hampshire has done something about it. He is Lord Montague of Beaulieu. Buying a 'Schools' class engine, he has set it up in the grounds of his estate which also includes a valuable vintage car museum, and added to it three of the Pullmans of the 'Belle'. With headboards and the interiors preserved just as if lunch was about to be served shortly after departure from Waterloo, the train is a nostalgic reminder of the gracious days of rail travel to the Hampshire Coast. Over in the West of England at Hereford, five 'Belle' Pullmans survive in the capable hands of BULMERS cider, who attach them to the preserved G.W.R. engine King George the Fifth.

Two other 'Belles' appeared for a short while as a post-War project by the then not-so-long nationalized Southern Region. These were the 'Thanet Belle' and the 'Devon Belle', both steam-hauled rakes of lavish Pullmans in their chocolate and cream, the former running from Victoria to Margate, Broadstairs and Ramsgate on the Kent Coast, taking ninety-five minutes for the seventy-eight miles, and the latter from Waterloo to Exeter and Ilfracombe on the North Devon coast, covering the 210 miles in four and a quarter hours. The 'Devon Belle' had a specially built observation car at the rear in which drinks were served to passengers in armchairs who could sit and watch the receding track and scenery through huge windows. It was the first express train to run through Salisbury without stopping since a violent accident destroyed an up Ocean Mails express in 1906 which took the dangerous curves and points through the station much too fast. The 'Devon Belle' only ran on another two miles, though, to a stop for an engine change at Wilton, Wiltshire.

Both these Southern Region 'Belles' had short careers, the 'Thanet' disappearing before the onset of Kent Coast electrification in 1960. Some of their Pullmans passed to the 'Golden Arrow' for its London to Dover run, and the observation car from the 'Devon' went to Inverness to work over the Skye Line until 1967. Why a 'Canterbury Belle' never appeared on the line amazes me, especially as the 'Golden Arrow' stock makes only one return trip to Dover in a day, but I suppose it is the reluctance to have outstanding trains among the standard equipment.

As we advance into 1971, the 'Brighton Belle' motor Pullmans enter their thirty-ninth year of service and the writing is on the wall for them. Southern Region have announced they will not be replaced after reaching their fortieth birthday, a decision which has aroused a storm of protest not only in London and Brighton but all over the British Isles. The railways say it would not be economic to build more high standard equipment of this kind with the large catering staff to look after passengers paying only a nominal supplement for the fifty-one mile run. But powerful voices are raised in the protest, not least being that of Lawrence Olivier (Lord Olivier) the famous actor, who 'saved the kippers' on the train a few years ago when austerity menus were threatened. This Belle may be fading but it is not yet extinct. . . .

11

Great Northern of Ireland Memoriam

An onlooker standing beside the double track railway line that runs from Belfast to Larne would have seen heavy freight trains with two engines at the head and often one at the rear panting along in the direction of Greenisland. He would have seen hundreds of these steam-hauled trains up to the end of the 1960s; perhaps he will see one or two for some little time to come. The romantic beat of the engines symbolizes the death throes of a railway literally digging its own grave. On the sides of the Derby built 2–6–4 tanks (known locally as 'jeeps') are the letters N.I.R. (Northern Ireland Railways).

These goods trains are filled with spoil and gravel dug from the quarries over on the shoreline of Belfast Lough. They are going to sidings not at a rail-head but at a road-head, for the material is for motorway construction. As each mile of motorway is completed with the essential help of the railway, so the life of the line is shortened. It can only be a matter of time before the northern Ireland Government, notably anti-rail during the past twenty years, calls a halt to the trains and forces all goods and passengers on to its new and expensive roads. Already the costly motorways of unhappy Ulster run from hardly anywhere worth noting to simply nowhere at all.

Not many years have gone by since the north of Ireland was served by a private railway company with a service and tradition second to none. It was known as the Great Northern Railway, with an 'Ireland' put in brackets after the name to avoid confusion with the line of the same name which existed in England until the grouping of 1923. Its network included a main line from Dublin to Belfast, 112 miles, another from Portadown (twenty miles from Belfast) over to Londonderry, and some secondary main lines to Clones, Enniskillen and the Donegal Coast. At a late stage in its existence, as recently as 1948, the Great Northern of Ireland had the fascinating distinction of operating four types of traction at the same time; steam, electric, diesel, and horse. Most famous and romantic of its scheduled services was the horse-drawn train (a tram of double-deck pattern really) which worked the branch line to Fintona from Fintona Junction, on the Enniskillen line. The mile and a quarter took about eight minutes and attracted tourists as well as regular passengers, and all regretted the day the service died. But it did not die because it was horse-drawn. The Great Northern had already passed into oblivion and an anti-rail administration closed the entire line to Enniskillen in 1957, so the horse-drawn branch faded with it. They took the vehicle to a place of honour in the Belfast Transport Museum.

Today you cannot get to Enniskillen, or to Fintona for that matter, by public transport unless you take a terribly expensive, infrequent, uncomfortable and time-consuming bus ride. But they expect you to drive. Rumour has it that the policy of rail destruction in Northern Ireland emanated from two civil servants who used to be held up at level crossings when driving to Belfast. They are said to have pushed forward the 'down with railways' idea through successive governments and sold their political masters on the loss-making qualities of trains. Because they are 'faceless' one cannot probe too deeply, but I have had private talks (outside Northern Ireland) with a likeable Ex-Prime Minister of that country whose words did not entirely disparage the rumours, although he was certain his small country could afford neither trains nor motorways.

The Great Northern was the epitome of romance on the rails. It lived in the past and even in its closing years built engines which were from a design of elegant 4–4–0s laid down in 1911. The last engines it built were five rugged 4–4–0s with plenty of rivets showing on the smoke-box doors, somewhat after the style of the Southern Railway of England's famous 'Schools' class, designed in 1930. Only this was 1948. . . .

All passenger engines were painted a beautiful shade of blue. They hauled pretty brown carriages, quite fast at times. In the thirties they inaugurated an 'Enterprise Express' which ran in each direction without stopping between Belfast and Dublin, taking two hours exactly for the 112 miles. Today, a lighter 'Enterprise' set runs twice daily in each direction, hauled by imported American diesels burning imported oil. They take ten minutes longer. . . .

The Great Northern of Ireland enjoyed profits for fifty years up to the 1939–45 war, and spent its money wisely on good quality rolling stock and handsome light engines which were strongly built nonetheless, kept time (in contrast to other railways in Ireland) and were beautifully maintained. Adelaide Shed just outside Belfast was their last home, where some were still to be seen as recently as 1964, with touches of blue paint still showing through the grime and an odd name-plate or two (like 'Slievemore' and 'Boyne') fixed above the splashers. But by then they were no one's care, just relics belonging to an organization called the Ulster Transport Authority, now defunct and known as 'Ulster's Terrible Affliction' by all who came in contact with it.

It was the Second World War that in some ways proved to be the Great Northern's undoing. The steady profits of decades swelled to enormous proportions as it carried all the traffic that war-inflated industry created. Because so much of its operation was in Ulster and thus allied to Britain, it got supplies of coal and never had to rely on peat and wood like less-fortunate railways in Ireland. Often a Great Northern fireman on his locomotive in Dublin's Amiens Street, standing simmering alongside an unhappy Irish engine, would throw some shovel-fulls of coal across. The Great Northern kept going well, and fast throughout the War. It carried British troops to Londonderry on a route which took it outside the province but it made them change to civilian clothes when it went across the border. It moved passengers in vast numbers who had no choice because petrol was tightly rationed and buses few and far between. To conserve coal it put on a service of Drum-battery electric units on Belfast and Dublin suburban routes, and helped the Great Southern of Ireland to do the same on its line to Bray.

When the war ended the Great Northern was in better shape, physically and financially, than almost any railway system in Europe with the exception of the Swiss and Swedish.

Locomotives had taken a battering but being of sturdy construction they were far from worn out. The money in the railway coffers was more than had ever been known before.

Yet seven years later the Great Northern was dead, totally bankrupt, in its last months unable to find enough money even to pay the wages of its staff. The net profit for 1946 was two and a quarter million pounds, still colossal by any standards in its history. In 1947 this had fallen to just on one million pounds, in 1948 to £248,000, in 1949 to £36,000, and then came the critical years of loss; in 1950 a few hundred thousand, then two million and by 1952 it had to be taken over by a joint committee of the Ulster Transport Authority (formed by nationalizing the London Midland and Scottish Railway's Northern Counties Committee and the bus services) and the Coras Iompair Eireann (Ireland's State Transport system formed by nationalizing the Republic of Ireland railways). Its name soon faded and its lines dwindled, being operated by various 'experts' until the once proud system involving many hundreds of route miles in both North and South Ireland became a straight 112 miles of line between the two capital cities plus the Dublin to Howth suburban branch. This is currently jointly managed by the two Governments but the Northern Ireland part, at least, is digging its own grave by handling the spoil for the new motorway.

It is too late now for recriminations, but clearly the Great Northern of Ireland declared too big a dividend in each of its golden years and put too little, if any, to reserve. It lacked foresight, failed to recognize growing road competition, omitted to lobby in Parliament, failed in public relations, ignored what should have been valuable contacts in business and the civil service, and squandered money on new orders for equipment which was outdated before it was built. This was at a time when the tide was running against railways everywhere; the Great Northern built no defences of any kind with its surplus moneys and was swamped.

Two of its engines, restored to their former glory in blue livery, survive in the hands of Irish railway enthusiasts, a 0–6–0 tender locomotive and a 4–4–0 express passenger engine of the elegant greyhound type once noted for hurrying Belfast-Dublin trains past Dundalk at over eighty miles an hour. My last active connection with all that remained of the Great Northern was in November 1963, when I visited Adelaide Shed with two colleagues and found a dozen locomotives there. So pleased was the Shedmaster with this spark of twilight interest that he took out one of the two surviving big outside-cylinder 4–4–0s, No. 207 *Boyne*, had her cleaned up so that the once-proud blue paint caught the pale rays of late autumn sunshine, and rostered her for a local train from Belfast's Great Victoria Street Station up to Lisburn, seven and a half miles away. Two of us were invited to ride on the footplate and help coal her for the short, stopping-train ride.

It was a romantic journey, full of nostalgia, but I doubt if the dozen or so passengers who joined the train understood why their usual diesel unit or U.T.A. 2–6–4 tank engine had been replaced by something out of memory. We barked up the hill past Balmoral, never exceeding thirty miles an hour, and received a wave or two from the lineside. In twenty minutes the trip was over and the engine ran round its train to take it back to Belfast, but an elderly passenger on the platform did come over to us. 'I thought the old Great Northern was dead and buried', he said. 'Are you trying to dig it up from the grave?' But it was too late to try and do that. . . .

12

Night Ferry to Paris

The volume of passenger traffic between London and Paris is the greatest between any two capital cities in the world. It has been that way for a century or more, and despite political and financial complications and language difficulties the traffic continues to grow. Greater London and Greater Paris account for a total population of some seventeen million people at the present time, and even fifty years ago the links between the capitals could draw upon a potential of about half that many persons. When Blériot made his historic flight from the grassy slopes above Cap Gris Nez to the Downs near Dover in 1909, it was a pointer to the idea that Britain had ceased to be an island and the Channel could be vanquished from the air. Few people expected, however, that only ten years later the first commercial flights carrying passengers would be running between London and Paris, or that twenty years later aircraft so large that a bus load of travellers could be accommodated, fed, and served champagne would be linking the two cities several times a day.

The traditional rail-boat-rail links, sustained prior to the 1923 grouping in England and the 1938 semi-nationalization in France by a number of competing companies, had tried many schemes to beat the Channel. The nearest to succeed was the Channel Tunnel plan of 1883, when pilot diggings actually went under the sea from both sides but were stopped by military pressures. Another was a fast steamer with passenger decks balanced on gimbals, the idea being that these would stay motionless while the ship pitched and rolled. In the event, things were worse aboard this vessel than on a conventional one in bad weather. A twin-hull paddle steamer was tried with limited success, the forerunner of catamarans and bigger than any since conceived, but this met with complicated setbacks.

It seemed better to concentrate on the romance of the trip, the thrill of a fast run by special boat-train to the ship's side, the excitement of watching the white cliffs recede, the smell of France and the sights and sounds of the Calais railway scene, the novelty of the first meal aboard a French train. In 1928 the Southern Railway Company, in association with the Chemin de Fer du Nord, decided to mix some luxury and elegance with the romance by devising a 'Golden Arrow' service. This began running to a fast schedule involving a departure from Victoria Station at 11 a.m. in a train of lavish Pullman cars hauled by one of the latest 'King Arthur' or 'Lord Nelson' 4–6–0 express engines. The train reached Dover Marine, seventy-eight and a half miles, in ninety-five minutes, and 'Golden Arrow' passengers were whisked through formalities, up a special gangway aboard the fast steamer *Canterbury* and on to a reserved deck where they sat at tables arranged like those of a Pullman car. The ship cast off at 12.55 p.m. and thrashed across to Calais, being berthed at 2 p.m. Some passengers had lunch en route if conditions were good, but most waited until boarding the French train. This was standing beside the ship, three or four blue and gold Pullmans and some first class ordinary carriages behind them, plus a sleeping car or two, ordinary restaurants and baggage cars. Again a special quick disembarkation and into the train, French formalities being dealt with aboard while aperitifs were being served. At the head of the 'Flèche d'Or' stood a Nord Pacific steam locomotive of distinctive and impressive appearance, for many years a Chapelon 231E type being assigned. Paris was reached by the 'Golden Arrow' Service in 185 minutes from Calais, the arrival at the Gare du Nord being 5.25 p.m.

The important thing is that no one has improved on this smart 'Golden Arrow' schedule of the early thirties, despite electrification (to Dover, and from Amiens to Paris) and new ships. But even during the year of its inauguration, the all-first-class 'Golden Arrow' carried less passengers between London and Paris than the relatively primitive biplanes lifted over the same route. This uncomfortable fact became apparent to the wide-awake and progressive Southern Railway management of the period, who introduced second class Pullmans early on and improved the load factor of their train and ship, but the French express remained first class for a long time.

In 1935 the managements decided to sprinkle a good deal more romance on to the London-Paris mixture and to take away the speed element. The first International Sleeping Cars to be seen in Britain were going to carry passengers in leisurely style right through from London to the Gare du Nord. Travellers could either reckon that this took eleven hours, or no time at all, since they had to sleep somewhere and would therefore go to bed in London and wake up in Paris. This was achieved with the aid of four train ferries running on the Dover-Dunkirk route, a longer sea crossing complicated by the use of locks at each end. The sleeping cars, specially built in France to a smaller size than those normally seen in Europe so that they could clear English tunnels and operate under the tight British loading gauge, were parked in the bowels of the ferries between midnight and 5 a.m. If all went well, passengers slept unconcerned throughout the trip. There was a supper car on the train from Victoria which came off at Dover, while the French put on a Wagon-Restaurant between Dunkirk and the Gare du Nord. Timings were 10 p.m. to 9 a.m. when the clocks of Britain and France told the same time, and 9 p.m. to 9 a.m. when Britain reverted to G.M.T.

The 'Night Ferry' was an instant success when it began running early in 1936. It catered for a different kind of traffic from that using the 'Golden Arrow', and it cost even more, especially for a single sleeper. In those days, flying was hazardous at night and rarely attempted, so the new train got all the executive business traffic that was going. It dealt Imperial Airways, British Airways and Air France, competitors on the London-Paris air route, a series of devastating blows from which they had not recovered when everything came to an end with the outbreak of the 1939–45 war.

Soon after the end of the war vigorous efforts resulted in both the 'Golden Arrow' and the 'Night Ferry' services being restored. By 1946 they were running again, the only casualties being some of the Leeds-built French Pullmans for the 'Flèche d'Or' which were destroyed during the war and were never replaced. One set of the special Wagons-Lits for the 'Night Ferry' had been kept in England and the other in France, but somehow the latter escaped destruction and was found more or less intact. These vehicles are still running today, a little roughly in their advancing years, but adequately, and they must obviously run until some new major breakthrough, such as the Channel Tunnel, transforms the London-Paris surface route. Meanwhile the 'gimmicks' on the sea stretch continue, British Railways using the biggest hovercraft in the world to dash across to Boulogne just above the tops of the waves (provided these are negligible) in thirty-five minutes, and experimenting with a Russian-built hydrofoil of considerable capacity.

Flights between London and Paris have become mundane affairs by jet, with no food service or attention to the majority of passengers who are riding crammed together in Economy class seats. The actual flying takes about fifty minutes, and there are departures every half hour with B.E.A. and Air France throughout the day and part of the night. It is cheaper, basically, than the first class surface routes, but there are road transport charges and severe take-off taxes added when leaving Paris. At busy traffic times, when Friday evening traffic jams clog the road to London Airport and choke Paris, it is slower, city-centre to city-centre, than it used to be in the early thirties when the flying part took two and a quarter hours by ungainly biplane but the road sectors were done in barely half an hour, to Croydon and Le Bourget.

The 'Night Ferry' has changed its tactics to seek different business. It maintains its atmosphere of romance, although it is in the charge of electric locomotives throughout its journey on rails, and diesel shunters handle the sleepers at the ferry berths. There is a through sleeper to Brussels, detached at Lille, and from December to March a through sleeper has been run to Geneva, also being detached at Lille. Only about five of the blue and gold vehicles go all the way to Paris, and passengers in the two-berth compartments enjoy big fare reductions, making the actual cost in money less than it was, despite massive inflation, back in 1936.

A journey with this train, the only one which starts from a British station and ends up at a continental one, remains a pleasurable experience. The timings are the same except that Britain and the Continent kept to the same clock arrangement for three years, so that departure from Victoria is at 10 p.m. and the arrival at the Gare du Nord always at 9 a.m. In the reverse direction it is 10 p.m. to 9 a.m. The traveller on approaching his train at Victoria cannot see the blue and gold Wagons-Lits, for they are hidden by a screen. First he must pass through Immigration and customs, and then go through a door on to the platform where the sleeping section of the train is drawn up. All the day-coaches on the rear will come off at Dover, their occupants walking to the ferry to bed down for the five-hour passage in lounges or dormitories.

Once aboard the sleepers, the traveller has only to fill in a French immigration form and leave his passport with the attendant (these men are all French), then he will not be disturbed until arrival in Paris. It is as well to request the attendant to buy duty-free goods aboard the ship, a commission he is usually willing to undertake. The Southern Region electric locomotive hums powerfully as it starts the heavy train rolling, but it always has a struggle up the steep 1 in 78 bank out of Victoria to the Grosvenor Bridge across the Thames. After this the going is fast, if noisy, and Dover is reached in ninety minutes. There is a restaurant car in front of the sleepers to serve drinks, coffee and snacks and hot suppers, but most passengers will have turned in and put their lights out before the train arrives in Dover. Shunting is not as smooth as it used to be, and the men who fit heavy chains to the wheels in the rail deck of the ship no longer seem to have the consideration which marked those Southern Railway employees in the 1936–39 period who took such care not to awaken sleepers.

Without air-conditioning and double-glazing, both noise and heat are troublesome during a summer crossing, but in cool weather, or in winter, circumstances favour the sleeper. He can and usually does slumber on without being aware of spending five hours stuck in the bowels of a ship. At Dunkirk, with re-marshalling, he is lucky to sleep on without a heavy bang or shout to sit him upright in his bunk, but if all goes well (and the stock runs smoother over French track) the first thing he will know about is the call shortly before Lille. If he is alighting at Lille, the attendant will bring coffee and rolls; the main restaurant serves both Continental and English breakfasts between Lille and Paris as the train takes the all-electric line to Amiens and Creil. After breakfast the attendant will return passports and negotiate the settlement of duty-free goods obtained during the night; then, on arrival at the Gare du Nord, the passenger can leave the train without any formalities of any kind, fresh (one hopes) and ready to keep an early morning appointment in the French capital.

At Claridges, in June 1971, the Joint Director General of S.N.C.F., M. Huter, went on record as saying that train schedules from London to Paris via the projected Channel tunnel had already been worked out with British Rail's Southern Region. Overall journey time would be three and a half hours: expresses would operate at breakfast time, lunch time and dinner time.

With the completion of the Channel tunnel, the leisurely Night Ferry to Paris will almost certainly become redundant.

13

First across the Alps: the Semmering

The great mountain wall of the Alps has presented a barrier to Man for countless decades, affecting trade, influencing thought and politics, making natural borders for nations and languages. Even today, more than 115 years since the Alps were first crossed by the relative ease and safety of railways, and fully a century after the driving of the Gotthard Tunnel, ethnic barriers are clear-cut. You enter a tunnel where the language is Italian and the way of life Mediterranean. Emerge ten miles in as many minutes later and the language is German, the outlook—and the climate—North European.

Railways had been in existence in Europe for a good twenty years before the first successful crossing of the Alps was achieved. It happened in 1854 a long way to the east, by a line whose achievement has often been overlooked because it did not drive any killer tunnels or link two different cultures. The Austrian Empire's Südbahn built it, due south from Vienna, and the route chosen took the line over the Semmering Pass.

The Alpine wall ranges through Switzerland and into Austria, staying high and rugged through the Vorarlberg and the Tirol. All the passes have been known and used since Roman times, some of them—witness Hannibal and his crossing with elephants over the Great St. Bernard—featuring in Carthaginian history. By horse, by mule or on foot, the passes had a finite season, never being considered possible for travel during more than six months of the year, and often only for three to four months. Winter travellers faced appalling hardships, particularly before the days of skis, and a high proportion of those who thought they had to make the trip perished en route. This was still the state of affairs when Austrian surveyors under Karl Ritter von Ghega started work on a possible line which would shorten north-south transit and make it possible, despite a big detour, at all seasons of the year. Work commenced in 1848 and was to last six years.

From great Imperial Vienna, already in 1848 the glittering capital of the richest land empire Europe had known since the Romans, a railway was pushed southwards through gentle country to Baden, watering place and major army barracks, and then on to Wiener Neustadt, thirty miles from the capital. Here it paused while men looked up at the Alps having their last real fling before they faded out well to the east and flattened into the Great Hungarian Plain. They needed to raise their line 3,000 feet to Semmering, seventy and three-quarter miles from Vienna, an easy journey for horsemen in summer, but in those days, before mountain railways had been built and a decade before the conquest of the Rocky Mountains by Union Pacific, the project was new and daring. A man named Fell from England was known to have a system which he employed on a temporary line over the Mont Cenis from France to Italy, and was later to employ with limited success in New Zealand, but this involved special equipment, steep gradients helped by ropes, cost a lot more money than Austria wanted to spend (or ever did spend) on its austere railways. Besides, it detracted from a main line character.

So the engineers built the first adhesion main line through mountains, ascending on steep but acceptable grades, twisting through short tunnels and over viaducts, doubling back on itself in a way that was to become much more famous when the Swiss did it on the approaches to Gotthard. Rails reached the Semmering in midsummer, 1852, and the Austrian Südbahn (Southern Railway Corporation) erected a vast hotel on a ridge overlooking the station. It was called Panhans, and it still stands today, one of the biggest hotels in Europe. In the main lounge is a painting of the first train coming up the Semmering.

The Südbahn carried on over the 3,250-foot pass dominated by Schneeberg rearing to 6,800 feet, but tunnelled the last mile below the summit at 2,920 feet, then on falling gradients reached Bruck-an-der-Mur, where a junction was constructed. One line went on to Graz, capital of Styria, while the other took a tortuous but fairly fast route down into Carinthia, to Klagenfurt and Villach and through to Italy. From Graz construction continued through Slovenia and Croatia and then towards what was still Turkish-occupied Serbia, contributing to the uprising which drove out the Turks as the railway reach Belgrade in the mid-sixties.

Whether or not the Austrian Südbahn enjoyed the full fruits of its ten-year monopoly over the Alps is questionable, for it became famous later more because of its link to the Dalmatian Coast and the warm-water lakes of Carinthia. But British travellers of the early sixties are recorded as using it on journeys to Trieste, Bosnia and Carinthia, one route chosen being from London to Harwich, then by ship to Rotterdam, then trains to Vienna. Once the railway over the Brenner Pass was opened in 1864 a much shorter more direct route existed, with Munich and Verona joined by 277 miles of line, only 112 miles of it being in Austria. Alois von Negrelli began to build the Brenner Railway in 1863 and the Südbahn took over the running from Wörgl to Bozen (now Bolzano).

My first acquaintance with the Semmering line was on a bright spring day in 1956, only a few months after the Austrian Peace Treaty had removed Soviet occupation troops from Vienna and the eastern parts of the country. The British Zone began at Semmering, the station being a sort of frontier between British and Soviet troops. The former had to travel by way of the south of Austria and up over the Südbahn, an extremely roundabout route. Now all was clear and Austria was opening up Vienna, the Semmering and Carinthia to tourism. I had been invited to visit and record some impressions of the travel potential of the area, as it had been nearly twenty years, when the Anschluss enveloped Austria in 1936, since the only tourists in any strength had come from Britain and Western Europe.

Boarding the 2 p.m. Südbahn express at Vienna's South Station, my destination was Semmering and a room at the Panhans Hotel, now open for normal business after nearly ten years as a British officers' billet on a grand scale. There was steam haulage throughout, although electrification had already reached Austria in a big way, the lines in the Tirol, over the

Brenner, through Salzburg to Linz and Vienna, and from Villach through the Tauern Tunnel to Salzburg being already under the wires. There was talk of the Südbahn being next, and in fact this came to pass by 1961. However, we left Vienna, a long and heavy mail train with first, second and third class coaches, a buffet and a diner, and baggage vehicles, in the charge of a powerful Südbahn 2–8–0. We stopped at Baden, then, about fifty-five minutes out of Vienna there came a longer stop at Wiener Neustadt, thirty and a half miles, with its large engine shed. A seventeen mile run to Gloggnitz followed, where a large stud of banking tanks resided. Two of these small but sturdy tanks attached themselves to the rear of our train and off we went in fine style, climbing and twisting towards the shimmering snows ahead. The exhaust was most satisfying, rousing the echoes from the approaching mountains, while white smoke billowed into the fir trees. This was a romantic railway ride over the Alps, the last of its kind. There were thirteen miles of 1 in 47 to climb, with stretches of 1 in 40 beyond Payerbach.

Shortly before we reached Semmering and the summit, after about twenty minutes' climbing from Gloggnitz, I collected my bag from the rack, got my camera ready, and walked right through the train to the last door in order to be ready to alight and photograph the banking engines. Once stopped at Semmering, which, like all Austrian stations outside the great cities, has no platforms and no shelter beyond the central building, I got out and took pictures from the rear as the engines simmered down. I became conscious of a brass band at work, and noticed a number of costumed men, led by a fat, jolly band leader wearing a hat with a chamois brush, gay leather jacket, and *lederhosen* shorts, playing vigorously to the train in the region of the restaurant car and first class coach. Assuming this to be part of the 'freedom from occupation of the Semmering' festivities, by which they welcomed the afternoon mail train from Vienna, I strolled up behind them and photographed them from the rear, then from a slightly side view, getting them in the foreground of a picture including the powerful train engine. Then the bankers detached, the train engine whistled, and the express, on level track now and about to begin a gentle descent towards Bruck-an-der-Mur, the next scheduled stop, puffed attractively out of Semmering Station.

I humped my bag across the lines to a waiting taxi, although I could see the huge mass of the Panhans Hotel rearing above me. However, it was quite 200 feet above the station level and the road wound a good deal to reach it. The driver spoke good English, a residue of the long years serving British troops here, and I asked him if the band always played to the mail trains. He said he had not seen it before. Just before we started off, the band could be seen coming away in disorder, the fat leader no longer jolly but waving his arms in some distraction, almost in tears. As they came near the taxi the driver called out to them in German, receiving an answer enhanced by gesticulation. He turned to me and translated: 'It seems they are waiting to greet an *Engländer Reisejournalist* (travel writer) called Westcott Jones, but he does not come. . . .'

14

Through the Lötschberg to the Brünig Pass

The largest and most important privately-owned railway company in Europe using standard gauge tracks, and the only railway system on that Continent making an annual profit and paying a sound dividend, is the Bern-Lötschberg-Simplon. This famous line has many advantages, not least being the fact that it has a complete monopoly through its long tunnel and cannot be competed with by road traffic. It links Central Switzerland with the big cities of Northern Italy and carries heavy freight loads, while at the same time it is eagerly sought by tourists. It was ahead of its time in development when it was built as an all-electric railway in 1913, using the best of materials and resources and the pick of Europe's craftsmen at a time when such men were at their peak of pride and effort.

The Lötschberg story began to take shape in 1909 when the people of Bern and North-West Switzerland wanted rail access to the newly-opened Simplon Tunnel linking the Valais with Italy. There was no road pass and the only direct route lay over the dreadful Gemmi Pass, still to this day a foot pass suited only to the intrepid traveller. Investments in a company were forthcoming from businessmen and traders of the Swiss Federal capital and the communities in the north-west Cantons, aided by some banks. All the problems were concerned with engineering, for, unlike so many railways, the money never ran out. The men worked to expand an existing line to Spiez and up the Kandar Valley to Frütigen, then they blasted the Lötschberg Tunnel for some nine miles under the main wall of the Alps at an altitude of 4,000 feet above sea level. Wisely, they built the great tunnel double-track at the time, having the vision to see traffic growth greater than their contemporaries predicted, for today the tunnel is used by eighty trains a day.

Bringing the fine main line down from that height in a few short miles to meet up with the Simplon line down on the floor of the Valais where it follows the Rhône was one of the masterpieces of engineering of this century. It has been done in such a way that heavy trains can ascend at speeds averaging over forty-five miles an hour, yet it wastes no space and has done no aesthetic damage to the natural beauties of this mountain wall. Electric locomotives ordered for the B.L.S. have always been of the highest quality and efficiency, frequently rating as the most powerful engines in the world.

Although its actual main line is only forty-six miles long, from Spiez on the Lake of Thun to Brig at the entrance to the Simplon Tunnel, the Bern-Lötschberg-Simplon Railway owns 154 miles of standard gauge line, having set up subsidiary companies, later to be absorbed, or built branches. The twenty-six miles from Bern to Neuchâtel are its second most important, and Spiez to Interlaken the busiest tourist route, totalling thirteen miles. Two other lines of lesser but growing importance which it wholly owns are the Spiez-Erlenbach-Zweisimmen (twenty-two miles) giving connection with the Montreux-Berner Oberland and Lake Geneva to the west, and the Gürbetal-Bern-Schwarzenburg (thirty-two miles). The B.L.S. also owns steamers on the Lakes of Thun and Brienz. Its headquarters are in Bern, capital of Switzerland, and it employs a total of 2,100 persons. Particularly interesting is the way in which its profits are added to by the increase in road traffic—a complete opposite to the usual situation facing railways in most parts of the world. Hauling cars and trucks on flat-cars through the Lötschberg Tunnel from Kandersteg to Goppenstein and vice-versa, which is the only possible way road vehicles can travel from the Valais to Central Switzerland, the B.L.S. has noted the numbers rising, from a mere 225 vehicles in 1950 to 13,718 in 1960 and no less than 127,600 in 1967. By all accounts the year 1971 should see the railway carrying over 200,000 private cars and lorries! During Easter 1971, it hauled 10,000!

Let us take a journey from Brig over the B.L.S. to Spiez

then to Interlaken and on one of its ships to Brienz. Let us then
go on with the Brünig narrow-gauge railway (now owned by
the Swiss Federal system) from Brienz over the Brünig Pass to
Lucerne. Oddly enough, of the three journeys I have made
with the Lötschberg Railway, only one was in conventional
garb on a conventional train. The other two were very special
occasions. The first was to mark the centenary of Thomas
Cook's first tour of Switzerland (an anachronism so far as the
B.L.S. was concerned for it did not exist in those days), when
the company put on a special steam train, which no one knew
they had, for the occasion. The other time was in April 1968,
again in costume, as part of the Sherlock Holmes Tour of
Switzerland. For this latter trip, the company provided a
special two-coach electric 'Blue Arrow' set to obviate a change
of train at Spiez, and also commissioned their magnificent
paddle steamer *Lötschberg* a month early for the navigation
across the Lake of Brienz. Even the 1863 reconstruction trip
had had a watery finish by the provision of a paddler called
Beattus dating from 1868 to cross the Lake of Thun. This was a
vessel held back from scrap for the Centenary celebrations by
the B.L.S., who had acquired it on their formation in 1910
from almost forgotten predecessors who had conducted navigation on the Lake of Thun in mid-Victorian times. They also
celebrated their own Golden Jubilee in 1963.

It is slightly difficult, therefore, for me to associate journeys
over the Lötschberg Railway without thinking of high collars,
spats, top hats and crinolines, which is romantic nonsense since
the true image of this railway is as modern and progressive as
any in the world, perhaps more than almost any others outside
Japan. One has only to see the incredible 8,800 horse-power
electric locomotives ascending the steep gradients, 1 in 27, at
forty-six and a half miles an hour with 900 tons of train behind
them. Nowhere else in the world can performance like this be
observed, and it is small wonder that freight traffic over this important line has risen from 1,600,000 tons in the year 1938
through 3,900,000 tons in 1961 to over five million tons in
1967. Passengers, too, are steadily rising, to close on ten million persons a year.

A B.L.S. train will be waiting at a long platform on the north side of Brig station, headed by a powerful electric locomotive in distinctive brown livery. It is not concerned to pick up many passengers from the community of Brig itself, but from express trains which come thundering out of Italy through the Simplon Tunnel, and also from local Swiss Federal trains rolling up the Valais with passengers from Zermatt and Visp wanting to change for Central Switzerland. Many expresses from Milan will detach through coaches and Wagons-Lits and switch them to the Lötschberg Express, for the B.L.S. hauls through coaches from Calais bound for Stresa and Milan, and from Hamburg to Rome. By the time the train is due to start the weight behind the engine will be considerable indeed, and a rake of some variety will be on show, the dark green B.L.S. rolling stock merging with the blue of Wagons-Lits, the two-tone brown of Italian vehicles, and perhaps a French S.N.C.F. shade of green, while it is possible that a red Swiss diner of the Swiss Dining Car Company will be on the train to serve meals as far as Bern.

All this weight means nothing to a Lötschberg engine, probably a 2–6–6–2. Ae 6/8 202 class built between 1939 and 1942 (Switzerland was of course neutral during those war years). The official wheel formula for these engines is 1 Co+Co 1, rated at 5,300 horse-power. Only the Ae 8/8 engines, introduced in 1959, are more powerful with 8,800 horse-power, the most powerful locomotives in the world today.

The start at Brig is smooth, the heavy train gathering speed quietly and quickly behind the locomotive as the line junctions to the right and a steep climb begins. It is almost like ascending in an aircraft of pre-war days, gaining height with piston engines at a relatively slow rate. Within bare minutes of the start, the Lötschberg train is high up on a shelf dug out from the wall of mountains while the great valley of the Rhône falls away beneath, flanked by its mountain ranges. At forty-five miles an hour, one is climbing a vertical distance much quicker than the average elevator in a building. The views become more and more breathtaking, especially as we pass high above Visp and the entrance to the valley in which stands Zermatt under the dramatic Matterhorn. This great peak can be clearly seen on all but cloudy or hazy days.

It was of the Lötschberg Railway, and this section of it in particular, that Gustav Ranker, the well-known Alpine poet, wrote in his novel published in 1950: 'The idea is perhaps dawning upon passengers travelling in the luminous and fine coaches of the struggle between railway and mountain nature, speeding as they do between tunnels and protection sheds along the Lonza Gorge; a gorge still under the burden of the first day of creation, like an Act of God that, seemingly, has happened only a short while ago. But, as soon as the train emerges from the Hohtenn Tunnel into the boundless spaciousness of the mountain's southern flank, and as soon as the traditional "ah" sounds at the sight of the depth so suddenly torn open of the Valley of the Rhône, you feel like gliding on plumes along the sunny slopes of the Valais. In the landscape with its translucent air, with its vegetation, there is an inkling of the South, and everybody and everything feels liberated, full of suavity in the enchanting fullness of light and frankness.'

Ranker was, of course, writing of the romantic journey in a southbound direction. The descent is so steep and fast that one's ears click as with a plane. Going north this is not destined to happen until after Kandersteg beyond the Lötschberg Tunnel. The change from a southern aspect with the touch of Italian in the air to a northern climate and the German language tends to create an opposite effect, especially as most passengers are returning from a holiday in the South of Europe.

The express climbs higher and higher above the Valais, so that before the Lötschberg line finally turns in to tackle the towering mountain wall it is riding over 3,000 feet above the silvery Rhône and the towns of the Valais are strung out in view just as if one were flying above the region in a non-pressurized piston-engined aircraft. Once the turn-in is made, rocky walls and short tunnels, viaducts and snow-shelters replace the broad aspect. There are only halts along the sixteen miles of line between Brig and the mouth of the Lötschberg Tunnel, but just before entering it, the train comes to a stop at the busy, mountain-enclosed station of Goppenstein. Here the road comes in and expires, cars and vans being loaded on to flat cars for rapid rail haulage through the tunnel. It is a quick and painless business for motorists, who remain seated in their vehicles. Charges are modest considering the service and speed, about twenty-two Swiss Francs for the car and driver, and a few francs more for each passenger. The cars are let off their flat wagons just short of Kandersteg station, ten miles away in distance but a world away in atmosphere.

Immediately on leaving Goppenstein, the heavy Lötschberg express plunges into the double-track tunnel and gathers speed to reach the summit of the line, 4,067 feet, about half-way through. The tunnel took six years to build, between 1906 and 1912, and is Switzerland's highest standard gauge railway tunnel. It was built double track and although its construction took some toll, as is inevitable with any major engineering achievement employing large numbers of men for long periods, it avoided the disasters and floodings which caused serious losses of life and equipment in the Gotthard and Simplon Tunnels.

There is no perceptible increase in speed once the summit is reached and passed, for the train will have accelerated to about fifty-five miles an hour up the grade and will not exceed sixty going downhill. It takes a fraction over ten minutes to run through the tunnel and then the express bursts into the light at the north end, into a world of white-clad mountains, glaciers, and dark green valleys. To the left and high above the train, the awesome mountains rearing above the difficult footway over the Gemmi Pass stand out boldly. Kandersteg Station, an important stop, is some 1,200 yards beyond the tunnel exit, and the train comes to a stand forty-one minutes after leaving Brig, twenty-six miles away. There is only one express each way every day which passes through Kandersteg without stopping, although the car sleeper trains to Brig running in summer on a once-weekly basis omit the stop.

From Kandersteg there begins what many travellers regard as the most scenic and fascinating part of the Lötschberg Railway, the descent of the Kander Valley and the negotiation of the spiral tunnels. Some of this section is still single track, requiring halts to wait for ascending traffic—and the sight of a thousand tons of freight train coming up the 1 in 37 at over forty-five miles an hour is spectacular as it thunders past. But doubling and automated traffic control over the stretch from Hondrich to Frütigen in 1964 has eliminated a daily total of twenty-four halts for crossing purposes. I had the extremely rare experience of riding down from Kandersteg to Frütigen through the spirals on the footplate of a 2–8–2 steam loco-motive in July 1963 (as part of the Cooks Centenary Tour), hauling four elderly four-wheeled carriages. This was the first time a steam passenger train had run through the spiral tun-nels, and it was destined to be the last, for the engine, retained only for urgent work on avalanche-damaged catenaries, has been broken up and replaced by powerful battery locomotives. But I have also made the run down from Kandersteg to Spiez in the cab of a two-coach electric unit, and the feeling of sliding down into bottomless depths is even more apparent.

Frütigen is a large station, eleven miles from Kandersteg and thirty-seven from Brig. After leaving this winter sports centre the line levels out through fruit-growing country to the shores of the Lake of Thun, where the mountains are softer, the snow slopes still visible but more distant. Spiez is the headquarters of the Lötschberg Railway, and before running in to the large, clean station, workshops and sheds are passed on the left. Going north, it is necessary to change for the run eastwards to Interlaken, as the expresses run on to Bern, but southbound trains detach sections for Interlaken at various times of the day. Some of the two-coach units reverse at Spiez and run to Interlaken. It is forty-six miles from Brig, with another twelve to go to Interlaken East, and twenty-five to Bern.

All the way from Spiez to Interlaken the train is within sight of water, clinging to the lakeside or passing through tunnels. There is a Lötschberg steamer on the lake as an alternative, which docks about two miles from the centre of the resort. In just under twenty minutes, Interlaken Station is reached, a big place with several tracks where porters from the various hotels wait with their trolleys. Trains of the Swiss Federal Railways have running powers into this station from Bern; they bring large numbers of holidaymakers both in summer and winter from Zürich and Bern. It is another two miles of fairly slow travel, however, through the long strung-out resort (with good views up the Lauterbrunnen Valley to the famous Jungfrau, over 13,000 feet, and its sister peaks, Mönch and Eiger), before Interlaken East Station is reached.

Interlaken Ostbahnhof, to give it the full title, is shared by trains of the Lötschberg Railway, the Berner Oberland Bahn, and the narrow gauge Swiss Federal Brünig Line. The B.O.B. trains, in their distinctive brown livery, go off up the valley to Grindelwald, and some of their coaches, also of metre gauge like the Brunig Line, are worked over that route all the way from Lucerne. But there is another half-mile before the Lötschberg tracks finally end on the shores of the Lake of Brienz at the harbour of Boningen. Here a Lötschberg steamer will be waiting, either a diesel vessel or the gorgeously decorated, elegant paddle steamer *Lötschberg*. In the busy summer season it is usually the big-capacity paddle steamer, built in 1914 and kept in superb condition, to be found working the lake.

In fine weather the ten miles across the Lake to the town of Brienz are a delight, especially aboard the *Lötschberg*. A call is made at Giesbach, where a tremendous waterfall roars down into the lake from the brooding mountains. The time to Brienz landing stage is about forty-five minutes, and then a short walk brings passengers to the metre gauge Brünig Line station. Until the Swiss Federal took over the Brünig Railway in the twenties, Brienz was a terminus, but then the line was extended round the lake shore for twelve difficult miles to Interlaken Ost. Prior to this opening, the Lötschberg steamer service was a vital transport link; today it is a trip for pleasure and variety. Brienz, famous for its wood-carvings, is also the terminus for one of Switzerland's few remaining all-steam railways (the only all steam cog line), the Brienz-Rothornbahn, a rack and pinion line which climbs to the summit of the 8,000-foot Rothorn.

Swiss Federal trains over the Brünig are neat and modern, with specially designed Brown-Boveri metre gauge engines. It is the only narrow gauge line operated by the Federal system, forty-six miles long from Interlaken Ost to Lucerne. Immediately on leaving Brienz the train swings round to the head of the Lake of Brienz and travels up the Haslital, the wide valley which later narrows and becomes shut in by high passes closed by snow for nine months of the year. At first the journey is on the level, a fast stream rushing past to the right of the train. After seven miles, the train runs into the station of

Meiringen, once headquarters of the Brünig Railway. Meiringen is a pleasant little town, serving the whole valley of the Haslital, and set on the floor of the valley below the famous Reichenbach Falls.

It was here on the first day of May 1968, that the 'return of Sherlock Holmes' was celebrated when the famous detective, in the guise of Sir Paul Gore-Booth (now Lord Gore-Booth), then head of the British Foreign Office, arrived with a huge retinue to re-enact Conan Doyle's classic story of the fight to the death between the great detective and Professor Moriarty on the lip of the Reichenbach Falls. For this special occasion, Moriarty was played by Mr. Charles Scholefield, Q.C., Master of the Middle Temple. The entire population of Meiringen turned out at the station to meet the train, and again to see the party off on its way to Lucerne two days later. 'Sherlock Holmes' was granted the Freedom of Meiringen, and any travellers arriving in the town on May 2nd in future years will find most premises closed and the townspeople *en fête*, for this has been declared 'Sherlock Holmes Day' and is now a holiday!

The train cannot proceed further up the narrowing Haslital (although a tiny battery railcar on a ninety centimetre gauge does go up a few more miles for the benefit of the farming community) so it reverses direction, then swings to the right of the tracks over which it has come from Brienz. At once it engages a rack and tackles the steep Brünig Pass in full face, with no twisting and turning. The coaches tilt, the clanging of the rack and pinion drowns the sound of the wheels, but with the power of the special electric rack engines, speeds of thirty miles an hour are maintained up this fierce incline, while the valley drops away below as if from a climbing aeroplane. As the trees close in near the summit the train swings away from the Haslital and turns north, slowing to disengage the rack before running into Brünig Station, three and a quarter miles from Meiringen. The journey will have taken about twelve minutes overall, which compares with half an hour at the turn of the century with a steam rack banker pushing, and twenty minutes in the late 1930s when some powerful steam banking engines were built for the line. These took the head, the centre, and the rear of heavy trains going over the Brünig, and were still in busy use in 1949, when I first went over the Pass. In fact, the last two were not officially withdrawn from service until the end of 1965, when one went to a private buyer and the other was preserved in splendour under a canopy on Meiringen Station.

With the Brünig Bank conquered, the metre gauge Swiss Federal electric is now free to cruise down past Lungern with its beautiful lake through the high country of Central Switzerland towards the Lake of Lucerne. This huge body of water, known as the Vierwaldstättersee or 'Lake of the Four Cantons' was the cradle of the Swiss Confederation, formed in the fifteenth century. At Sarnen, the train runs along the shores of the Sarnersee, and views can be obtained of bold 'pre-Alps' like the Stanserhorn, Pilatus, and Rigi. Some thirteen miles remain to be travelled after leaving Sarnen, and soon Lake Lucerne is reached. At Alpnachstad there is a ferry landing and on the other side the terminus of the world's steepest rack railway, the line which climbs direct to the 7,300-foot summit of Pilatus. A new railway line, not built until 1963, crosses the shallow lake by a causeway split by a swing bridge close to Alpnachstad. This is the Lucerne-Engelberg private electric line, which has much reduced travelling time in winter for the thousands of people going to the popular snowsports resort.

About three miles from Lucerne, with views across the arm of the lake to the abrupt Burgenstock and the Hammetschwand lift near which lie some of the world's most exclusive hotels, the Brünig Line swings inland, running through some short tunnels and past a few Lucerne suburban backyards before entering the busy terminal station. Its magnificent Germanic roof and buildings were destroyed by a fire which got out of control during February 1971, and will no doubt be replaced by some functional modern design, but being Swiss it will have many useful features and improve—rather than detract from—the lot of the passenger. The thirty-five difficult miles from Brienz will have taken about 105 minutes by stopping train, and only ninety-two by express, but almost all those minutes will have produced varied and often breathtaking scenery.

Above. The author on the footplate of *Boyne*, former Great Northern of Ireland 4. 4. o. leaving Great Victoria Street in November 1963.

Below. A former Great Northern of Ireland 4. 4. o. heads a Londonderry train out of Belfast in early 1964.

[*Photographs by Brian Haresnape*]

Above. The beautiful paddle steamer *Lötschberg* owned by the B.L.S. railway company plies up and down the lake from Interlaken to Brienz.

Below. An electrically hauled express on the narrow gauge Brünig railway, near Lucerne.

[*Photographs by Tony Hudson*]

Steam on the oldest line over the Alps. The Vienna-Klagenfurt express coming
up through the Semmering Pass before the line was electrified.

[*Photograph by courtesy of the Austrian State Tourist Dept.*]

Right. The 'Warsaw-Sofia Poloma Express' at Breclav in Czechoslovakia hauled by a 4.8.2. locomotive.

[*Photograph by W. Solch*]

Left. A modern Czech 4. 8. 2. Type
498.1 at Brno station, Moravia, heading
the Balt-Orient express.

[*Photograph by Tony Hudson*]

Engineer Jan Stefanic, 27 year old technical graduate opens up his 4. 8. 2. No 035, as she pounds up the grade from Çeska Trebova, with the author on the footplate.

[*Photograph by Tony Hudson*]

A quiet ride for the fireman on class 498.1 No. 035 which is fitted with a mechanical stoker.

[*Photograph by Tony Hudson*]

A dramatic view of two Czech steam locomotives thundering along in the same
direction on parallel tracks necessitated by the accident referred to in the book.

[*Photograph by Tony Hudson*]

15

Czech Journey

Home of some of the most modern and impressive steam locomotives remaining in Europe, Czechoslovakia is attracting more and more railway enthusiasts from far afield to its internal network of lines. Although many routes have been electrified, express steam is likely to be kept in action until at least 1975, and the condition in which the engines are maintained gladdens the hearts of all interested observers. Even the Czechs themselves, dour sturdy people not normally given to romantic notions, have begun to recognize that they have 'got something' and that Dvorak (their great composer) might not have been mad after all for loving steam engines.

During the autumn of 1967 I was in Czechoslovakia with my colleague, photographer Tony Hudson, and after contact with the Minister of the Railways in Prague we were issued with footplate passes valid for steam engines. We planned to use them on the most famous train in the country, which crosses Czechoslovakia on its way from the Baltic Coast at Stettin to the Black Sea at Constanza, the heavy and popular 'Balt-Orient Express'. We knew the train was electrically hauled for the first part of its journey from Prague, as far as Çeska Trebova, but there steam took over for the run to Brno and Bratislava.

Early on a sunny autumn morning in Prague, the first for several days, we took a short taxi ride from our hotel to the classical Main Station, and boarded the waiting 'Balt-Orient Express' with only minutes to spare before it left at 8.10 a.m. The train had been drawn into the high-roofed, late nineteenth century 'Czech-Renaissance'-style station by a Pacific-type steam locomotive from Decin on the Czech-East German border at 7.34 a.m. The heavy 'Balt-Orient', beginning its long journey as a short train from Stettin, picks up a number of coaches and sleepers at Berlin Ostbahnhof, whence it departs shortly before midnight to make an overnight run across East Germany, calling at Dresden at 2.40 a.m. and then crossing into Czechoslovakia just after four o'clock in the morning.

As we pulled out of Prague behind an electric locomotive picking up current from 1,500-volt overhead wires, the formation was sixteen coaches, a red Mitropa diner riding next to the baggage car behind the engine, and another diner, Czech C.S.D. this time, at the rear of the train. In between were first and second class coaches of East German, Czech, Hungarian and Rumanian systems, couchettes and sleeping cars from each administration. The 1,100 tons or so seemed too much for the single electric, which promptly stuck at the platform end and waited with motors humming for assistance on the bank leading up to a bridge near the State Park. This came in the form of a second electric unit and the double-headed train got under way, only to come to a stop while the pilot engine was uncoupled and the E.499 class unit was left in sole charge. There is a more powerful type of electric known as E.699, which should be rostered for this heaviest of all passenger trains to run in Czechoslovakia, but for unknown reasons none was available on this occasion.

It is 102 miles from Prague to Çeska Trebova, a railway junction in Moravia, and the run is supposed to be made without a stop in two hours eighteen minutes, at an average speed of forty-five miles an hour, reasonably fast by Czech standards (and by Eastern European standards for that matter). But due to the bad start and a long delay at signals followed by some 'wrong-line' running at a point beyond the big town of Kolin, we took a total of two hours, forty-eight minutes to Çeska Trebova, arriving thirty minutes late. There had been one or two bursts of speed at between sixty-five and seventy miles an hour, shortly after passing Çesky Brod and again near Chocen where the hilly country of Moravia starts, but the running was not spectacular. Due to the Brno Fair being on, the train was packed, and a large proportion of travellers in first class were businessmen going to this important autumn sales occasion which, in East Europe, ranks with the Leipzig Spring Fair.

Arrived at last at Ceska Trebova, my colleague and I alighted and went to the head of the train armed with a small but impressive-looking footplate pass and letter in Czech signed by the Minister of the Railways. We were in time to see two massive and spotlessly clean 498 class Skoda-built 4–8–2 locomotives backing down on the train. We chose the leading engine, showed our document to a surprised driver, and climbed into the high, spacious, and well-protected cab. Language difficulties were encountered, but with a smattering of German it was possible to gather that the handsome young driver was Jan Stefanic of Bratislava, a graduate of the Slovakian Technical School. We learned later that he was married to a doctor, but it was already obvious that he was no traditionalist of the footplate.

It was the first time I had ridden the footplate of a double-headed express and the signals between drivers proved to be interesting as the powerful engines opened up and blasted away up a savage 1 in 70 grade which climbed for three miles out of Çeska Trebova into the Moravian hills. An electric line, the main route to the east, reaching to Kosice, went off to the left. Our young fireman was more of a technician than a stoker, for his main job was to watch and operate the worm-drive automatic stoker and keep the gauges at the right level. Exhaust beats were musical and powerful as the 'Balt-Orient' was heaved up the gradient, achieving twenty-eight miles an hour by the summit. The switch-back line to Brno via Svitavy is fifty-seven miles, double track and laid for the most part with new concrete sleepers and long welded rails. Normally, time allowed is one hour and thirty-four minutes, but we had no sooner got up to forty-five miles an hour when adverse signals were sighted and we came to a dead stop. There were people on the track and a good deal of hand signalling as the 'Balt-Orient', for the second time on its journey from Prague, was switched to 'wrong line' working. It was a curious sensation to be charging along double track on the wrong line overtaking a train going in the same direction!

But more hand signals were ahead and steam was shut off as Jan Stefanic applied the brakes and signalled to the train engine to do the same. We crawled forward to the station at Svitavy and soon saw what was causing the trouble. A passenger train had crashed, the wrecked engine being embedded in the partially demolished station building, while the coaches, all but one derailed, presented a dismal picture of buckled ends and smashed windows. We heard later that two people had been killed on the train and two on the station, with about thirty injured, during the derailment which had occurred in the small hours of the morning.

We still moved slowly forward well beyond Svitavy to some points where more men were hand-signalling trains, and here we switched back to the correct (right-hand) side of the line. By this time the 'Balt-Orient Express' was more than forty minutes late, and there appeared to be no hope of improving on this situation. However, Driver Stefanic opened up the massive throttle and with joint whistles in agreement it was a case of giving the big engines their head. After passing another breakdown train with a crane and some gangers' trolleys, we left all signs of disaster behind and tore along the track, the thunder of our combined exhausts echoing from the surrounding hills. We burst through short tunnels and hurtled round curves, the speed rising to sixty-five and even seventy miles an hour. There was a speedometer of large size, apparently quite accurate, on the driver's side, and another on the fireman's, both giving the speed in kilometres per hour with a thick red warning line cautioning against exceeding 120 k.p.h. (seventy-five miles an hour). Soon the needle was touching this line and it held that position for three very fast and rocketing miles when it was difficult to stand without holding on as the big engine shouldered at full speed into curves. Letovice Station shot past, dust rising from the platform in our wake. The sight of this great train would have warmed the hearts of thousands in Britain and America, but the Czech passengers on stations or people seen in fields scarcely spared us a dour glance. It appears to be a case of familiarity breeding contempt, but the time will come when—as this romantic sight becomes rare—they, too, will hanker after the sight and sound and smell of a fine steam express. Already, in 1971, enthusiasts' specials are being run behind a preserved pacific.

Through Skalice we tore at sixty-eight miles an hour, over a stretch of line carrying a 100 k.p.h. restriction (sixty-two and a half miles an hour), and the leading engine was registering the bumps. But we held on and went like the wind. I looked back from time to time to see our smoke merging with that of the train engine and whirling high over the long train. A succession of nine short twisting tunnels through the last of the Moravian hills slowed us only very slightly, and at Adamov on the Svitava River we could already see the towers and spires of Brno dead ahead. The signals were clear for an unrestricted approach and both engines, their huge driving rods clanking musically as they echoed through the cutting, slid through the approaches to the city and entered the station, rolling to the platform end and a stop at exactly 12.30 p.m., only twenty-eight minutes late. We had not only completed the troublesome run from Çeska Trebova in ninety-two minutes, two minutes less than schedule (despite the restrictions imposed by the Svitavy crash) but had recovered two minutes of the time lost by the electric and picked up at least twelve minutes on the section from Svitavy to Brno. It was an amazing demonstration of modern Czech steam power and the technical competence and courage of our driver.

We left the footplate here, having eaten part of a picnic lunch and drunk a bottle of Pilsen beer, leaving the 'empty' in the tender. The remainder of the journey, back in the comfort of the train, took us along the level, straight line to Bratislava with one stop at Breclav, an eighty-seven mile run, in two hours exactly, saving eight minutes on schedule. The 'Balt-Orient' was only twenty minutes late as it pulled into the Slovak capital.

Until the end of November 1967, the Brno-Bratislava line was the busiest steam route in Europe, but it has now passed 'under the wires'. For some years to come, massive engines of the 498 class (which have slight variations and are known as 498.1, 498.2, and 498.3 according to the differences) will handle traffic on the Moravian section to Brno, but there they hand over to electrics of E.499 and E.699 classes. Bratislava engine shed, to which our friend Jan Stefanic belonged, lost most of its allocation of these relatively new Skoda engines, but because lines to the east and north from Bratislava remain steam-operated, there are plenty of engines of various types, including the 'Albatross' type 475 4–8–2s, left in the shed. The line going to the popular Tatra Mountains north from Bratislava on the Danube is steam-hauled as far as Zilina, 126 miles, where it meets the main line from Prague via Çeska Trebova, Olomouc, and Ostrava which is already electrified, and it carries on 'under the wires' to Poprad-Tatra (junction for the mountain electric railways) and Kosice.

16

Benguela Railway

Surely the most romantic and enchanting railway of any major size appealing to the enthusiast of all ages is that long single line which prods deep into Africa from the Angolan coast and links up with all the railways of Central Africa. The Benguela Railway, or Caminho de Ferro Benguela to give it the Portuguese title, is not only a pleasant system on which steam reigns supreme but one of the most efficient and profitable railways in the world. It is unique, too, for its use of special fuel—eucalyptus logs cut from beside the track out of forests deliberately planted from Australian seeds imported fifty years ago.

Big modern wood-burning engines are a rare and spectacular sight, and the Benguela Railway has nearly a hundred of them on its 838 miles of line. Before anyone gains the impression that they are quaint, let me point out that thermal efficiency has been developed locally to a point where only fifty-eight grammes of eucalyptus wood have to be burned to move a ton-kilometre. The hefty Beyer-Garretts can and do haul 450 tons of train up formidable gradients of 1 in 50 and even 1 in 40 on some sections at a speed of eighteen to twenty miles an hour. This is achieved on fuel available in abundance along the system and delivered into the locomotive tenders at a cost of barely three dollars (£1.25 Sterling) per ton.

The Benguela Railway is unique in other ways, too, not least by its retention of quality and service belonging to an age long past in many countries. Sampling the overnight train service in 1969 I wrote that it was like going into a long established merchant bankers, using the gold-embossed leather blotters, and meeting an extremely courteous, efficient teller. There are old-fashioned practices in this part of Africa, but they work and they pay dividends. In 1970 the Benguela Railway's net profit was over £2 millions, a half million more than the year before.

The first class carriages on Benguela main line trains are exquisitely comfortable, and when made up as sleepers at night have no betters anywhere in the world. They are like the best of Pullman Standard craftsmanship in the U.S.A. during the thirties. As well as wash basins of the latest type in the cabins, there are showers at the ends of each coach. Varnish and gloss are evident in the corridors and cabins, while brass and aluminium are shining. The dining cars (the Company owns five) are amazing examples of carriage building art, clerestoried, carpeted, only 24 chairs in a big space, silver and napery gleaming, and Pullman-type lamps glowing aided by small overhead chandeliers. Fortunately the food and service match the decor, and all visitors agree that the best hotels in Angola are the sleepers and restaurants of the Benguela Railway. To be honest, they do not have much of a standard to beat, especially in the matter of food.

An Anglo-Portuguese Company, with its head office in Lisbon and a London Committee, the Benguela Railway is part of a vast concern known as Tanganyika Concessions which nowadays has its head office in Nassau in the Bahamas. Its prime profitable function is the long-haul of copper and other minerals to the port of Lobito for shipment to Europe. This copper comes from Zambia and the Katangan copperbelt of the Congo. Due to political problems in Rhodesia, the route westwards is preferred by African leaders in those countries to the older-established outlet through Rhodesia to Beira and the South. New lines are being built in Africa at a greater rate than at any time since the turn of the century, and the long-term future of the Benguela is threatened by a Chinese venture being built for Zambia to be called the 'Tan-Zam' Railway. This will be a thousand miles long and will carry Zambia's copper to Dar-es-Salaam when it is completed about 1977–78. A second threat comes from a project in the Congo to extend the line at present reaching Port Francqui on the Kasai River (where trans-shipment is made on to the steamers of the Otraco river system) all the way to Kinshasa and the Congo port of Matadi as well as the 'Brazzaville-Congo' Republic's South Atlantic port of Pointe Noire. But there are certainly eight years of prosperity left in the Benguela system as an international carrier, viewed at the time of writing, and these should be years when it attracts an increasing amount of interest to its unique and happily steam-powered operations.

The idea of a railway through Angola, which had been a Portuguese African province since the latter part of the fifteenth century, was evolved by a certain Robert Williams in 1902. He thought in terms of a line starting at the rather exposed port of Benguela and running inland to join up eventually with railways then being built in Southern and Northern Rhodesia. The first lines were laid in 1904 but there were savage earthworks to erect and a brutal escarpment to overcome requiring the railway to be lifted from sea level to nearly 6,000 feet in a comparatively short distance. It was 1912 before the line reached 250 miles inland to the Province of Huambo and expired at a township then called Huambo where workshops were sited. This became a sort of latter-day Nairobi but did not grow to any extent in its first two decades, although the summit of the line, at a station named in honour of the Railway's founder, became a well populated place.

The First World War stopped further construction, and after that it was difficult to raise more money in the economic conditions of the period. Sir Robert Williams (a Baronet by this time) still had his ninety-nine year concession, and remained adamant that the completion of the railway was a necessity for the giant mining enterprise, Union-Minière du Haut-Katanga, which he had helped to create. Finance eventually came from Tanganyika Concessions, and track construction was resumed in 1920, pushing through the highlands of Angola to reach the border with the Congo in 1928. Here it had to wait for completion of the B.C.K. system (Bas Congo et Katanga) whose linking line, called the K.D.L. (Katanga, Dilolo and Lakes) arrived in 1931. Then, at last, through railway connection on the 3 feet 6 inches gauge existed all the way from Lobito Bay to Cape Town, a distance of 3,610 miles.

Success came almost immediately as shippers realized the value of this short cut. Compared to the existing route from Lusaka in Northern Rhodesia via Beira to London, the

Benguela Railway offered a total distance of 6,725 miles, saving 2,160 miles. For Union-Minière's copper shipments out of Elizabethville to Antwerp the saving was much more dramatic, 6,434 miles instead of 9,330 miles, although the mixed railway and river route through to Matadi only called for 6,160 miles (but with a good deal of trans-shipment).

Passengers sought the new way into Central Africa and soon the Belgian mail ships running weekly from Antwerp brought their Katanga-bound passengers to Lobito for a comfortable through boat express to Elizabethville. The Union Castle Line's intermediate ships from Southampton to South Africa began calling at Lobito once a fortnight and a through first class carriage was attached to trains to provide a fortnightly luxury trip to Livingstone and the Victoria Falls, a five day land cruise. From here, of course, passengers could make their way to Salisbury, Bulawayo, and even Johannesburg, saving time and distance compared with sailing all the way to the Cape and training upwards, through the Karoos to the Rand.

Things went extremely well for fully thirty years, but with the change of status in the Congo, and later in Northern Rhodesia (which became Zambia), coupled with political animosity towards Portuguese Africa, international passenger traffic fell away. The Belgians departed from the Congo and only a nucleus of skilled engineers remain in the Katanga, almost all of whom fly to their destination. The mailships of Compagnie Maritime Belge are no more, two of them having been sold to the P & O Group. Union Castle no longer call at Lobito, and in fact have disposed of their intermediate liners, concentrating on express mail runs taking eleven and a half days to Cape Town. Passengers and tourists going to the Victoria Falls mostly fly direct to Zambian airports, or come up by road and rail through Rhodesia.

With all this, any lesser organization might have gone into decay, but the Benguela Railway, fortified by increased receipts from mineral loads forced over its system by the same political factors that bar the way for through passenger trains to Central Africa, maintains its high standards. Today it serves Portuguese passengers almost exclusively, but its overnight trains from Lobito to the highlands, and even those going right through to the last Portuguese town before the Congo border, are models of luxury and solidarity for first class passengers, affording, too, very sound standards for those in second class. By the time these words are in print, through carriages could well be running again over the K.D.L. to Lubumbashi (formerly Elizabethville) following urgent requests for them by some Congolese, and a diplomatic thaw.

Let us take a train to the interior, as I did fairly recently (in August 1969) from Lobito. There are four passenger trains a week, two of them going as far as the developing town of Silva Porto on the highlands, and two making their way for two days and nights to Texeira da Sousa close to the Congolese border. Lobito Harbour, with its famous three mile long sandspit forming a natural breakwater, is busier than ever with ships loading copper, but the only big mailships coming in now are the weekly Portuguese liners from Lisbon, plus a quarterly call by Holland-Africa Line. The main passenger traffic is from the coast to the big city of Nova Lisboa, which started life as Huambo, had its name changed in 1928 when the railway was completed to the border, and has been booming ever since. With a population of over 100,000 living at a healthy 5,700 feet, it is the equivalent of Nairobi in many respects.

At Lobito the Benguela Railway maintains not only wharfs and workshops and an attractive engine shed (in which two classic Baldwin 4–8–0 locomotives live) but a fine hotel called the Terminus. The Company's palatial offices face the wide, airy terminal station and look out on the preserved 0–4–0 tank 'General Muchado' mounted on a plinth and numbered 001. This was the Benguela's first engine, a contractor's machine, retired honourably some forty years ago, and it is worth noting that no Benguela engines have ever been scrapped. None, of course, are very aged, and as they are superseded on main line work they are put on shunting or cane traffic, or in some cases become stationary boilers in works and sheds. Four of them are at Luso, fed by 45 tons of wood a day to work the town's electricity plant. The present (1971) engine stock stands at 109, more than half of them Beyer-Garretts.

All trains stop at all stations and passing loops, so it would be wrong to refer to the long, handsome train waiting to leave

Lobito at 5 p.m. (four days a week) as an express. It is no use selling speed in Africa; comfort and security take its place and this train acts as the best dinner, bed and breakfast venue in Angola, almost incidentally rolling from the coast to the high plateau overnight. On the Benguela, maximum speed is confined to 70 k.p.h. (about forty-four and a half miles an hour) a speed rarely attained in practice.

There is a sizeable population living along the twenty-mile coastal strip between Lobito and Benguela, including the town of Catumbela in between. Some suburban trains are operated on this line, and all engines employed on this level stretch, as well as those in the Lobito yards, burn coal imported from South Africa. At the head of the train for the interior will be a shining 'Mountain' class 4–8–2 built by North British Loco in 1956, one of a batch of six. These are divided between the coastal region where they are coal burners and the highlands where they burn eucalyptus logs. As an alternative one of the big 4–8–0 North British built engines, an earlier production, may be heading the train. In any case, it is only required to take the ten or twelve coaches for twenty miles to Benguela, and this it does, with stops at Catumbela and Damba-Maria, in just under fifty minutes.

Once arrived at Benguela there is frenzied activity on the platform, for most passengers join the train here, especially those patronizing the third and fourth classes at the front of the train. All passenger trains are made up the same way—a postal car behind the engine, then two or more fourth class coaches (handsome on the outside but with long benches of wood running down the centre and sides as the only accommodation) followed by two or more third class coaches. These latter are fitted with wooden shaped seats and would support mattresses if brought aboard. Two or three seconds are next in line on the train, rather like South African seconds with compartments and leather seats making up into berths for four or six people by night. A crew car with berths for train attendants and restaurant car staff comes next, attached to a lavish restaurant car, and behind that, at the very end of the train, one or two first class coaches, luxuriously appointed and finished in glossy veneer. All engines and rolling stock are beautifully maintained at

Nova Lisboa workshops, where they can do almost everything short of building a locomotive new (only the special steel for coupling rods and a few other units defeats them).

By 6 p.m. the train for the interior is ready to depart from Benguela, headed now by a special oil-fired Beyer-Garrett of the 10 C or 10 E classes, turned out in the late fifties. Nine of the latter were acquired from the Rhodesian Railways in 1965 after some dieselization had occurred there, and while some were converted to wood burning, the others were kept for the oil section. Owing to the sanctions against Rhodesia and a current oil shortage, the Rhodesian Railways have been heard to regret the sale and are thinking of trying to get these engines, or similar ones, back on to their system. Oil is considered necessary for the hard section from Benguela up to Cubal, a distance of 102 miles with many twists and turns and a ruling gradient of 1 in 40. In the first thirty-nine miles up to Portela the line climbs the coastal escarpment to reach 3,000 feet above sea level. Work has started on what is called the 'Cubal Variant', an easier route avoiding the worst of the escarpment. The 'Variant' should be opened by late 1972.

It is pleasant to listen to the engine pounding up the grade as the train works its way round the curves through spectacular scenery. Darkness is falling before Monte Saoa is reached, seventeen miles out from Benguela, but the fine Commander Alvaro Machado Bridge will have been crossed before the light fades. Dinner gongs sound at 7 p.m. and the lighted restaurant car is a welcoming sight, reminiscent of a sort of 'Cafe Royal on wheels'. Service of wine and good food is a ritual, and by no means costly. One has the feeling that the Company is kicking back some of its big profits when the bill for a five course dinner, washed down with Portuguese wine and topped off with a good measure of that country's brandy, comes to under a pound Sterling.

Returning to one's compartment shortly after 8 p.m. it is to find the bed made up and luggage stowed away, a bedroom on wheels with soft lights and only gentle sounds, thanks to three types of window covering pulled up. Here one might find the provision of a club car, American style, desirable, but in its absence the restaurant car can be used, or a stroll in the corridor with its windows opening fully might suit for a while if a pipe is to be smoked. With oil fuel, and later wood fuel, there are no smuts and the windows can be open without detriment.

The train stops at all stations and loops because there are no signals on the Benguela Railway. Every train obtains its clearance by the Company's own telephone system, and the driver is issued with a key for his section. No collisions have ever occurred, and no accident involving the loss of life of a passenger has ever been noted due to railway operations. Action near the Congo border by terrorists and insurgents led by Chinese guerrillas is excluded from this statement, but these attacks have mostly been on freight trains and in any case have not occurred very often. The Company has a spotting plane which flies over its exposed eastern tracks. It also runs armoured trolleys in advance of passenger trains eastwards of Luso.

Despite the stops and starts, which are handled extremely gently by the Portuguese driver, the passenger in first class— and second class for that matter—should sleep extremely well. I awakened only because an unfamiliar, pleasant smell assailed my nostrils, and getting up at about a quarter to four in the morning, found we were behind a wood-burning Garrett. The eucalyptus smoke reminded me of the lounge of a big old hotel in Australia I had stayed in one winter! Showers of minute sparks emerged from the engine's funnel but these did no visible damage and relatively few fires are caused along the way, so there is no call for spark arresting chimneys. The outside air was cold when I put my head out, and I found the altitude was little short of 5,000 feet.

On only one thing can other railways in Central, South and East Africa score over the Benguela, and that is the provision of early morning tea. The Portuguese have not yet got around to this pleasant custom so you sleep undisturbed, unlike South Africa where it comes at 6 a.m. whether you want it or not, or East Africa where the tea-boys start making a noise from 6.30 a.m. onwards. I awoke naturally with light coming into my compartment at about 6.45 a.m. Going along to the shower, which mercifully proved empty on first try, I saw curious rock shapes looming above the high plain and guessed we were nearing Lepi, 229 miles from Lobito and 5,300 feet above the sea.

The sun was burning off the early morning cloud and mist and it promised to be a warm dry day, normal for August on the Angola highlands.

The breakfast gong sounded at 7 a.m. but I gathered it was possible to go in any time up to 8 a.m., although language difficulties once away from the coast seem considerable. Portuguese is the only language, and even those who can speak a smattering of English rarely seem to understand what is said to them. At one time, when there were many Belgian passengers on the trains going to and from the Congo, French was widely spoken but this had dried up by 1969. British influences were very apparent, though, once in the restaurant car, for breakfast consisted, not of coffee and rolls, but fruit juice, fresh pineapple slices, ham and scrambled eggs, toast, coffee, rolls and marmalade. Even tea was available. The bill was just 30p.

A sharp climb brought the train to a stop at Vila Verde about 7.20 a.m., 6,000 feet above sea level. From there we rolled down to Robert Williams, now quite a big town named in honour of the Founder, and after that it was an easy run through the cattle studied highlands to Nova Lisboa, 265 miles, reached exactly on time at 8.30 a.m. Here most passengers alighted and the scene on the long platform was of bustle and excitement and emotional greeting. Our sturdy Garrett came off and was replaced with a sparkling North British 'Mountain', Number 405, for the final run of 141 miles to Silva Porto, the destination for this particular train.

I mounted the engine armed with a special footplate pass, and met my driver, Senhor Albino Nunes of Nova Lisboa Shed. We had two young African firemen, one of whom trimmed the wood in the high tender, bringing it down to within easy reach of the other, who opened the Agate firebox door from time to time and threw in—with an easy forward motion—the neat smooth logs weighing some 20 lbs. He would fire every three minutes or so, putting about twelve logs on the fire in different places, and this sufficed to keep boiler pressure at between 170 and 190 lbs per square inch. The smell on the footplate was very pleasant and the atmosphere clean. Apart from fuel the eucalyptus are used for track sleepers while the leaves go into boiled sweets made by the Company's associates. We ran easily and climbed the stiff bank up to Vila Nova, at 6,063 feet the absolute summit of the line 313 miles from Lobito. After that it was mainly downhill and Driver Nunes coasted his train along at between 60 and 65 k.p.h. (thirty-eight to forty-one miles an hour). At Chinguar we made a ten minute stop for wood and water, coming to rest alongside a huge towering mound of eucalyptus. One fireman hurled the logs down into the tender aided by a workman stationed there, while the other fireman saw to the water. These engines burning wood are gentle on water consumption partly because of the comparatively low pressure at which they work. While all this was going on, Driver Nunes did some oiling and wiped any nearly invisible specks of dirt from the gleaming sides of his perfectly maintained locomotive.

The train finally pulled into Silva Porto, past the growing industrial estate of this new highlands town, exactly on time at 2.19 p.m. I had been back in the train and enjoyed a lunch which matched the previous night's dinner, but until I was back again in a Benguela train I was not to find a single meal pleasantly edible. There is a long way to go before Angola is suited to tourism, but to be fair, it has problems towards its eastern boundaries while the deeply ensconced colonial Portuguese in the cities and along the coast, with 500 years of tradition behind them, are loathe to accept change or ideas from outside.

With the aid of the Governor of Bie Province's private Cessna aircraft, based on Silva Porto, I was able to fly along the line of rail, to see big game moving in the bushveld country towards Cuemba, and to photograph from low altitude two magnificent waterfalls, on the Cuemba and Luando rivers which, if they were easily accessible, would be in the front rank of world tourist attractions. Perhaps the one on the Cuemba will be one day, for the Benguela tracks are not far away and the Company's concession extends to twenty kilometres either side at this point. If any opening up of tourism is to be done they are the ones to do it, for as I hope I have shown, they know the right way to run a railway. . . .

17

Rails of South-West Africa

Just outside Windhoek Station in the middle of the square
there stands a tiny narrow-gauge steam locomotive dating from
1902. It is probably the only engine in the world which has
been declared a National Monument in both its own country
and a neighbouring one and yet was constructed in a third one!
The Germans built it at the turn of the century as part of a
back-to-back o–6–o plus o–6–o and delivered it to the raw, bar-
ren coast of South-West Africa to work on construction and
later to haul the first train to run from the coast to the high
capital. It is credited with doing more to open up South-West
Africa and creating the city of Windhoek than any other thing
or person.

Since 1920, South-West Africa has been mandated territory
administered by South Africa, and nowadays the Republic (as it
has been since leaving the British Commonwealth in 1961)
runs 'South-West' almost as part of itself. The edict making
'The Little Locomotive' a National Monument ranking with
President Kruger's house at Pretoria and Groote Schuur in
Cape Town was issued in South Africa itself and repeated by
the Administrator of South-West Africa in 1953.

Up in the highest part of the already mile-high city of
Windhoek, beside a 1912 statue known as the Horseman
Memorial (commemorating the part mounted troops of the
Kaiser played in the Herero Wars of 1903–07) is a handsome
2–6–o tender locomotive built in Britain shortly before the first
World War. This, too, is a National Monument, although it
was still in use on the very narrow gauge lines in the northern
parts of South-West Africa until 1962. Coupled to it are some
elderly carriages, a goods wagon and a brake van, the whole

10—RR

complex sprawling rather attractively on track laid above the Horseman Memorial between the wonderful new Administrative Building, the old Tintenpalast (former German headquarters) and the High School sports stadium.

South-West Africa is a vast area of wilderness, desert, rugged mountains, gorges and savannahs, the most sparsely inhabited region in Africa (Sahara notwithstanding). It stretches over 317,000 square miles between the Orange River and Angola and less than half a million people of all races live in it. As the official guide book says, 'South-West Africa is not a pretty country nor is it a gentle one'. It is close to the heart of the old Africa of legend, awesome, grand, spacious and even terrifying at times. It contains the largest game reserve in the world, Etosha, with 38,000 square miles where teeming game herds roam free and safe. But there are plenty of animals even outside the reserves, and a recent count by farmers added up to 110 black rhinos, while leopards are so numerous they can be seen at night in car headlights within a dozen miles of Windhoek.

It was to this great empty land where a few tribes were engaged in local and destructive fighting that the Germans were invited in 1885, Queen Victoria's Government having already declined the invitation to add one more big area to its African Empire. 'Only sand and rock and wild animals' read the report of a British survey party who advised against taking it on as a Protectorate. Oddly, it was about that period in British Imperial history that attempts were being made to shed commitments and pieces of unwanted Empire. Uganda was a case in point, because before this newly-explored, fertile Central African land became a British Protectorate the reluctant British Government tried to give it to the Jews as a National Homeland. This nearly succeeded, and if it had not been for the powerful Return to Zion movement ('Israel and only Israel is our Homeland') the whole balance of Africa, and the problems of the Middle East, would have been very different. However, on the evidence and with the survey equipment of the time, the British were probably right in not wanting South-West Africa added to their burdens.

But the German Emperor, seeking expansion and colonies,

accepted the invitation from war-torn Herero leaders battered by raiding Hottentots to be Protector. As with so many rugged, empty parts of the world at that time, a railway was the only way to open it up, and this practice continues today. Despite roads and airways, it is likely that the first requirement even in the distant future will be a railway to lay the basic foundation of development and supply—witness Labrador, North-West Canada, Arabia and part of South America, to say nothing of Zambia's coming link with the Indian Ocean (the Tanzam Railway) being built by the Chinese.

The Germans began laying a railway of 2 foot 6 inch gauge from the cool, cloudy but eternally dry coastline at Walvis Bay to the high, dry plateau on which their designated capital Windhoek (meaning 'windy corner') stood. They pushed their line through the worst desert in the world, the Namib, devoid of moisture and cursed by winds which shift monster sand-dunes so that all sense of direction is lost. Once through the Namib the going was better, across hilly, sunny country which does at times receive rain and where subterranean supplies of life-giving fluid can be found. By 1904 they had forced their shaky line up to Windhoek, where the station is 5,488 feet above sea level. This immediately led to the growth of the city, to settlers, and to reliable communication with the coast. The line is 256 miles long, and in those days a train took at least twenty-four hours to make the journey, but this was very much better than a doubtful eight days on horseback across waterless country.

Working on ballast improvements in 1907, a German rail-way foreman named August Stauch was handed a large pebble picked up by one of his men at a place called Kolmanskop, ten miles out of Lüderitz Bay, the second port of South-West Africa. A new line was being built inland to Keetmanshoop, south of the capital, as part of a developing network. Overnight Stauch became a millionaire, for there were other pebbles in the sand and they were all diamonds of unparalleled magnitude. Prospectors descended in their thousands in 1908, but soon a wise but controversial clamp-down on diggings was enforced. Despite changes of government and world situations, the clamp remains as tight as ever, and this is essential if the value of diamonds is to be retained. In that brief period when prospecting was a free-for-all, diamonds poured on the markets and prices fell to absurd levels. Today, this is the 'Forbidden Coast' and security control is operated from that same Kolmanskop Station. No one may enter the vast sandy areas along the coast of South-West Africa, or for about seventy miles inland, unless for very special reasons and then under heavy security guard. Every woman in the world, however compassionate she may be, would support this restriction if she understood the reasons in full, for her engagement ring would be as worthless as a Woolworth's paste ring (possibly lower in value) if all those real diamonds were to flood and destroy the markets. Mankind must have some guiding values, however artificial, and gold and diamonds serve in this respect.

If you happen to be a passenger in a train running along the 227 miles from Keetmanshoop to Lüderitz, especially over the last twenty-two miles between Rotkop and Lüderitz, you may be looking at diamonds among the pebbles in the desert. You may not freely alight to find out if they are. Lüderitz Bay itself is an open town, even with motor cars about, but to drive southwards along the apparently good coastal road running towards the Republic of South Africa border is beyond the power of almost any person except security officers. When I was in South-West Africa in August 1968, only one 'non-essential' person had been granted this privilege within the past few years, and he was a Swedish artist who, under escort, was going to Rock Arch, a fantastic erosion on the windy desert coast, to paint the lonely scene for hanging in the hall of the Administration Building at Windhoek.

People confuse the 'Forbidden Coast' with the 'Skeleton Coast'. The former is a vast diamond area of sand and desert running south from about the Kuiseb River near Walvis Bay (a river that is dry ten months of the year) to the Orange River mouth at least 350 miles away marking the border with the Republic of South Africa. Anyone found without permission or valid excuse (genuine castaway or crashed plane) is likely to disappear due to security reasons. But the 'Skeleton Coast' lies north of Cape Cross above Walvis Bay and runs to the Angola border, a wild and hopeless region of pounding seas, wind, and totally dry conditions. There are no diamonds, and no points of access. Ships going ashore cannot be assisted. The shifting sands and huge breakers smash them to pieces, and the bare skeletons of many wrecked ships, some of them quite large liners (like the Blue Star liner lost there in 1944), can be clearly seen by anyone flying a light plane low up this terrible coast. Even four-wheel drive vehicles could not get across the shifting, blowing sand dunes to the rescue and small boats cannot manage the surf. Today, rescues of human beings are possible, thanks to helicopters flown from Walvis Bay, but visibility can be bad for days on end due to sand in the wind and chances are never very high.

So the whole immense length of coastline of South-West Africa can be reached in only two places, by rail from Windhoek to Walvis Bay and its nearby holiday beach resort of Swakopmund, and by rail from Keetmanshoop to Lüderitz Bay (the train sealed over the last part of its run), also by roads which parallel these railway lines. Walvis Bay and its surrounding territory is officially part of the Republic of South Africa, an enclave in the Mandate.

German colonization of South-West Africa lasted only thirty years, for in 1915 General Botha, at the head of a brigade of South African troops coming up from Cape Province partly by train, took the city of Windhoek and accepted the German surrender. The country was jointly occupied by British and South African forces, and Walvis Bay became a British naval base and fuelling station. After the Treaty of Versailles, when Germany lost her former colonies, South-West Africa was mandated to South Africa (just as Tanganyika became a British mandated territory). The South Africans at once began to improve communications and built a railway up to Windhoek from De Aar Junction on the main Cape Town-Johannesburg line through Upington in north-west Cape Province and Keetmanshoop to Windhoek. This was built to the South African 3 foot 6 inch gauge. Opportunity was taken in stages to convert the former German lines to this gauge, work being completed when the Otavi-Tsumeb and Otavi-Grootfontein lines in the extreme North of the country reaching into the game areas became 3 foot 6 inches in 1962/63. The Germans had pushed a line up to

Tsumeb, where they had a fort built to control the fierce Ovambos. Today it serves the important Tsumeb copper mines and the nearby Etosha Pan, eighty miles of salt flats where hundreds of thousands of animals in the Etosha Reserve come to lick. Grootfontein is a pleasant town in fairly good pastoral country, near the site where the second biggest recorded meteorite landed, somewhere about 1876 to 1886.

Rich in minerals, South-West Africa enjoys tremendous prosperity and no one, not even the remotest tribal African, is poor by the standards of the Continent. If mining glittering diamonds is banned, except for the occasional carefully guarded Corporation release of a few, rearing 'black diamonds' goes on all over the grazing areas of the land. This is a name given by farmers to the Karakul sheep industry, producing 'Persian lamb' pelts. This began around the shores of the Caspian Sea and depends upon killing a new-born lamb within twenty-four hours of its birth. Because sheep in such dry country have to rush about from bush to bush to find food (in parts of South-West Africa it is considered good grazing if one sheep can be sustained on a hundred acres) their pelts become smooth and patterned, the animals thin. There is one lamb a year, but its pelt sells for between twelve and twenty U.S. dollars (the currency of South-West Africa is the same as the Republic, the Rand, 1.71 to the £). This is far more than a New Zealand farmer gets for the meat of his lambs, and almost all farmers with their big holdings are rich in South-West Africa. Most of the pelts go to London and New York, where a full length 'Persian Lamb' coat fetches from $500 to $1,000, some twenty-four pelts being needed to make it. Train-loads of pelts are to be seen making their tortuous way to the coast or down to the Republic, while copper trains move over the same route. Inland from Walvis and Lüderitz Bays trains with refrigerator cars filled with fish come up to Windhoek and the interior towns, for the fishing wealth of the coast with its cold South Atlantic current is unbelievable.

There are passenger trains on all lines open in South-West Africa but the enthusiast has to accept the fact that all traction is by diesel locomotives. The last steam engines were retired in 1965, not because of 'modernization' (the excuse put out so often in Europe and America when the real reason is pressure by oil salesmen) but because of the worsening water situation. In fact they were transferred for useful work in South-East Cape areas. All too often, as industry and more population called for water supplies, trains had been reaching watering points to find them dry. Diesels have solved this problem in the totally arid areas. General Motors and General Electric diesels, with their strident hooters, can be seen and heard at work in the dry country, and if they have detracted from the romance of the rails in this raw and awesome part of Africa, they have speeded things up by omitting long water stops.

Every night an 'express' leaves Windhoek for Walvis Bay, and vice-versa, doing the 256 miles in eleven hours, all compartments being sleepers. The line falls away steadily from Windhoek on a comparatively gentle descent, to the half-way mark at Kranzberg, junction for Tsumeb, where the altitude is 3,243 feet, nearly half a mile lower than the capital. The remaining 125 miles to the coast are among the driest in the world, totally devoid of human habitation or even of plant life, until Swakopmund is reached. There is a hut and siding called Namib, forty miles from Walvis Bay.

The Windhoek-Walvis Bay line has a relatively frequent service, for no real air competition exists except for a three times weekly five-seater Aztec plane, and there is only a tour bus over the road occasionally. There is even a day express on Sundays, returning on Fridays, while goods trains with one or two passenger coaches hooked on the rear make the trip every day. But Lüderitz Bay gets only three trains a week from Keetmanshoop, taking thirteen hours for the 227 miles, and the 142-mile-long Gobabis line, running east from the capital, has an 'express' on Thursday afternoons only, taking eight and a quarter hours, plus a goods train four times a week with two passenger coaches, taking nine hours. Tsumeb has a strong service, partly because copper trains attach passenger coaches and partly because tourists going to the Etosha Game Reserve require service. There are expresses on Thursdays and Sundays taking about seventeen hours for the 375 miles, plus a daily train making a lot of stops over the northerly part of the line which takes fully twenty hours for the trip.

The link with South Africa is tenuous and long by rail. Diesel traction may have speeded it up by some hours, but they have taken away some of the interest and the scenic attractions are limited. All is well over the 500 miles from De Aar Junction to Cape Town, which is steam-hauled as far as Beaufort West, and soon after that passes through monumental scenery. Windhoek has a new airport called 'J. G. Strijdom', built on level ground beyond the mountains some thirty-five miles east of the capital, and from here direct flights by South African Airways go to Europe twice weekly, and to Johannesburg and Cape Town several times a week. But not everyone flies, and as the Union Castle mail ships no longer call at Walvis Bay on their weekly runs between Cape Town and Southampton, there is rail connection by through train once a week from Walvis Bay through Windhoek to Cape Town. The train is called the 'South-Wester' and it leaves Walvis Bay on a Sunday evening at 5.30 p.m., Windhoek on a Monday morning at 11 a.m., to arrive in Cape Town at 2 p.m. on Wednesdays, just two hours before the Union Castle mail ship leaves her berth. One other train leaves for De Aar Junction from Windhoek (connections from all other South-West Africa lines having fed into it) at 10.30 p.m. on Fridays, reaching De Aar Junction at 10.30 a.m. on Sundays, having taken exactly thirty-six hours for 882 miles. Connections eventually get away from here to East London, Johannesburg, Port Elizabeth, Durban and Cape Town. There are South-West African dining cars on the 'South-Wester' and on the Friday night train. As with all African (East, West, or South) long-distance trains, all berths are sleepers, made up at night with mattresses and bedding.

At the beginning of June 1971, Union Castle broke an 83-year-old tradition by scheduling their mailships from Capetown to Southampton to leave at noon instead of 4 p.m., thus forcing a retiming of the South-Wester.

Despite its slow trains and diesel traction, there is something majestic and romantic about South-West Africa to attract the determined traveller, and make him (as it makes me) want to return one day. The crisp air is dry, and while temperatures are fairly high by day even in winter, reaching over 80° Fahrenheit at noon, the nights are very cool and even frosty by dawn. Rain does fall on the uplands between January and April, but it is predictable and never dangerous, while the dry expanses suddenly bloom after every shower. Rain, however, has *never* yet been known to fall in the Namib desert, and Swakopmund—unlike its opposite number of Arica in the Atacama Desert of South America—has no monument to a rain-drop!

18

'Orange Express' and 'Blue Train'

Committed as they are to a narrow gauge system of 3 feet 6 inches to serve almost all parts of the vast country, South African Railways have never concentrated upon speed. They have made rail travel comfortable, interesting, leisurely and scenic. People who are in a great hurry will fly, which does not worry the railways for they own South African Airways as well, and that airline has a monopoly of flights within the Republic. Other people will dash off in their own cars, or someone else's, doing a journey with some discomfort and not a little risk in about half the time a train takes. But a high proportion of South Africans, whose effective travelling population totals about five and a half millions, seem to regard rail journeys favourably, since the 1967 statistics showed that twenty-seven million long distance trips were made by train, against about one and a half millions by air during that year. The seventies began with a small increase on both figures.

Very much in the North American style but with a distinctive African atmosphere, South African train journeys over long distances give passengers the 'hotel on wheels' treatment. Every seat makes up into a bed at night, four persons being accommodated in a first class compartment, two in a first class coupe, and six in a second class compartment. Bedding stewards come round to provide mattresses and sheets and blankets at nominal cost, stewards call with tea or coffee in the early morning, there are pretty chimes sounded for meal-times in the dining car, and full meals are also served in the compartments. The best trains have observation bar-lounge cars, and most new coaches are equipped with showers. There are nice long stops at main stations for walks, local sightseeing, engine viewing and meeting friends. Overall average speeds are between twenty-eight and thirty-nine miles an hour, but on long level stretches behind powerful steam locomotives, seventy miles an hour is by no means unknown even on the narrow gauge with 1,200 tons of train!

The romance of South Africa's rails is heightened by the tendency to give crack trains colours. There are now four colours at work, one of which, the 'Blue Train', has attained world standards and is eagerly sought by tourists and South Africans alike, with the result that its ninety spaces are always fully booked, sometimes for three months ahead. The 'Orange Express' is another pleasant train, running over a longer journey, while the 'Brown Train' substitutes for the 'Blue Train' over the same route five days a week, although its official title nowadays is 'Trans-Karoo Express'. Lastly there is the 'White Train', built for the visit of King George VI and Queen Elizabeth in 1947 and now used by the President of the Republic.

When I first saw it in 1946–47, the 'Orange Express' was a train of comparatively mundane coaches and diners painted flaming orange, running from Durban to Cape Town through the Orange Free State. Today it is composed of the latest rolling stock in the standard colours of South African Railways, a sort of mauve-brown and off-white, and the name tends to signify its route through the Free State and across the life-giving, all-important Orange River. The Brown Train has had similar treatment, becoming the 'Trans Karoo Express'. Only the 'Blue Train' is so called because of the special colour of its coaches, and two new Blue Trains were under construction in 1968 for final completion in 1972, also painted blue. The "White Train', of course, only appears on ceremonial occasions, and is not available for public travel.

For the tourist wanting to see a good deal of South Africa, and the railway enthusiast who enjoys the latest in powerful steam haulage (very difficult to find in many countries at the beginning of the nineteen-seventies), the 'Orange Express' can be rated the best value journey in Africa. It is steam-hauled over 698 miles of its 1,300-mile journey, with heavy electric units coping with the rest. Some of the cities and towns it calls at are historic and fascinating as it links the Indian Ocean with the Atlantic and climbs from sea level to 5,755 feet at Kreuzberg, stays nearly a mile high all day, and comes down to sea level only in the last hour of its journey.

The 'Orange Express' (or 'Oranje Schneltrein' as it is called in Afrikaans) runs twice a week in each direction, leaving Durban for Cape Town on Mondays and Saturdays, Cape Town for Durban on Mondays and Saturdays. It is necessary to book some time in advance; you cannot expect to go to the station half an hour before departure and hope to get aboard, although of course a cancellation can occur. While everyone obtaining a seat automatically has a sleeper, some short-distance passengers can be taken seated in the observation car, subject to the discretion of the conductor in his three-ring uniform or his assistant, who wears two rings on his sleeve.

Departure from Durban's arched-roof station (built in traditional British style and dating from the turn of the century) is at 4.30 p.m. As a rule there are sixteen coaches behind an electric engine taking overhead current, and the weight is about 1,120 tons tare, which with passengers and baggage and mail, crew and stores, comes to close on 1,200 tons loaded. Speed is never more than about forty miles an hour out into the Durban suburbs because the train is climbing all the time and by the time Pinetown is reached, only seventeen miles out, it is already 1,125 feet above sea level. The names of the stations in this warm, sub-tropic part of Natal are partly very English (like Sea View, Poet's Corner, Glen Park and Hillcrest) and partly Zulu (such as Inchanga, Umlaas Road), reflecting the troubled mid-Victorian history of Natal and the Zulu Wars.

The scenery is predominantly upland, with vistas of rolling green hills and copses, some with Zulu kraals in clearings. To the right of the train (on the north side) can be seen the Valley of a Thousand Hills. Numerous curves, cuttings, and short tunnels are experienced as the train makes its way uphill to Natal's capital, Pietermaritzburg, a charming educational centre seventy-three miles from Durban, 2,218 feet above sea level, the first stop. The 'Orange Express' is scheduled to take two hours and twelve minutes for this run, the same time that the daily 'Trans-Natal Express' is allowed.

The line continues to climb steadily through the foothills of the Drakensbergs after leaving Pietermaritzburg (a fifteen-minute stop) and while first dinner is being served and darkness begins to gather the train pulls through wonderful scenery. Some stations have Afrikaans names, although most are still English to the Natal border. The 3,000-foot mark is passed at Sweet Waters, eighty-one miles from Durban, and 3,500 feet just after leaving Merrivale, junction for the spectacular Howick Falls served by a three-mile-long branch line. At 112 miles out from Durban, the train is passing Balgowan and tops 4,000 feet. Climbing seems to be effortless behind the electric engine, although speed is steady and modest. The first stop for the 'Orange Express' after leaving Pietermaritzburg comes at Mooirivier, a township famous for the battle in Boer War days when it was called Mooi River. It was from an armoured train on the line near here that Winston Churchill as a young war correspondent was captured in 1900. The stop is only brief at the pleasant, cool station 4,556 feet above the Indian Ocean, then the going is downhill as the hardest part of the Drakensberg climb is left behind. Estcourt, one of Natal's larger provincial towns, is reached at 9.5 p.m., 159 miles from Durban. Five minutes are spent here then the express curves through hills on a descending gradient, passing Colenso where another Boer War battle was fought, and reaches the famous city of Ladysmith, scene of the great siege of 1899–1900, at 10.14 p.m. The train is now 3,284 feet up, having dropped some 1,500 feet from the high point on this section at Hidcote, sixty-seven miles before.

Ladysmith is the junction for the line to Johannesburg, and the one the 'Orange Express' takes through the Orange Free State. The train spends thirteen minutes here before setting off again, still behind the same electric unit, and starts another long climb, this time on to the high veld up Africa's great escarpment. A non-stop run of 131 minutes lifts the express up 2,037 feet in sixty miles to Harrismith, on the Free State border. Sir Harry Smith was a former Governor of Natal; the town is named after him and Ladysmith after his wife. The stop at Harrismith, while most passengers are asleep, lasts twenty-two minutes, and during this time the electric unit comes off to be replaced by a large and powerful steam engine usually a 15F. 4–8–4. Steam now stays with the 'Orange Express' for more than twenty-two hours, all the way to Beaufort West in Cape Province, and this is likely to be the welcome situation for some years to come, for the three key factors which make steam haulage worth while are there in force—abundant supplies of labour, local coal and water. It is the latter which may weaken, but soon the Orange River dam projects should improve water supplies and a large fleet of powerful modern steam engines available in South Africa should be able to cope with the heaviest trains for at least a decade.

The 'Orange' takes the line to Kroonstad via Bethlehem. Leaving Harrismith at 1 a.m. it runs nonstop across high veld country, passing Afrikastop (5,603 feet) and Kreuzburg (at 5,755 feet the highest point on the line) before reaching the important junction of Bethlehem, Orange Free State, in exactly two hours for the sixty-five miles. Some twenty-five minutes are spent here, which most passengers, deeply asleep in the comfort of their soft mattresses, rarely see, although an engine change is carried out. The next engine, probably another 15F., gets away at 3.25 a.m., takes the 'Orange' nonstop to Arlington (thirty-seven miles in seventy-eight minutes) then on to Kroonstad (fifty-three miles in a hundred minutes). It is now 6.35 a.m. and stewards will have awakened everybody with tea or coffee. In the early daylight, keen risers will see another engine change effected by the huge and busy shed at this industrial Free State city. Kroonstad is a junction for Johannesburg and the Rand; it lies 4,491 feet up on the veld, 443 miles from Durban.

There is a line from Bethlehem to Bloemfontein, capital of the Orange Free State, which goes by way of Fouriesburg and Ficksburg, fringing the border of the mountainous independent Kingdom of Lesotho, formerly the Basutoland Protectorate. It is, however, shorter, smoother and busier from a passenger point of view to take the Kroonstad line, which the 'Orange' does. Leaving Kroonstad at 7 a.m. it rolls across well farmed, high, but rather uninteresting country, calling at Henneman, Virginia, Theunissen, and Brandfort before entering the big station of Bloemfontein at 10.55 a.m. The 128 miles will have taken five minutes under four hours, with the four intermediate stops.

Bloemfontein is Judicial Capital of the Republic of South Africa, a well-laid-out city which is steadily expanding. It is the Centre City of the Republic and its biggest railway centre, where 14,000 men work in the sheds and workshops. It is the world's largest remaining stronghold of steam, with 175 engines of many classes from express passenger to shunting locomotives based at the mammoth shed. On the twenty-ninth parallel of latitude, Bloemfontein is 4,568 feet above sea level with a dry, invigorating climate, the winter (May to September) mornings almost invariably being frosty while midday temperatures top sixty degrees Fahrenheit. Summer is the rainy season, but there is plenty of sunshine and nights due to altitude are cool. The flowers which gave it the name, coupled with hot springs, are in evidence everywhere, and a long flat-topped hill, called Naval Hill, dominates the city. This is a game reserve, the only one in the heart of a city in the Republic of South Africa, and springbok, kudu, and eland roam as they used to do when their herds were ten thousand strong a century ago.

There is another engine change on platform two at Bloemfontein, when a 23 class 4–8–2 usually takes over from the 15F. These engines date from 1956 and are among the fastest and most powerful in use. Now the 'Orange' takes the line to Kimberley, rather than going down south by way of Springfontein and Noupoort, which may seem at first glance the obvious route. It is fast double track to Kimberley, and the 106 miles, all gently downhill, take three hours and ten minutes. Sometimes there is a stop at Petrusburg, but although it is clearly marked in the timetables, the last time I took the express (in September 1968) we rushed through just as in 1947. The track is in very good condition and lunch can be enjoyed to the full, the typical South African Railways lunch of five courses costing only seventy-five cents (about 35 n.p.). It should be mentioned at this point that the 'Orange Express', like all main line trains, carries a section for passengers of non-European race who are served the same meal at tables in their compartments following the 'Apartheid' system. Stewards in the dining car are white; bedding assistants and those serving the non-white carriages are Coloureds or Bantu.

The last three miles before Kimberley, up from Beaconsfield Junction, are steeply uphill, and the engine's beat comes romantically loud to all passengers as the train labours up a 1 in 50 grade to the Diamond City. At 2.35 p.m. the 'Orange' is at rest in the long platform of Kimberley Station, and direction is reversed. Another engine comes on at the other end, this time a 25 class 4–8–4. If it is winter this will probably be a non-condensing type, but in very dry or hot weather a 25 of the condensing tender type will be used, capable of doing long hauls across the dry Karoo without much consumption of water.

Leaving Kimberley at 3 p.m. the same way as it came in, the 'Orange' glides down the steep hill up which it laboriously struggled half an hour before. Overhead electric wires are everywhere, for the main line from Johannesburg via Potchefstroom is under the wires as far as the Diamond City. The 'steam gap' is between Kimberley and Beaufort West, a distance of 311 miles, about a third of the total journey between the Witwatersrand and Cape Town. The all-steam Mafeking and Bulawayo line comes in at Kimberley as well as the electrified route from Johannesburg.

Kimberley is 4,012 feet above sea level, and can claim to be the sunniest city in the world. More than 3,200 hours of bright sunshine are experienced in an average year, yet it is rarely too hot, due to dry conditions and altitude. Huge grey mounds all over the place show how hard the ground has been worked to get at the diamonds, but the famous 'Big Hole', nearly a mile deep, is now a tourist attraction in the centre of the city, working having been abandoned in 1915. Huge mines and excavations seen to the left of the train as it leaves the station are often confused with the 'Big Hole' but they are in fact either quarries or extant diamond workings.

The fastest part of the journey now begins as the powerful 4–8–4 at the head of the train gets into its stride. These engines are kept in fine condition at Kimberley Shed, where each engine is still allocated to a named driver in the highly successful manner once adopted in Britain. The 'Orange Express' thunders along dead straight double track with only slight

A wood-burning 4. 8. 2. of the Benguela Railway, (one of six delivered by the North British Locomotive Works in the mid-fifties), heads an Eastbound train away from Nova Lisboa, 6,000 feet up in the Angola Highlands.

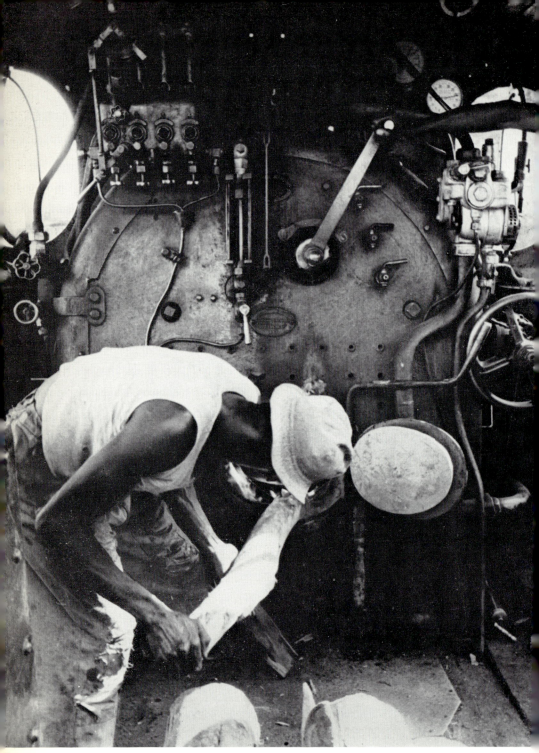
Firing with eucalyptus logs, on the Benguela railway.

Above. A train from Lobito to the interior passing the vast eucalyptus plantations which provide its fuel.

[*Photographs by courtesy of C.F.B.*]

Below. A typically luxurious restaurant car on the Benguela railway.

The Dawn Chorus: eucalyptus burning Garretts of the Benguela Railway near Cubral, Angola.

[Photograph by courtesy of C.F.B.]

Above. The Little Locomotive, designated a National Monument in southern Africa. The tiny o. 6. o. stands outside Windhoek station.

Below. A diesel hauled freight train from the Coast approaches Windhoek station.

Above. A mixed train passing through the savannah grasslands of South West Africa.

Below. With a change of engine at Bloemfontein, the 'Orange Express' headboards are changed.

Above. The 'Blue Train' headed by an electric locomotive, in the Hex river valley, Cape Province.

Below. The station approach and yards at Johannesburg.

[*Photographs by S.A. Rlyes, H.B.*]

Above. The eastbound trans-Siberian train headed by a Class P36 locomotive at Khabarovsk.

Below. The westbound trans-Siberian Express 'Rossia' stopped at Bira in Eastern Siberia.

gradients, keeping to an altitude of between 3,500 and 4,200 feet. The sweeping vistas are of rolling dry farmland with *kopjes* (small hills and rocky peaks) showing. Occasionally herds of springbok or other buck can be seen on the move, for many dry-country South African farmers encourage game herds on their land these days, making up to some extent for the slaughter their forefathers undertook.

It is seventy-seven miles to the next stop at Oranjerivier, and this is scheduled to take exactly two hours. I recorded a maximum speed of sixty-six miles an hour in 1968, and this with one engine on 1,200 tons of train on level track, but I am told of drivers exceeding seventy-five m.p.h., which must be nearly a world record for 3 feet 6 inch gauge. Running was very smooth in my case. There was a considerable downhill stretch approaching the famous Orange River, which we crossed on a high bridge. The water level varies according to the time of year, but even in the wet (summer) season the river does not impress people used to wide streams. However, it was magic to the early 'Voortrekkers', for whom it meant water, life and salvation, and the name of this long river, which rises in the Drakensbergs and flows into the Atlantic well to the north of Capetown, is perpetuated in all things South African. The Vaal is a tributary of it, and so is the Modder. Early in the nineteen-seventies the Orange River scheme will dam the stream in several places and make millions of acres of reservoir water available for irrigation and power.

The 'Orange Express' stops at Orange River station to take water from overhead gravity hoses. There are always two or three freight trains to be seen here, waiting their turn to go northwards. Gathering the water takes about eight minutes and at 5.10 p.m. the express is on its way again, to cover the seventy miles to De Aar Junction in ninety-five minutes, nearly equal to the 'Blue Train' and better than the 'Trans-Karoo Express', one of the fastest schedules in South Africa. It calls for an average of forty-four miles an hour, and means some steady running at sixty or more along track which is slightly against the engine, for the ground rises from 3,542 feet at Orange River to 4,278 feet at Houtkraal and 4,079 feet at De Aar.

The biggest junction in South Africa and a world-famous place among those who have studied geography, De Aar is a railway town with vast marshalling yards and a huge shed with more than 120 locomotives in it. De Aar was the name of a Boer farm on which the various lines coming from the coast and the north, all met. Diesels are to be seen here for they come in with trains off the arid line from South-West Africa. Lines go off to Bloemfontein via Noupoort, to Port Elizabeth, to East London, to Kimberley and Cape Town, and to Upington and the north. There is a stop of only ten minutes, during which time an engine change is made, another 25 class 4–8–4 (condensing or otherwise) taking over. Immediately on leaving the engine starts working hard up a stiff climb, rousing the echoes across the wide Karoo as it tackles three miles at one in seventy to lift the train up to 4,217 feet at Britsville summit, less than five miles from De Aar.

By this time the darkness may be falling, depending of course upon the time of year, and a second night aboard the 'Orange Express' begins, with passengers playing cards in the lounge, drinking at the bar, talking or changing in their compartments, or taking the first dinner in the brightly lit and extremely comfortable restaurant car with its sideboard full of fruits and cheeses. Even dinner, a five-course meal, costs only 90c. (50 n.p.) and a half-bottle of good Cape wine to wash it down can be had for 50c. (30 n.p.). Coffee comes free, and a big glass of local sherry to start the meal costs 10c. (5 n.p.).

It is exactly two hours from De Aar across the Karoo to Hutchinson, junction for Calvinia, a run of eighty-two miles. In contrast to Natal, the names of the tiny Karoo halts and sidings are almost all Afrikaans, but this is one exception. Hutchinson is at 4,176 feet and in winter this can be a bitterly cold spot, with steam rising in the chill air from the trains and engines. The long Calvinia branch has been dieselized and the train leaves before the 'Orange' which is taking water.

Not many years ago, when South African coaches had open ends, the Karoo was a hated region, for all the dust in creation blew into the compartments. Today, with modern sealed stock, there is no discomfort. The express pulls away from Hutchinson at 9.7 p.m. on what is to be its last run behind steam, affording some romantic sights for enthusiasts as the fiery glow lights up the sky and white smoke soars above the train to be lost on the wide, rolling, arid plains. Exactly two hours and one minute are allowed for the eighty-one miles to Beaufort West, reached at 11.8 p.m., and here the locomotive pants to a halt beneath the wires as a large brown and yellow electric unit towing a booster car backs down to take its place. Considerable altitude has been lost on this last stretch, Beaufort West being only 2,792 feet above sea level.

Most people put their lights out and retire for the night before the train leaves this important station at 11.16 p.m. Through the darkness the electrically hauled 'Orange Express' runs at a fair pace, downhill to Dwyka (only 1,570 feet above sea level) then up again to Ruiterskop (2,709 feet). The next main stop is Lainsburg, 126 miles from De Aar, covered in 188 minutes. After a five-minute halt, probably for crew purposes since no passengers are embarked or disembarked at this time of night and no water is needed, the train runs on to Touws River, 53 miles in 103 minutes over a line which has climbed again to 3,500 feet and fallen back to 2,551. There is another stop soon after this, at Matroosberg, where it is at 3,148 feet, but then the line slides downhill all the way to Cape Town. Shortly before reaching Worcester in the dawn, the train enters the spectacular Hex River valley, and passengers called early with the six o'clock tea or coffee round will be rewarded with gorgeous mountain views and a sparkling sunrise over some of the most dramatic mountain shapes in Africa.

Worcester, for long the end of the electric line up from the Cape, is stopped at from 6.13 to 6.15 a.m. The scene is of attractive white Dutch farmhouses, rich green fields, high mountains, foaming waters, and in winter some snow on the peaks. Through the Hex Pass, twisting and winding, the train makes slow progress to Wolseley, twenty-four miles beyond, and then over another pass, this time the Tulbagh. Wolseley is reached at 6.51 a.m., and just after leaving, the chimes for first breakfast will be sounding through the train.

An hour of delightful scenery follows, through valleys and over rivers, with the striking mountains ranging away in confusing directions. The pleasant town of Wellington is reached at 7.56 a.m., set amid vineyards. This was the terminus of the first railway opened in Cape Province and the second in South Africa, in 1863, coming up from Cape Town over forty-five miles of track which took four years to lay.

After Wellington comes Paarl, only thirty-six miles from Cape Town, the main centre for South African wine, a charming Cape Dutch town with enchanting white-gabled farmhouses all around. As it is 8.21 a.m. when the 'Orange Express' makes its stop, a few Cape Town-bound commuters try to board, a few being lucky but they must either stand in the corridors, sit in the lounge, or take coffee when the last breakfasters have left the restaurant car. In some cases, they may be invited to sit in the compartments by people whose beds have now been dismantled. The outlook from the train is now rich farmland giving way to rich suburban villas and later industry in the form of Bellville, the huge new development area twelve miles from the city.

South African trains are punctual in the extreme, and the 'Orange Express', allowed sixty-nine minutes for the comparatively easy thirty-six miles from Paarl, will take things slowly for the last few miles through busy suburbs so as to approach the enormous new station of Cape Town dead on time at 9.30 a.m. It uses platform 23, which number in itself indicates how large and well served the magnificent station is, with its extensive electric suburban services and main lines. Unexpectedly, although there are no steam engines allowed into the white acres of terminal, the steam shed just outside holds no less than 172 engines, the second largest number in South Africa, although most of them are for dock shunting and the numbers were recently increased to cope with extra work caused by the Cape route taking over from Suez. Only a few of the Cape Town locomotives haul passenger trains, and then not from the terminal but from Salt River or Bellville.

The twice-weekly arrivals of the 'Orange Express' are always an occasion as the fully laden train disgorges passengers into the arms of friends, relatives and porters. But once a week on Tuesdays, and twice a week in summer, the 'Blue Train' rolls into platform 24 to an even more animated welcome, although it carries fewer people. The 'Blue Train' arrival is a social event in South Africa, to gain a berth in it a cachet. I must make it clear that despite influence and application long in advance, I have not been able to obtain a reservation. My acquaintance with the famous express is limited to walking through it from end to end once it has disembarked its passengers at Cape Town, seeing it at speed behind a 25 class on the Karoo, and noting it in the yards at Pretoria.

The 'Blue Train' leaves Cape Town at noon on Wednesdays for Johannesburg and Pretoria, arriving at the former at 2 p.m. next day, and at Pretoria (exactly 999 miles from Cape Town) at 3.38 p.m. In summer there is an extra departure, on Mondays, to the same timings. In theory, one of these services is primarily intended as a 'boat train' for the weekly Union Castle mailship between Cape Town and Southampton, but since two sailings out of seven now carry only twelve passengers, the priority Union Castle passengers once had on the train has been discontinued. The second 'Blue Train' does carry a priority, for it aims to serve members of Parliament when that body is sitting at Cape Town from January to June. During that period of the year, South Africa has two capitals, Cape Town and Pretoria.

Coming south, the 'Blue Train' leaves Pretoria all year round at 8.40 a.m. on Mondays, and Johannesburg at 10.30 a.m., to reach the Cape at 11.30 a.m. on Tuesdays (Union Castle mailships now leave the Cape on Wednesdays at noon). The 'extra' service leaves Pretoria on Wednesdays with its parliamentary and diplomatic priorities. The express, fully air-conditioned, with carpeted compartments sleeping two persons or coupés for single occupancy, all first class plus a fifteen per cent supplement, higher than usual meal charges but with an extra course, showers at the ends of coaches and even a bathroom, is steam-hauled from Kimberley to Beaufort West, as are all trains over the line. The rostered steam locomotives carry a blue circular headboard and have a blue tint in the paint on their smoke-box doors plus two golden springbok emblems. The speeds are the highest in South Africa and, as it happens, the highest on the African Continent (despite the fact that some countries have standard gauge). From Kimberley to Orange River, one hour and fifty-two minutes is allowed for the seventy-eight miles, and from there on to De Aar, seventy miles, only ninety minutes are scheduled, making an average of forty-six and a half miles an hour. On the electric section between Johannesburg and Kimberley, there is a run of exactly two hours from Klerksdorp to Bloemhof, eighty-nine miles, giving an average of forty-four and a half miles an hour. All this is with one engine at the head of the train, be it steam or electric, and in fairness to the electrics with their lower average speeds it must be said that, generally speaking, they work on the slightly harder sections of line. The hefty coaches with their air-conditioning plant add up to a total weight of just over a thousand tons.

One is left with an impression, after journeys in South African trains, that the railway system is still on the upgrade, operating with a conscious sense of service, grace, romance and interest. There is no running-down of any form of traction and cleanliness is paramount. I have noticed a cut-back in compartment equipment in the ten years which passed between my visits, such as no towels or soap being issued ('We stopped doing this because most passengers pinched them,' I was told) and a small charge being made for plastic cups. But the fares remain relatively low and the future is bright, not only because of the two new Blue Trains under construction. . . .

19

Through Siberia from the Far East

In a previous railway book I have given, as many authors before me, a second hand account of the Trans Siberian Railway. Reviewers in the National and Provincial Press made great play with the fact that 'the Author had watched the train depart from Moscow but had never been on it'. Now, at last, I have made the journey, and can point with some satisfaction to having crossed all the Continents by rail.

The Trans Siberian express train 'Russia' still leaves Moscow's Yaroslavl Station every day at five minutes past ten during the summer season, and four times a week in winter. It goes to Vladivostock and it takes eight days (seven nights on the train). Foreign visitors to the Soviet Union cannot enter the Vladivostock Zone, but use the port of Nakhodka, about fifty miles to the North East, reached by a short branch line from Ussurisk. They must, however, change trains at the major Far East city of Khabarovsk, leaving the 'Russia' after seven days and staying some twelve hours (during which time they are taken on Intourist trips around the area) before joining a special de luxe double diesel hauled boat train which runs overnight to Nakhodka in connection with the steamers on the Japan-Hong Kong service.

It is 5,778 miles to Vladivostock from Moscow, and 5,865 to Nakhodka. The first 3,509 miles, from Moscow to Ulan Ude, beyond the Lake Baikal region, are under electric wires, by far the longest electrified main line in the world. The wires were energised as far as Selanga, on the southern shore of Baikal, and it is here that electric locomotives were changed at the time of my journey, in April 1969, for steam engines. At the Pacific end of the line, electric wires reach from both

Vladivostock and Nakhodka to Ussurisk, seventy miles from the former and 130 miles from the latter. Eventually, probably by 1975/76 winter timetables, the wires will be linked and stretch from end to end of the world's longest railway, but multi-current locomotives will be needed as two types of electrification (3kV DC and 25kV AC) are used.

The Trans Siberian is double track throughout, has colour light signalling and centralized train control. It carries a fully fitted, fast freight train every twenty minutes, running to passenger speeds, and its total *daily* volume of traffic today exceeds its *annual* total just after it was built at the turn of the century. It is highly modernised and efficient, with firm track and massive bridges, bearing no relation at all to the rickety line that was hastily flung across Siberia so many years ago, when for the first few years no train ever managed to complete the journey without a derailment. The 1905 Russo-Japanese War lent urgency to track and bridge improvement and things were better by 1907, but it is only since the Nazi invasion of the Soviet Union, when so much heavy industrial plant was transferred behind the Urals, that the track was brought up to the peak of condition, in which it is now maintained. Even so, spring thaws in Siberia inevitably bring some bridge and track damage in their wake, and closures of sections for two or three days are annual occurrences.

I made the trip from East to West, beginning in Khabarovsk on a warm sunny day in April when the ice was breaking on the mighty Amur River and the breath of spring was flowing up from the Pacific through the Far East valleys. Foreign visitors have their own well appointed waiting room in Khabarovsk Station, maintained by Intourist, and the check-in proceedure is not unlike that at an air terminal, with the desk clerk talking into an internal communicator, then issuing a boarding card. Australians are the principal English-speaking users of the Trans Siberian, followed by Britons (many of them bound to or from Hong Kong).

The westbound train (Number One) was due in at 1.40 p.m. local time which is 6.40 a.m. Moscow Time. The Soviet Railways (S.Z.D.) maintain all services on Moscow Time in all parts of the country, and it is up to the individual passenger to

ascertain the local time, as with some United States long distance trains which keep Eastern Standard Time.

Precision time keeping is essential on the Trans Siberian if
the intense freight service is to work, and the 'Russia' came in
exactly to the minute. Station stops range from eight to seventeen minutes and are shown on notices in every carriage. Average speeds are not particularly high but having regard to the
distance and the stops, and also to the fact that freight trains are
running to the same schedule, they are quite creditable. On the
eastern section, with steam power, the overall average is
thirty-two miles an hour, and on the western section with electrics the speed goes up to thirty-nine miles an hour in Siberia
and forty-three miles an hour in European Russsia.

Khabarovsk merits a fifteen-minute stop, to cover an engine
change and a check-up of train facilities such as water for the
toilets and ice for the restaurant car.

Khabarovsk is a major railway centre and houses a railway
engineering institute. Locomotives and rolling stock are maintained in spotless condition, immediately apparent to me on
seeing the engines and carriages in the station. Our new train
engine backed on, a P.36 class 4–8–4 of the post-war design
once known as 'Stalins' built at Lugansk between 1949 and
1952. It was No. 0098, painted green with cream lines, the
wheels and rods outlined in red, while the traditional red star
carried by all steam locomotives in most of Eastern Europe,
and Communist countries in Asia, was worn on the smoke box
door. Below it was a decorated portrait of Lenin, protected
against wind and weather. Most surprisingly, a twin diesel unit
of the ubiquitous T.33 class (used for freight trains on the
Trans Siberian) was being pushed by the steam engine down
on to the train. I heard later that it was being worked forward to
Bira for positioning but it played no part in haulage, the one
massive steam locomotive handling the dead diesel plus eleven
heavy coaches.

Accommodation on the 'Russia' is not as good as that on the
special boat trains between Khabarovsk and Nakhodka. There
are no de luxe sleeping cars with two berths and a shower
shared by each three compartments, although this facility may
well be introduced within two years. The train consists of three

green painted modern steel coaches for station to station travel, equipped with long benches for overnight journeys when sleeping is possible with a hired mattress, followed by soft class coaches equipped with nine four-berth compartments, then a modern hard class car with ten four berth compartments, a restaurant car, another soft, then hards and a crew and baggage car.

My soft class car was well upholstered and carpeted, smooth running due to its 56 ton weight on very well designed bogies, and rather too warm owing to a stove kept well stoked up by the attendants on a bright, sunny day in a winter-sealed train. My 'cabin mates' were two Russian electrical engineers going to Chita, and it seemed we had one berth empty which meant the compartment was not too full. The attendant, a girl called Tanya from Omsk, brought my bedding and linen, and pointed out how big suitcases were put into a space below the bunk. There was a table with a reading lamp, and each bunk had an individual reading light above the pillow. . . .

Although I could read the Cyrillic Alphabet (a 'must' for any travellers on long trips in the Soviet Union) I had only a very few words of the language. Nevertheless, by the time we reached Chita, forty-six hours later, my two companions had taught me quite a lot and I could name the trees and animals of the forest, and even talk haltingly about trains.

The train made a very slow and dignified exit from Khabarovsk and rolled through the outskirts of this city of half a million people, founded by Erofeye Khabarovsk on his trek eastwards in 1858. A monument to him stands in the station square, welcoming travellers. After about four miles we came to the great bridge across the Amur, nearly two miles long and supported in the middle by pillars sunk into an island. This bridge was not completed until 1917, when the Trans Siberian Railway was brought around the Russian side of Manchuria— a construction that has proved a blessing today. Previously, Vladivostock was reached by way of Harbin and Mukden over the lines of the much disputed and never very reliable Chinese Eastern Railway.

If there were a bridge actually going straight across the wide Amur from the Khabarovsk waterfront it would lead into

China, for the Manchurian border starts not far from the bank opposite Khabarovsk where the Ussuri tributary goes off. One of the islands in the Ussuri, Damasky, was the scene of bitter fighting early in 1969 when Chinese troops crossed the ice and attacked a Soviet garrison, inflicting serious casualties and killing the commanding officer. When I reached this area in mid-April the ice was fast melting and no further attacks across the river were thought likely. Great stress was being laid by the authorities in Khabarovsk on a large painting in the city museum depicting a Tsarist Russian Grand Duke pointing on a map while watched by a Chinese Manchu delegate following severe border disputes in 1905. The Ussuri region is noted for its huge Siberian tigers which roam the forests under complete protection (unlike the 'paper tigers' of Mao, I was informed).

Crossing the river where we did means remaining well inside Soviet territory, although for many hours during the long journey to Chita the hills of China remain clearly visible to the south of the train. The Amur River is one of the five great rivers of the world, navigable by large vessels all the way from Blagovyeschensk to its mouth at Nikolaevsk in the Sea of Okhotsk, more than 2,000 miles. Pleasure steamers begin running in May and continue until the end of September. Blagovyeschensk is the terminus of a branch line from the main Trans Siberian, and it stands right on the river facing Chinese Manchuria (without a bridge).

Despite the heavy weight of the diesel running dead and the train of 600 tons behind that, the steam locomotive made a fair job of hill climbing and ran easily on the level stretches, although no great speeds were touched on downgrades, perhaps fifty-five miles an hour but no more. At the first water stop, a place in the wilds simply called In, I got out for a walk as the train halted for ten minutes. An hour and a quarter later, we made our second stop, at Birobaijan, capital of a small autonomous Jewish Republic within the Soviet Union, but here we only had four minutes, so my next 'exercise' had to wait until Bira, 135 miles from Khabarovsk, a run we completed in three hours, thirty eight minutes. Here the engine was changed and the diesels taken away to a siding, while P.36 Number 0172 backed on to the train. Another coach was added to the rear, giving us a formation of twelve with a total tare weight of 639 tons, probably about 685 tons loaded, which the one engine handled without difficulty.

The journey progressed gently and pleasantly through warm spring sunshine giving way to a balmy evening with the temperature close to 20° Centigrade (68° Fahrenheit). There was still some ice on rivers and lakes but no traces of snow. But the Russians do not regard this region as Siberia; they call it the Far East and associate it with a much milder climate.

In the train I had made the acquaintance of a very helpful and friendly lady in charge of service in the restaurant car named Anna Stepanovna. The menu she proudly presented was in six languages, and she herself had a few words of German, but later I was able to ask for basic necessities in Russian. She worked extremely hard, for the restaurant car opened its doors every morning at nine and did not close until ten in the evening. Russians are big and frequent eaters, sometimes having four heavy meals a day (breakfast is often not just ham and eggs but a meat soup and sausages as well). She and her male assistant, and the cooks, not only had to cope with train passengers coming in throughout the thirteen hour day but also with visitors at station stops, who would come aboard to buy chocolate, cakes, bottles of drink, and even cigarettes, for at some remote places the restaurant car passing through was a far better 'shop' than any in the village. I have seen this sort of thing in parts of Canada, particularly on the Northern Ontario lines. Prices in the restaurant car were extremely modest considering the weight and size of meals. A typical lunch or dinner, consisting of a 'Moscow Borsch' (red soup with large pieces of meat and sour cream in it), a rump steak (well done with breadcrumbs on one occasion) with chipped potatoes (never tasty), compote of fruit, washed down with half a litre of red Georgian wine and coffee costing about one Rouble, ninety Kopeks (2.16 to the Pound or 95 Kopeks to a Dollar). The refrigerator space was inadequate so little or no ice cream ('Morezhno'—at which the Russians are expert) was forthcoming, and supplies of cold beer loaded in Khabarovsk soon ran out.

The train ran on comfortably, night fell, and one settled into a routine of eating, resting, reading, watching the scenery going by, getting out at station stops for a walk, and writing up notes. The last exercise I took that first night was at Achara, 443 kilometres (275 miles) from Khabarovsk, which we reached at 10.37 p.m. Far East Time, after a run of eight hours, forty minutes including stops. Here we again changed our engine, receiving another P.36 but I could not see the number in the darkness beyond the rather weak station lamps.

In the 'soft' carriage the attendants changed over. I found they worked twelve hours on, twelve hours off. On retiring they happily brought along some tea in glasses from the samovar, and also offered cocoa, which I tried on the first night. I must admit I slept extremely well in the comfortable bed, aided by the comparatively gentle motion of the train and the fact that my 'cabin mates' did not snore! The next morning they expressed themselves delighted that I had not snored, either!

The attendant brought in tea, with lemon on request, and packets of lemon biscuits, soon after 8 a.m. Washing facilities were not very good in the male washroom at the head-end of the carriage, but hot water could be obtained from the attendant. Plugs for electric razors were set into the bulkheads out in the carpeted corridor, and there were fold-down seats by the windows so that one could shave and watch the scenery.

Still maintaining the gentle but reasonable average of thirty-two to thirty-three miles an hour inclusive of stops, we carried on all day through well forested hill country with rivers or lakes often in sight. The ubiquitous silver birch trees of the Siberian forest were becoming more and more apparent. The Russian name for these is 'beriozhka', which is used also for a famous dance ensemble and for the chain of souvenir shops. Other trees always in sight were larch ('listvinitza') and pine (sassna) with some Siberian cedars ('Cairdre'). We had a fifteen-minute stop at the important town of Skovorodzino, 1,218 kilometres (756 miles from Khabarovsk) where I saw P.36 Number 0078 back on, an engine fitted with two whistles, one of which—used in stations—gave a rasping blast from compressed air, and the other a most melodious note when in motion, by steam pressure. Just before leaving every station, the compressed air whistle was sounded at length to call back strollers and those buying fresh fruit and trinkets at the stalls on the stations called 'Bazaars'. The carriage attendants checked carefully to see that passengers belonging to their vehicle were safely aboard before pulling up the steps. Because there were often stragglers all starts were gentle and slow. I was always aboard before the whistle, not being anxious to get left behind in the middle of Siberia while everything I possessed, including Passport and tickets, moved away towards Moscow. On the occasion of my trip, the 'Russia' was not running daily, and it would be forty-eight hours before another westbound passenger train came this way.

All morning on the third day, which was brilliantly sunny and fine, with a definite warmth in the air, we ran beside the Shilka River, Manchuria away to the South of the train. I had made acquaintance with three young ladies in the next compartment, all of them dressed in the latest gear. With some difficulty, I learned they came from Magadan, in the Arctic Far North East of Siberia beyond the Kamchatka Peninsula. They had flown the 1,600 miles down to Khabarovsk and were bound for a month's holiday in Moscow, their first visit to the Russian capital. For two of them, this was not only their first train journey but the first time they had ever set eyes on a train! I noticed they had a considerable affinity for ham, which they bought in large quantities at station bazaars, and for Soviet 'Cognac' which they obtained by the bottle from the restaurant car, preferring it to my Scotch!

Just before noon on the third day, we stopped at Chita, the big city and junction for what used to be the Chinese Eastern line to Tsitsihar and Harbin through Manchuria. There is still a once weekly through train to Peking by this route, but until recently most Moscow-Peking expresses took the new short cut which goes off at Ulan Ude in the Baikal region, passing through Ulan Bator, Outer Mongolia's capital. This service is now also once weekly, since relations between the Russians and Chinese are so strained there is little traffic outside the diplomatic field. I bade farewell to my Russian engineer friends here, and found that no new passengers had boarded the train so that I had the whole compartment—suddenly seeming to be very large and spacious—all to myself.

Soon after pulling away from Chita we began to climb, gently at first but more steeply later. We ran through the station of Amazar where I noticed serried ranks of condemned steam locomotives, 2–10–0s of the 'Ea' class predominating. Shortly after this the sun disappeared behind high cloud which got thicker, and when we stopped at Yablonovaya (where there were more dead steamers) it was bitterly cold. Here we attached a second train engine, No. 0066 aiding No. 0166, and also a banker, an Ea class 2–10–0, one of the few survivors kept rostered for what turned out to be a spectacular banking duty.

We pounded off into the cold grey afternoon, twisting and turning as the double tracks rose out of the fringes of the Gobi Desert and climbed towards the high Central Siberian Plateau of the Baikal Region. The mountain range we were driving up was the Yablonoi, rearing in parts to 8000 or 9000 feet, and little known to Western travellers. It marked the start of Trans Baikalia and the territory to the South was now the Independent People's Republic of Mongolia.

The three great engines could be heard, even in the sealed train, barking away splendidly, a sound to thrill the heart of any railway enthusiast. Their white exhaust thrust into the cold air in majestic patterns as we stormed the 1 in 60 gradient. There are not many great railway banks left in the world where steam still reigns, although Mr. George Behrend, in his new book *Yatakli Vagon—Turkish Steam Travel*, tells of the passage of the Taurus Express through the mountains (after which it is named) behind three engines. There is a three-engine banking operation out of Port Elizabeth in South Africa but I am at a loss, in 1971, in recalling other examples with steam.

I suppose we were about 4000 feet up when it began to snow. The wind increased from the East and soon a real Siberian blizzard was howling round the labouring train. But it made no difference to progress uphill, and in any case these engines and their crews are used to winter conditions when they must make this journey—and keep time—in 100° Fahrenheit of frost. At last the summit appeared, clearly marked—as are all points on the Trans Siberian Railway—at 6,000 feet. We stopped to detach the banker and the pilot engine at Mogzon, where the snow was lying thick and deep. There was no conspicuous descent to follow the climb for this was mainly high plateau country with plenty of forest. It looked and felt wintry but the carriage was kept warm enough by the frequent stoking of the stove by Tanya or her colleague.

The big station of Petrovskin Zavod gave us a fifteen minute stop just before I went along for dinner, but apart from a quick look to see P.36 number 0110 back on, I did not stay outside the train for long. The large town had a forlorn, snow-blown look, a scene out of Tolstoy, and fur hats and big boots were much in evidence. I suppose it was about ten below on the Centigrade scale (about 14° Fahrenheit).

I had turned in for the night when the train stopped at the important junction of Ulan Ude, where the line to Outer Mongolia goes off. Here the last steam change of our journey was taking place but by now the P.36 coming on for the short run to Selanga will have been replaced by an electric locomotive capable of running right through to Moscow. Suddenly my door was flung open and three men stamped in with snow on their boots. They were journeying to Novosibirsk, and all at once the compartment seemed rather crowded, especially as they had to be given new bedding. It was midnight before the lights went out and quiet descended on the moving train. However I slept well, awakening soon after six o'clock due not to noise but to cold. My blankets were not enough, and I threw over a coat.

Getting up first, before my new 'cabin mates' had awakened I saw a bright dawn on a frozen lake, then a sparkling river with running water. The temperature outside, in the ice and snow, was minus fifteen Centigrade (about five Fahrenheit). While I drank my tea, the train ran beside the Angara River and towards the outskirts of Irkutsk, one of Siberia's biggest cities. The Angara is the only river to flow *out* of Lake Baikal, deepest lake on earth, into which no less than 336 rivers and streams flow. The lake, really an enormous inland sea, freezes in late December and is rid of its ice by early May, but because of its mile of depth and a narrow lip out of which the wayward Angara escapes, the latter rushes with such pressure that it remains ice free, to be dammed twice (at Irkutsk and at Bratsk) providing vast quantities of electric power.

Our train was under the wires and was hauled by a single VL 8 Bo-Bo electric engine, which stayed on the train during the fifteen minute stop at Irkutsk.

Thus ends the really interesting and romantic part of the Trans Siberian rail journey. From Irkutsk to Moscow the way lies through endless forests, across great rivers (the Yenisei, the Ob, the Irtisch, the Tobol, the Ural, the Kama, and eventually the Volga at Yaroslavl), and through big cities, like Krasnoyarsk, Novosibirsk, Omsk, Sverdlovsk, and Perm. The only mountains are the relatively low Urals, rising to about 3000 feet but marked with ravines and gorges because they contrast strongly with the low plains. An obelisk beside the track near Perm shows Europe one side and Asia the other. I had stopped at some of these cities while making the plane journey to the Far East with Aeroflot, spending two days in Novosibirsk, three in Irkutsk, and a brief halt at Omsk. The electric engine does not need water stops and increases the pace of the train progressively to forty-three miles an hour average, but the maximum permitted speed on any part of the Trans Siberian line is seventy-five miles an hour. There are several sections when the train runs non-stop for 150 miles or more (Moscow to Yaroslavl, Buce to Sharya, Balezino to Perm, Tuomeni to Ishum, Omsk to Barabinsk).

All the way from the Pacific Coast to Moscow you know exactly where you are, for posts mark every tenth of a kilometre, and larger ones at the kilometre give the distance from Moscow. In all, there are ninety-one stops in the east-west direction and ninety-two in the reverse, which, added together, total fourteen hours. Although popular conception has it that the train goes through Omsk and Tomsk, the latter place is 103 miles off the main line and hapless travellers to this 'Northampton of Siberia' (which got left behind the general progress when the main line avoided it) must change at Taiga. The whole effect of riding this train for a week is that of voyaging with a small passenger ship up the Norwegian coast or around

12—RR • •

Iceland or on the Newfoundland-Labrador services, for the 'cabins' are about the same size and the feeling of cosiness is somewhat similar. However, the train does not pitch violently when exposed to blizzards and gales! All in all, it is a great experience, well worth doing once, and perhaps twice, in a lifetime, and on reaching the end of the line, many passengers leave the train with regret.

20

'Northern Express' to Chiang Mai

Every evening at five minutes past five, as the fierce heat of the sun begins to ease and the great city of Bangkok comes off the boil, a smart express train pulls away from the bustling Central Station of Thailand's capital and starts its 473-mile journey to the dry, cool hills of the Southern Shan States. This is the 'Northern Express', crack train of the Royal State Railways, and its accommodation is first and second class only, with the emphasis on sleeping cars. To travel with it requires advance booking and the payment of a supplement amounting to 20 baht. It takes seventeen hours to make the trip, at an average speed of twenty-eight miles an hour, inclusive of stops, which is creditable over narrow gauge.

When I applied for a ticket on the 'Northern Express' in February 1968, 20 baht was two-fifths of a pound sterling, almost exactly one American dollar. Travel is cheap in Thailand, and the tickets I managed to obtain, after waiting at the booking counter for nearly half an hour in humid heat, came to 226 baht covering a second class single, single occupancy of a section in one of the new Japanese Hitachi-built sleeping cars, and the express supplement. I noticed with appreciation that this spotlessly clean country lived up to its reputation even in a station booking office, for after each transaction a little man came along with a brush and swept the pigeon-hole!

Two hours later I joined the train, a long rake of brown and cream coaches not unlike the colour scheme of the old Great Western. Two special luxury vehicles on the rear of the express attracted my attention. They were in genuine G.W.R. colours and bore the insignia of the Malaysian Railways. One turned out to be the private saloon of His Highness the Sultan of Selangor, and the other was the special sleeping car for his retinue. The Sultan, it turned out, was on an official visit to Thailand and his rolling stock had come all the way from Kuala Lumpur attached to the International Express which makes its way up through the jungles of Malaysia and the narrow Siamese Isthmus to Bangkok. Accompanied by his family, including the Crown Prince, and a large retinue of officials, he was travelling north to Chiang Mai, the northern terminal and railhead for the Southern Shan States.

The crossed flags of Thailand and Malaysia decorated the front of the highly polished yellow and brown General Motors diesel locomotive, and various flags and banners were out on the platform for the arrival of the Sultan and his party. We left exactly on time, a load of twelve coaches behind the engine, and moved very slowly into the hot late afternoon. Thailand's gauge is 3 feet 6 inches, the popular gauge of East Asia, but the very slow running for the first few miles appeared to be due to the lightly protected crossings and the heavy road traffic that was, during the rush hour, trying to get over the railway. There were also groups of people on the line, waiting to get a glimpse of the royal visitor.

Within ten minutes we had come to our first stop, at Nonthaburi Station. As we left a minute later, a line went off to the left. This runs for about thirty-two miles westwards to the town of Nakhon Pathom, home of Thailand's most famous Golden Pagoda. The line carries on into the jungle for about twenty-five miles beyond that great tourist attraction, and, twenty-one miles northwards, reaches big cemeteries in which lie many thousands of British and Australian soldiers. The reason is soon determined, for the railway crosses a bridge and then becomes overgrown, no longer operated to the Burma border. The bridge is one of those over the River Kwai and its tributaries, made famous by the film based on fact. Visitors wanting to cross the only remaining railworked bridge on this river system should book to Kanchanaburi.

The 'Death Railway' is the one dark period in the history of Thailand, a country which until the 1943–45 period had never been occupied, colonized or dominated by any foreign power.

The average Thai is gentle, quiet, courteous, charming and capable, with no arrogance and no 'chip on the shoulder'. He has never had to be an inferior person, and does not now regard himself as superior to any foreigner. It is an excellent country for the Western visitor, whether on holiday or on business. The Thais acknowledge a long-established equal business partnership with Denmark through the East Asiatic Company, and Scandinavian Airlines, who fly the fastest route to Bangkok with only one stop at Tashkent on their way across the Soviet Union from Copenhagen, have a working arrangement with Royal Thai International Airways.

It seems to me that the main reason why Thai men are so pleasant to deal with, no matter in what walk of life they are encountered, is that they have had to spend a few months in a *Wat* (Monastery) compound. This is a sort of religious conscription, and affects everyone from the King to the humblest subject. During the period in the *Wat*, usually a rainy season when a young man between sixteen and twenty years of age, the devotee studies, wears only a simple robe, has no money at all, and spends much time in reflective contemplation, dependent upon others for his food. Apart from Ceylon, Thailand is the purest Buddhist country in the East, practising the exact teachings of Buddha without the variations introduced elsewhere, but with richer decoration than in Ceylon.

Six minutes after leaving the junction of Nonthaburi, travelling in leisurely fashion with tall palm trees beside the track, a road on one side and a *klang* (Thailand canal) on the other, we stopped briefly at Bang Sue for no apparent reason. It was here that I caught my first glimpse of a Royal Thailand State Railways steam locomotive, in the form of a spotlessly clean 2–6–0 Mogul working in the yards. But after leaving the station we passed the engine sheds containing a number of engines in steam, mainly 2–6–0s and 4–6–0s, and mounted on a plinth was an early 0–6–0 tank whose inscription I could not read.

Fifteen miles out of Bangkok we made our third stop, this time at Da Muang, station for Bangkok's International Airport. Not many travellers arriving by air realize that this airport is rail-connected, and I imagine few taxi-drivers, porters and limousine operators are likely to tell them. In any case the train service is somewhat infrequent, but for those people arriving by air and going north, the direct link to the train can be invaluable. As it was, a few passengers, including Americans, did join the train with their baggage at this station.

I thought the 'Northern Express' would begin to live up to its name as soon as Da Muang was left behind and the last of the straggling outer urban evidence of the big city of Bangkok had disappeared. But at 5.50, forty-five minutes after departure from the Central Terminus, we pulled in to a station called Klong Rang Sit, 28.5 kilometres (18 miles) from Bangkok for our fourth stop. This well-kept, flower-trimmed station produced few passengers, but a considerable army of young ladies appeared and marched up and down the train carrying boxes of chicken, sweetmeats and fruit for sale. They only had two minutes for any transactions, for we left sharply and with determination, this time keeping going through rather low-lying hot country with fields and canals and low trees. Plenty of water-buffalo could be seen at work or wallowing, and occasionally a farmer or a group of children would wave to the passing train, which was now making about forty miles an hour on the smooth yet narrow gauge track.

We kept going until the sun went down in a veil of red dust and mist and a city loomed up ahead, the last rays glinting on the inevitable golden *prangs* of a *Wat*. This was Ayutthaya, for 417 years the capital of Siam. It was just after half-past six when we stopped and the ready army of food vendors went into action. I was more interested in a parcels and freight train standing in another platform headed by a spotless, gleaming 'MacArthur' steam locomotive. These engines, built by the American Locomotive Company at Schenectady between 1945 and 1946, are so called because they were part of a programme instituted by the American General at the end of the Pacific War to rehabilitate transport in the lands affected by the Japanese occupation. Most of those allocated to Thailand are still in service, well kept, and used mostly on first division freight trains and some passenger services.

Again the stop was of only two minutes, then we were off for a run of twenty-six minutes through rapidly darkening tropical countryside to Ban Phachi, junction for the Eastern Line (to Korat and the border of Cambodia which is or was at the time closed due to disputes over the Vietnam situation). We had embarked a passenger in our sleeping car at Ayutthaya, and I noticed that an attendant hurriedly appeared with a mop and bucket to wash the floor and the step beside the door where the 'intruder' with possibly dirty shoes had trod!

Leaving Ban Phachi at two minutes past seven, the train gathered speed in complete darkness and I made my way forward two cars to the restaurant, from which came enticing smells. Some passengers were being served at their seats, on small tables set up by the attendant, but I wanted to select from a menu reported to be available in English in the diner. There were no spare tables at first, but after a wash and brush-up in an ultra-modern 'men's room' with aluminium bowls, mirrors and strip lighting in true contemporary Japanese New Tokaido Line style, I tried again and got a table. My information proved to be only partially correct—drinks were in English but food was in Thai script and in Danish (one more indication of the frequency with which East Asiatic Company officials and employees travelled in Thailand). But the waiter spoke a smattering of English and I managed to order a rice dish with tomatoes, beer (quite expensive although a local brew) and bananas.

At other tables groups of men, some in what looked like British Army officers' uniforms, were talking away in English. I soon joined in, to learn they were part of the personal staff of the Sultan. His aide-de-camp was a Brigadier, retired after thirty years in the Malaysian land forces. There was an official photographer to the group, a Malaysian-Chinese, who had his son, a newspaper correspondent, with him. Two Thai security men, quite good speakers of English in a land where they find pronunciation of English words very difficult, sat round and talked with the retinue.

I was offered 'Mekong Delta Whisky'. This turned out to be more like Chinese rice wine than harsh spirit and was not so potent as it looked or sounded. A bottle of it cost 10 baht, less than a bottle of beer! As we were drinking, a young man in a silk dressing gown came into the restaurant car. We stood up, I because the others had suddenly gone quiet and started to rise. It was His Highness the Crown Prince of Selangor. He spoke perfect English in an easy, casual and colloquial way, and when I was introduced he said he had read some of my newspaper articles. The explanation, he told me after seeing my surprised expression, was simple. He had been in London three years, training as a photographer at the Guildford College which specializes in this subject, and had studied various newspapers thoroughly. But only three weeks previously, his father had summoned him back from London to take up his station in life. This Royal Tour of Thailand was his first State mission, and he was not enjoying the restrictions placed upon him. Before he went on up the train, still dressed in his silk night attire, he offered to arrange an audience with his father the next morning after breakfast.

Several Americans going to Chiang Mai joined in the general talk after the Crown Prince had left, delighted at having seen royalty in an informal setting. They were due to see some more, for the door opened and in came the brother of the Sultan. He sat down and had a glass of 'Mekong', telling us that he was paying his own way on this fourteen-day State Visit. Then the Crown Prince returned, looking delighted and leading a young couple, obviously from England. It seemed he had found them in the 'sit-up' accommodation forward, and they were going, like so many before them, to Chiang Mai for International Voluntary Service. Apparently the Crown Prince had known the young man in London.

All this time the train had been running through the night, fairly smoothly, although the diner was not up to the running condition of the new Hitachi sleepers. Speeds of about forty-five to fifty miles an hour were being maintained and stops were fewer—unidentified, I fear, but I was otherwise occupied with the gathering at the tables.

At about half-past ten I returned to my sleeper, to find it made up and window closed with metal blinds covering it. Having drawn the curtains it felt extremely hot, but I dropped off to sleep almost at once, and had one of the most complete night's sleep I have ever had in a train—a tribute to the well-kept track and the Hitachi sleeping car, aided perhaps by

Mekong Delta 'Whisky'. It was half-past six when I awoke, to find people getting up, an attendant milling about with cups of something, and a sort of opaque dawn breaking. Opening the window, it felt distinctly chilly, and a mist wreathed about the train which was moving slowly uphill and round some curves. There were now two diesels, both of the same Co-Co General Motors type, at the head of the train, and as the sun came up and began to burn off the mist, it was revealed that we were cleaving through mountainous jungle.

Dressing and then going to the washroom, where I found that the Japanese coaches had missed one detail—there were no sockets of any kind for electric razors—I arranged for breakfast to be served at the seat which was now rapidly replacing my bed. Orange juice, scrambled eggs and coffee materialized quickly and cheaply, to be consumed in civilized comfort as I watched the growing light outside reveal teak forests and mountainsides. From time to time, in clearings, glimpses were obtained of elephants hauling teak logs. Thailand has frequent trained elephant parades and ceremonies, having domesticated nearly half the elephants in her borders. Since Burma, the silent neighbour to the west, shut herself off almost completely from all contact, even with the Soviet bloc, Thailand has become the world's main source of teak.

At 7.15 a.m., just as I was finishing breakfast, we stopped at a big junction station called Muang Lampang. The now familiar army of young ladies appeared, marched up and down the train and offered breakfast fruits, meats and various delicacies, while some had hot coffee on tap, the containers being carried on their heads. Two coaches were shunted off the train here for haulage up a branch line, and I alighted for a stroll in the fresh mountain air. Several members of the American tour party were up and about in their first class side-corridor sleeping car. Most had spent a good night, and I heard favourable comments about the train: 'That was a painless night,' said one, and another added: 'I'm glad we didn't fly.'

Pulling away from Muang Lampang the going became steeper and the curves very severe, with sometimes the diesels and the rear of the train (with the Sultan's coaches) showing at the same time. Progress was slow, but apart from glimpsing colourful birds there were no sightings of wild life in the jungle. This is country famous for its large and ferocious tigers, its Asian bears, deer of various kinds, and of course elephants. Of the wild kind, so easily seen from trains in East Africa, there was no trace, but one got used to the trained variety with their harnesses and decorations, soon coming to treat them like water-buffalo or horses.

At 8.35 a.m., with the sun up amid some light clouds and the day already hot but dry and free of the sticky damp that characterizes the region around Bangkok, we pulled into the station of Khuntan, the summit of the line. A notice board on the platform pointed out both in Thai script and English that the altitude was 578 metres (1,910 feet) above sea level. This is not very high by East African, Rocky Mountains, or Indian hill station standards, but it was enough to give a change of climate and let some freshness into the air. A southbound train crossed us here, full of people, while a big steam banking locomotive detached itself from the diesel-hauled train. We had not taken a banker owing to the double-heading, and I rather imagine it would have been avoided at all costs, since the Sultan's observation saloon with its large windows would have faced directly into the locomotive's smokebox door!

A few minutes before nine, as the train was running smoothly down the single line, the Chinese-Malaysian photographer came to see me and told me of the audience. I walked back two cars with him, through the ordinary first class, then he unlocked the door leading into the first class sleeper containing the Sultan's retinue. Here the aide-de-camp greeted me, followed by the young Crown Prince, who asked me to sit in a compartment with him for a few moments until a further summons came, when we went into the personal carriage. Cabin doors were locked and I gathered that the ladies of the Sultan's retinue were remaining out of sight! Then we entered a very luxurious carpeted compartment, air-conditioned, with armchairs, tables and a divan. This, I saw, led into a small and elegant personal dining room, and beyond that were half a dozen arm chairs facing aft towards the big observation windows. The Crown Prince spoke in English and addressed his father as 'H.H.'. "This is the British writer, H.H.", he began.

The Sultan spoke excellent English and we talked about various aspects of travel and the royal itinerary, as well as touching on British newspapers. Then the audience was over and the Crown Prince led me back to the aide's corridor and I was escorted through the train to my sleeper.

Shortly after I had sat down the train reached the town of Muang Lamphun, which is also spelt Lampoon and may have some connection with the type of satire. This city dates from the Mon civilization of the thirteenth century, whose capital it was until taken by the Thais two hundred years ago. A walled historic city of some 10,000 people, it lost its importance in 1921 when the railway was built, all the trade and commerce passing to Chiang Mai, the terminus and railhead just twenty miles further towards the Shan States.

The last twenty miles, over mainly level track across a warm dry plain surrounded by hills, took the 'Northern Express' thirty-three minutes and we pulled in to the spacious, clean and flower-filled station of Chiang Mai two minutes early, at 10.03 a.m. A big shining Pacific steam locomotive waited simmering to take the rake of coaches away to the cleaning sheds. A big crowd lined the platform to greet the Sultan and his party, who alighted with dignity and walked the length of the train while all the other passengers stood back, gathering their baggage. The American tour group found their escort and a waiting coach, while others passed on into the city noted for its silver and leather work, its schools, and its exceptionally pretty girls—most of whom today ride around on Japanese motorcycles. Directly opposite the station is the brand new Railway Hotel, the best in northern Thailand. Others went sightseeing, including me, and a drive to the hills a few miles away led to a climb up 365 steps to the Doy Sutp Temple with its golden pagoda flashing in the sun. From here the view extended to the mountains of the remote Burma border which no man has crossed legally for two decades. . . .

21

The 10.40 to China

Kowloon, on the mainland of China, is a huge, thriving, bustling place with buses, ferries, traffic jams, tall buildings, glamorous hotels and the finest maritime terminal ever constructed in the world. There is also a railway station, a terminus, the most southerly on the Chinese mainland. But although this is China in essence, in character, in appearance, and of course from the ethnic point of view, it is actually Britain in the Far East, a remnant of Empire which has been caught up in the maelstrom of international big business. Kowloon is a British-run city in China, part of the Colony of Hong Kong. It has been British since 1841, and part of it, up to a boundary wall, is due to stay British for as long as one can foresee, or as long as it can be held usefully. Beyond the boundary, the territory is leased from China, and that lease expires in 1997.

Kowloon faces south across the beautiful harbour to the island of Hong Kong and the skyscraper city of Victoria. Its business outlook points that way and its ferries thrash southwards across the harbour. All its traffic moves that way with one exception—the railway. Twin standard gauge tracks wind north from Kowloon, run through the New Territories, and enter China proper. The railway constitutes the only physical link between China and the British trading station. The tracks cross the frontier at what men have been calling the 'Bamboo Curtain' for nearly two decades, and a covered bridge at Lowu across which passengers walk from the Chinese train to the British train or vice versa is the prime route by which personal contact is maintained.

China is a vast mystery, inscrutable as always, and since the 'Cultural Revolution' fired off in 1966 no one can be certain what has happened or what is going to happen. 'China Watchers' all gather in Hong Kong to try and note the signs, and their information is often more accurate than that obtained by the few, tightly restricted foreigners allowed to stay around the embassies and legations in Peking. One thing is watched more than anything else, and that is the Kowloon-Canton Railway. If traffic is interrupted, this means something which has to be investigated in the best way available. During the height of the Red Guard disturbances late in 1966 and 1967, when Hong Kong was itself afflicted by troubles, no trains came from the Chinese side to the border for three weeks. This poses a serious situation for the Colony, because it grows only five per cent of its rice needs, and the Chinese population consume three-quarters of a pound of rice per head per day. Fully 95 per cent has to be imported, mainly from China and from Thailand.

In normal circumstances, there are three freight trains a day which make the through journey from Canton to Kowloon. The Chinese locomotive backs the freight cars across the Lowu Bridge, the vehicles pass inspection, and then a British diesel engine of the Kowloon-Canton Railway (British Section), takes the cars without ever having put its nose across into China and hauls them away to Kowloon.

When conditions were easier, during the years 1955 to 1965, and China was encouraging foreign tourists through its 'Luxingshe' organization, there were two passenger train departures a day from Kowloon to Canton. This facility was interrupted during the year-long troubles, and by early 1968 it was not properly restored, except that the 10.40 train from Kowloon to the Border carried through passengers to China, who were reasonably certain of finding, after their walk across the covered bridge at Lowu, a passenger train bound for Canton.

There is always a certain amount of traffic for China, because many Hong Kong Chinese still have their closest relatives in the big Communist country, while others do a good deal of trading. Two other ways exist of reaching Canton from the Hong Kong area, one by hydrofoil or ferry to the Portuguese trading station of Macao and then by bus through the Barrier

Gate, or up the Pearl River in a Chinese-owned junk. But the railway in normal conditions offers the quickest and most comfortable means, with a time of about three and three-quarter hours including frontier formalities. In any case, Europeans must travel by rail! It is only 111 miles between the two cities.

The railway has existed in part since shortly after the turn of the century. China was very late with railway construction and, during the era of the Emperors, foreign engineers were even less encouraged than they are today. However, a British company managed to extend the line that they pushed through the 'New Territories', leased in 1900 to expand the living space for Chinese residents of the Crown Colony, and to grow food. The Railway was opened throughout between Kowloon and Canton in October 1911. In early days, when there was freedom to come and go between China and Hong Kong, fewer people lived under British rule and food supplies grown in the New Territories catered for about half the demand. It is only since 1949 that the population—and the prosperity—of Hong Kong have gone up by leaps and bounds.

Once upon a time, and it was not so long ago that middle-aged people cannot easily remember it, a smart train stood waiting in the Kowloon Terminus with through Wagons-Lits sleepers for Shanghai and even a through sleeper for Peking for a brief period of tranquillity between the two Sino-Japanese wars of the thirties. Shanghai, then the Paris of the East and a vast trading city with a large international population living in privileged settlements, was the destination for hundreds of passengers off every P & O mailship coming to Hong Kong. Some stayed with the ship for its passage through the East China Sea, but others, satiated with sea life after about a month on board coming out from England, chose to shorten their journey by disembarking at Kowloon, spending the night at that traditional gateway to China, the Peninsula Hotel, and boarding the Canton-Shanghai Express the next morning. In three hours they were in Canton, and within twenty-four hours they had reached Shanghai, at least two days ahead of the ship.

The Peninsula Hotel is still there, just across from Kowloon Station, but it has had a face-lift and is now one of the best hotels in the Colony of Hong Kong. P & O ships still arrive in the harbour but less frequently, and they tie up to the superb air-conditioned Ocean Terminal with its two floors of smart shops, its restaurants and waiting-rooms. But the ships no longer sail for China. Australia or Japan is their next call and none of the passengers they will have disembarked is likely to be bound for Shanghai. Kowloon Station remains unchanged over the years, a bit the worse for wear and its facilities run down. But there are plenty of trains and the throb of heavy diesels has replaced the romantic simmering of steam engines. Oddly enough, it is Kai Tak Airport, the remarkable runway built out into the harbour by the Royal Engineers at the beginning of the nineteen-fifties to give Hong Kong an international airport in place of a flying boat base, which supplies most foreigners to the trains leaving the station only two miles from the airport terminal. A survey conducted by the Hong Kong Tourist Association for the year 1966 found that six per cent of visitors arriving by air made a train journey during their stay. In most cases, though, it is a trip within the New Territories, for the train is the quickest way to Fan Ling Golf Club!

When I walked into Kowloon Station on a cold bright day in the middle of February 1968, I saw hundreds of passengers trying to buy tickets from the booths marked First, Second and Third Class. The 10.40 to China was getting ready to leave and only third class tickets were still available. I bought one, at negligible cost. One of the former waiting-rooms at the station had been converted into a 'parcels for China' office where Hong Kong Chinese could send food and other essentials to their relatives across the border, who were by all accounts suffering from the ravages of the Red Guards and in many cases in a state of near starvation. Some of these parcels were being loaded into the baggage car at the head of the train.

There was a long rake of green coaches, with a scroll on the side in gold lettering 'Kowloon-Canton Railway, British Section'. One big General Motors American diesel was idling noisily, ready to haul the train for its twenty-two-mile journey to the border. No one may purchase tickets for Lowu unless they are going through into China; normal unrestricted traffic may go as far as Sheung Shui, about two and a half miles short of the 'Bamboo Curtain'. Most passengers, Chinese and

European, were in fact heading for the town and resort of Tai Po or Fan Ling. Trains run every half-hour up the line as far as Sheung Shui during busy periods of the day, and at least hourly the rest of the time. Only a few, plus the three daily freights, go through to the border station on the Sham Chun River.

The day I had chosen was a Sunday, which may not mean much from a religious point of view to the 97 per cent of Hong Kong's population who are Chinese, but it is a holiday because the Colony's rulers have long arranged it that way. So the train was longer and more crowded than it would have been on a weekday, and some passengers were making the day trip to Canton to see their relatives. Foreigners had not at that time any real prospect of obtaining a visa to enter China except for certain businessmen and technicians, but occasional day-permits were being issued by the Chinese People's Republic officials in Hong Kong for visits to Canton, in connection with the famous Canton Industrial Spring Fair.

At first four tracks, with sidings into carriage yards, the railway follows Chatham Road, with its busy traffic and huge double-decker buses, then it passes under the bridge at the roundabout where Gascoigne Road comes in and swings due north. The engine sheds and workshops are on the right as the train passes the Military Hospital then continues through the densely built-up inner suburbs of Kowloon. Over Waterloo Road, then Argyle Street, until, two and a quarter miles out of the terminus, the bridge over Boundary Street is crossed. Boundary Street, straight and quite wide, can be seen running right across the Kowloon Peninsula, from Kai Tak Airport buildings on the right of the train to the sea wall overlooking the harbour on the left. This marks the limit of Hong Kong Colony, the permanently ceded area; beyond it lies the New Territories, leased from China and due for return in the foreseeable future.

Packed into a third class coach, I had wedged myself at the end with a view out of both doors which had their windows open. I was glad that the weather was much colder than normal for the Hong Kong winter and pitied those who made the trip in these conditions during the hot and humid summer. The running was very smooth at forty miles an hour, but through

The cab and engineers of a class P36 locomotive, standing at Chita at the head of a westbound trans-Siberian express.

At the rear of the 'Northern Express' to Chiang Mai is the saloon car of the Sultan of Selangor, standing in Bangkok station.

Above. One of the railway bridges on the River Kwai, Kanachana-Buki Province, Thailand.

Below. A General Motors diesel locomotive at the head of the 'Northern Express' in Bangkok Terminus.

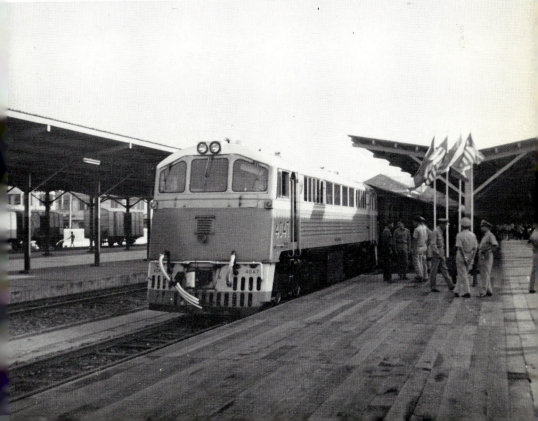

Right. Kowloon Terminus station in Steam days with a train headed by a British built 4. 6. 2. tank engine leaving for the Chinese border.

[By courtesy of the Hong Kong Tourist Association]

Below, The 10.40 to China stopped at Tai Pi Market station.

Below, right. The 10.40 to China passing through the New Territories.

[Photographs by courtesy of BOAC]

Above. The new Australian trans-Continental 'Indian Pacific'—one third of a mile of stainless steel.

[*By courtesy of the Department of Railways, N.S.W.*]

Below. The east and westbound 'Indian Pacific' meet at Gladstone, South Australia, and exchange crews.

While the 'Indian Pacific' stops at Port Augusta, South Australia, passengers admire the tiny *Sandfly* an o. 4. o. steam locomotive used by contractors to build the line to Port Augusta at the turn of the century.

The rear view of the 'Indian Pacific' halted at Kalgoorlie in the dawn, 408 miles out from Perth.

Unless otherwise indicated, all photographs are by the author.

the open windows I could hear the diesel snarling fiercely, its sound thrown back by the tall buildings and cuttings.

As the outskirts of Kowloon were dropping away the ground rose suddenly and a rocky cutting became higher, then we plunged into the two-mile-long Lion's Rock Tunnel. Until the mid-nineteen-sixties, the railway had a monopoly of route through this rocky mountain cutting off the Kowloon Peninsula. Wheeled traffic had to negotiate a tortuous track over the top, 1,521 feet, and so even senior British administrators and their wives bound for a day's golf at Fan Ling took the train. However, after years of work and a good deal of expense, a road tunnel more or less parallel to that of the railway has been driven, with inevitable damage to the first class patronage on the trains.

We took exactly three minutes to pass through the tunnel, which Chinese call 'Lion's Lock', and emerged into open country with a view of sparkling water, green fields and high rocky hills. The rice fields of Sha Tin came in sight, where some of the best rice in Asia is grown. In the days before Hong Kong (this name, incidentally, means 'fragrant harbour') took over the New Territories, the people of Sha Tin were required to send tributes of rice to the Manchu Emperors in Peking. Etched sharply against the sky overlooking Tide Cove is one of the most conspicuous landmarks of this mountainous region, the Amah Rock. A natural rock formation on its 830-foot summit looks for all the world like a Chinese woman and her child. It is not a momentary illusion, but keeps its appearance from whatever angle it is seen. The legend of Amah's Rock has been handed down from generation to generation and varies in detail but always emphasizes the same point—the constant longing of women for their men-folk who are away from home. The Amah is said to be Mei Ching with her child on her back, endlessly looking out to sea for her fisherman husband Wu Ying, whose junk was lost in a storm.

Sha Tin Station is the first stop, about eighteen minutes after leaving Kowloon. There are yachts and water sports available here, also a floating restaurant of less 'touristic' character than those in Aberdeen Bay on Hong Kong Island. A few people alighted here, slightly easing the pressure on space, but standing

13—RR * *

was still the order of the day. From Sha Tin the line kept to the edge of the sea-inlet for the next few miles, while inland the scene was pastoral, with the emphasis on rice fields, with high hills behind them. The next station was Ma Liu Shui, also marked in English as 'University'. All along the left side of the tracks the smart modern buildings of the Hong Kong Chinese University spread in an unusual campus, with sports grounds in between. This is not only attended by Chinese but by students from many parts of Asia and Europe, with some Americans.

Two more miles beside the sea brought the train to Tai Po, an important station for a bayside town and resort, where more people left the train. Turning inland in a north-westerly direction, the train stopped after another mile at Tai Po Market. This is an anglicized name meaning 'Big Market Market'. There are narrow streets packed with open-fronted shops selling all manner of wares, a place to which the conventional tourist who is said to adore picturesque markets would love to come if more was known about it.

There are three miles of pastoral country with deep green fields of rice and terraced hills before the train stops again, this time at Fan Ling, a small town to the left of the train with a view of the excellent Royal Hong Kong Golf Club beyond it. To the right, across a narrow stream, there is a view of an ancient Chinese stone bridge, the only original one in Hong Kong Colony. It is less than a mile then to Sheung Shui, where there is an almost complete exodus from the train. Here a ticket check of remaining passengers takes place, for the next station is the border and only through ticket holders can continue, except for military personnel and those having special permission to be in the touchy border zone. Photography is not allowed beyond this station.

Just under a mile and a half brings the two tracks to the Sham Chun River, some sidings, and the station on the southern side of Lowu Bridge. Here everyone must alight and pass through British formalities, which in the case of people going into China are cursory. Their check is much tighter for people, especially Chinese, coming the other way. Hong Kong Chinese uniformed police, customs and immigration officials, British officers, and Ghurka troops are to be seen at the station and on the southern end of the covered wooden bridge. One track remains in the centre of the bridge, and passengers walk on the right-hand side towards the red flags of China and some troops with red stars on their steel helmets.

It is exactly twenty-two miles from Kowloon and eighty-nine miles from Canton when one walks into the Lowu Station of the People's Republic of China. Circumstances keep changing here, and no one can honestly say what constitutes normal practice. In 1964 a friend and colleague of mine, the well-known photographic journalist Mr. J. Allan Cash, walked through on his way to an official visit to China with unlimited opportunities for taking pictures. He was warmly greeted at Lowu, met by 'Luxingshe' officials and interpreters, and taken to a luxurious first class compartment with observation windows at the rear end of the Canton train. Soft chairs, flowers in the compartment, refreshment on tap and spotless conditions awaited him. He was able to take a photograph of a large and shining Chinese 4–8–2 steam locomotive at the head of the train. His journey, in welcoming company, was pleasant and lasted just under three hours as the train meandered through rice-fields and hills.

Without company, unexpected, and as conspicuous as only a lone European can be among a multitude of Chinese, conditions are very different, especially in the hostile atmosphere of the late sixties. There is a language barrier beyond the border, where virtually no one speaks—or will admit to speaking—English and the station name boards are in Chinese lettering only. There are also problems of money exchange, since it is forbidden to bring out of China any local currency, not even small coins, and careful note has to be made on forms of what you take in and exchange. Transfer to second class on payment of a few yen improved travel conditions, but the train, with about 1,200 passengers once it cleared Lowu, and ten coaches headed by a steam locomotive, probably Chinese-built in recent years and a 4–8–2, seemed to contain only Chinese.

The Kowloon-Canton Railway was very substantially built from the start, and weights on bridges and viaducts are no problem. The most difficult and expensive section to build was that from Kowloon to the border, after which it is fairly level with no gradient worse than 1 in 150 and mainly flat country to traverse. The main engineering work on the Chinese section is Shek Lung Viaduct, heavily guarded by troops. A lengthy stop was made at Shek Lung, forty-one miles from Canton, a town on the East River. It was 2.37 p.m. when the train pulled in to Tai Sha Tou Terminus in Canton, a bleak station with wide clean platforms and only two running tracks. About five miles before reaching the end of the line, in a populous though ragged Canton suburb called Shek Pai, a line runs off to the north which goes round to the Wong Sha Terminus in Canton where the Peking-Hangkow Line (completed in 1932) starts. It was this which at one time made the Peking and Shanghai through coach system possible. For a brief period between the Japanese wars, approximately from 1933 to 1937, a train called the 'Flying Eagle Express' ran from Kowloon to Canton in two hours fifty-five minutes, with four stops, the fastest train in China. From all indications, everything has slowed up on that not very noteworthy schedule of three decades ago, and damage by insurrectionists and saboteurs seems to have interfered with rail communication in many parts of China since the Red Guards came on the scene.

It was with relief that the next, and in fact the only other train of the day, was taken back to the border and to Hong Kong, leaving at 5.15 p.m. Riding second class, surrounded by men and women in mundane garb, all with their little red books containing the Thoughts of Mao (I had bought one in English in Hong Kong) the only consolation was that £1 changed and completely spent in yen had bought better accommodation on the train, odd foodstuffs to eat while travelling, a mother-of-pearl cigarette case, a pair of black gloves and a hundred joss-sticks.

Suddenly during the spring of 1971 the Chinese warmed towards the West and in the rapid thaw they admitted more than a hundred business travellers plus a table tennis team from Britain. They also allowed in an American table tennis team, reopened the London-Shanghai telephone link, and spoke of reviving tourism. By now, as we go to Press, it is more than likely the 10.40 is not the only train from Hong Kong with connections at Lo Wu for China. . . .

22

The Indian Pacific

Trains take the tension out of travel, say the advertisements by
Railways of Australia, and their brand new, spick and span
streamliner 'Indian Pacific', which in 1970 became the first
coast to coast train on that Continent, lives up to those words.
Although a hundred and one years late by American construc-
tional standards, a through trans-continental train has come to
Australia with all the amenities of a first class hotel on wheels
operated as a land cruise.

There has been a rail link of sorts between the Eastern States
of Australia and Perth, capital of Western Australia, since
1917, but the gauges were different and until 1937 the journey,
whether for passengers or freight, required six changes of train
when going from Sydney to Perth. Western Australia made the
construction of a railway across the vast uninhabited wastelands
of the Nullarbor Plain a condition of entry into Federation,
reminiscent of California's demands for a pony express and
then a railway before joining the United States in the mid-
nineteenth century.

The lines in Western Australia were 3 feet 6 inches gauge,
while the 1,103 miles of Commonwealth Railway, built by the
Federal Government to secure the West's entry, were standard
at 4 feet 8½ inches. But South Australia had 3 feet 6 inches and
5 feet 3 inches, and Victoria held to 5 feet 3 inches. The
'Mother' State of Australia, New South Wales, had been standard gauge from the beginning of railway history on the
Continent. So the luckless passenger of the 1917–37 period
started out from Perth and then had to change after 360 miles
at Kalgoorlie into a standard gauge Commonwealth Railways
express. This took him to Port Augusta, where a change was

made to a narrow gauge line for the four hour run to Port Pirie Junction. Here he was turned out again and clambered aboard a wide gauge South Australian Railways express for three hours, by which time he was in Adelaide. Then came quite a good overnight run in another train, the 'Overland Express', to Melbourne. One more change, and a further wide gauge Victorian train took him to Albury for the sixth and final change—into a standard gauge New South Wales express which completed the run to Sydney, 2,779 miles from Perth.

In 1938 the changes had been reduced to five when Commonwealth standard gauge was extended from Port Augusta to Port Pirie Junction. Then in 1962, standard gauge went through with a flourish from Melbourne to Sydney, eliminating the long-dreaded change at Albury. Spending tens of millions of dollars, the Commonwealth system and the West Australian Railways built a new standard gauge line between Perth and Kalgoorlie, deviating widely from the old route to serve important new mineral deposits. Although 408 miles long it was much faster and did away with the Kalgoorlie change, so that by early 1969, the trans-continental passenger's changes were down to three.

Work went on in South Australia, converting part of a light narrow gauge line to standard and building a new route so that eventually Port Pirie and Broken Hill on the New South Wales border were linked. It only remained to upgrade lightly laid standard gauge track between Broken Hill and Parkes to complete the Trans-Continental, for the way from there to Sydney across the high New South Wales Central Tablelands had existed since the 1880s. All was set for the opening, on February 23rd, 1970, and a train of twenty-four stainless steel cars built in Australia under Budd licence started to roll across the Continent, carrying the Governor-General, Members of the Legislative Assembly, and representatives of the world's press. The great train, half a mile long, was officially named after the two oceans it linked, 'Indian Pacific'.

The coming of the "Indian Pacific" was declared a public holiday for the citizens of Perth. The sense of isolation and loneliness the city had always felt, despite fifty years of developing aviation and frequent jet services, had ended. By its very location, Perth seems the loneliest big city in the world. It is booming now, with the coming of the standard gauge and the new mineral and industrial uplift, and has added 100,000 to its population in three years, bringing it to the 750,000 mark. But it is still a long way to the nearest city with more than 30,000 people—more than 4,500 miles westwards (Durban), 2,500 miles northwards (Djakarta), 1,500 miles eastwards (Adelaide) and infinity to the South for it is open ocean to the Antarctic.

More than 16,000 people applied to ride the 'Indian Pacific' which meant a wait-list a year long. Only two trains have been built for the service so far, and they run twice a week, leaving Perth on Sundays and Thursdays, Sydney on Mondays and Thursdays. The direct journey is 2,461 miles long, and it takes sixty-five and a quarter hours, but most people seeing Australia with the train express a wish on completion of the trip that it had taken longer. This is no longer basic transportation; in Australia aviation was developed very early on, this sunny Continent being ideal for it, and in 1970 Qantas, Australia's State-owned Overseas airline, celebrated its fiftieth anniversary. If passengers want to get from Perth to Sydney, or Melbourne for that matter, in a great hurry, they take a jet which does the trip in five to six hours. But it says much for the appeal of the new train, and its associated 'Trans' Express running to Port Pirie with only one change for Adelaide that nowadays the uplift of people out of Perth by rail and air for the Eastern States is about equal. Ten years ago, for every train passenger there were seven by air.

It must be quite a historical landmark, and one that may amaze people in the United States, that 1970 saw the issue of special postage stamps, one commemorating the major State airline's fiftieth birthday and another the first year of trans-continental travel.

I had crossed Australia many years ago when a lot of changes were involved. It had always been a dream of mine to do it on a through train. Making application from Tokyo nearly a year before the line was completed, I obtained space out of Perth for the May 3rd, 1970, departure. This was no mean feat, for with all the publicity and the favourable reports from passengers, the 'Indian Pacific' was booked out a year ahead. Flying in on a

Qantas V Jet to a booming Perth, I made my way to the sparkling new Inter-State Terminal and found the gleaming hotel on wheels. Rather similar to the best of American streamliners, the 'Indian Pacific' consisted of twelve stainless steel air conditioned cars, but it was surely unique in that its social centre, for first class passengers, was divided into a cocktail bar, an observation lounge-cum-drawing room, and a music room complete with full sized piano! Pianos have long been a tradition of trains on the long haul across the semi-desert of the Nullarbor Plain to South Australia, but they were once tinkled in an open-ended car furthest away from a steam locomotive gasping for water on the arid flatlands. What with dust and heat, they needed frequent re-tuning. But no dust was ever likely to penetrate this new train's elegant music room.

Only 138 passengers are carried by the 'Indian Pacific', seventy in first class and sixty-eight in economy class. The first class compartments are not unlike those encountered in the U.S.A. but each one has a private shower in an annexe, while the single cabins are a large extension of a conventional roomette, equipped with double windows between which a venetian blind can be controlled, a good deal of carpeting, radio, and a private toilet. There are showers for men and women at the ends of the car. A large suite, comparable with an American drawing room, was also available for families.

An ingenious arrangement of curved centre aisles made it possible to allot more space for each cabin. There were no vista domes, for restricted tunnel clearances do not permit them. But the wellbeing of passengers is looked after in a way the rest of the world has not experienced since the days of the 'Twentieth Century Limited' at its best and the 'Orient Express' when it was an all-sleeper luxury train crossing Europe. Attendants bring round morning tea and biscuits, and in true Australian tradition afternoon tea comes as well, accompanied by pastries. Not only are these refreshments delivered to the cabins, they are free! A morning newspaper comes, too, and an evening one if there is such a thing published in the territory through which the 'Indian Pacific' is passing. Main meals are free, too, included in the fare, and these meals, to a set menu, are superlative, running to five courses. But both first and economy class passengers share the diner, which means meals have to be in three sittings (for naturally everyone eats right through the menu when it is free). It is hoped that extra diners, allowing longer and more leisurely dining, will be built soon, and that two new train sets will be coming along to help cope with demand soon after these words are read.

As for drinks, and cocktails especially, the barman on my trip was formerly at Scotland's luxury Gleneagles hotel, and his Martinis and gin and tonics were already well known. Unlike earlier Australian trains, passing through semi-dry States or places where a six o'clock swill was legend (drinking bars open only until 6 p.m.), service of drinks goes on aboard 'Indian Pacific' so long as there are passengers in the cocktail lounge requiring them.

There is a cafeteria bar-car with a lounge attached in the economy class, where such modest but comforting night-caps as cocoa or coffee or tea can be obtained. That was my beverage for the first night out, leaving Perth to the accompaniment of two thousand waving sightseers, at 9.30 p.m. I retired at 10.30 p.m. with the train rolling through the low hills of the Darling Range, and I awoke shortly before six o'clock next morning as the 'Indian Pacific' stopped at West Kalgoorlie marshalling yards.

This new standard gauge line is 408 miles long, compared to the old narrow gauge route between Perth and Kalgoorlie of 360 miles. It deviates considerably to serve new mining areas where powerful American investments have helped the yield from West Australia's depths. Only for short stretches is there mixed gauge on the old road bed; mostly the new line is many miles to the northward of the old, and it serves Koolyanobbing, a point from which ore trains of 2,000 tons have been running to Kwinana on the coast, helping to bed down the standard gauge tracks quickly. Despite the extra forty-eight miles involved, the speed possible on standard gauge makes a sharp timing contrast with the 3 foot 6 inch track. The 'Indian Pacific' takes from 9.30 p.m. to 6.30 a.m. to make the 408-mile run, while the existing 'Kalgoorlie Express', which runs over the narrow gauge, takes from 4.55 p.m. to 7.05 a.m. to cover 360 miles.

In the early dawn light I walked the length of Kalgoorlie's new platform, built in front of the old one where passengers used to have to change for the long trip eastwards. 'Indian Pacific' stopped half an hour while the West Australian Railway crews were exchanged (but not before they had made morning tea for all passengers and themselves) for Commonwealth Railways men. But the heavy diesel up front hauled the train on for three miles to Parkeston depot before coming off and being replaced by twin Commonwealth Clyde units in red and white livery.

At 7.10 a.m., just as the first call for breakfast was sounded, the train began to roll on its long journey across semi-arid lands towards South Australia. For over a thousand miles there would not be a hamlet or settlement larger than 200 people, and even those that exist along the line do so solely for railway purposes. For the first thirty miles or so, there are eucalyptus trees and rough grasses, for some rainfall is still experienced in this region. It is not enough for Kalgoorlie to live on, so a water pipe line brings the life-sustaining fluid from Mundaring Weir in the Darling Range, laid by an engineer named O'Connor as part of the Goldfields Water Scheme in 1903.

The trans-continental line is mainly single track but with occasional passing loops protected by signals and with an unmanned hut graced by a name. These names are taken for the most part from former Australian Prime Ministers, or figures of history, and there is no habitation around them. By the time we had passed Karonie, sixty-nine miles out of Kalgoorlie, what trees there were had become stunted and the country was obviously arid. Two or three heavy freights going in the other direction caused interest, for they were long and usually had up to a hundred motor cars in special wagons. While it is possible to drive from Western Australia to the Eastern States, the road is unsealed from the South Australian border and it is something of an adventure, undertaken during the cool season by about five cars a day. An Ansett Pioneer bus makes the trip, equipped with heavy tires and breakdown gear, three times a week, and sometimes private cars follow in its wake for safety. But even the best and most successful car crossings of the Continent do a certain amount of damage, the least ever reported being two punctures and a broken spring, so most motorists send their cars by rail, which is by no means expensive.

The 'Indian Pacific's' first official stop was at Rawlinna, 235 miles from Kalgoorlie and 643 from Perth, reached at 12.13 p.m. This only lasted five minutes and was simply for locomotive crews to change, our men going back to Parkeston Depot on a west bound freight. Most of these freights carry adequate passenger accommodation at the rear. The country was still well grassed, with clumps of saltbush, bluebush, and belts of myall. In fact the wide expanses of plain are always varied and quite fascinating, but one misses wild life, for there is simply no surface water. All the plants which survive out here do so by sending down very long roots, some stunted trees thrusting down as much as 130 feet. In steam days the Commonwealth Railways sometimes had to dig 1,500 feet for artesian supplies.

By 3.25 p.m. the train was passing Forrest, named after Lord Forrest, the West Australian who was instigator of the Trans-continental line. We were running on what is known as the 'long straight', no less than 297 miles of track without a single curve from Nurina to Ooldea. The running was, of course, very smooth, and a steady sixty-five miles an hour caused little or no motion aboard the express. The Nullarbor Plain proper (and this name is taken from the Latin meaning 'no trees') was going past, utterly flat and featureless, but the sky was cloudy and as the surface was dotted with odd clumps of saltbush the limestone plateau did not look so hostile on this autumnal day as it can in high summer, when to wander more than three miles from the line of rail is to be lost for ever.

The first real stop was at Cook, just across the South Australian border, reached at 7.15 p.m. Here clocks were advanced by one and a half hours to South Australia time, and the twenty-five minute stop enabled passengers to take a walk after dinner, ten minutes covering the entire township of railwaymen and their families, the cable office and the school. Mobile cinemas come twice a week attached to freights so that the local people can enjoy some entertainment. We were now

539 miles from Kalgoorlie and 947 from Perth, about half way across the Plain.

Into the night, which was completely dark, unrelieved by moon or stars or homestead lights, the 'Indian Pacific' rushed smoothly, itself a blaze of lights and civilization in the wilderness. Glasses chinked and the piano tinkled for a while, but most passengers turned in early, taking advantage of the smooth running to have showers before going to bed. There was one stop during the night that followed, at Tarcoola, where engine crews were changed. Tarcoola, with 198 people, is the largest settlement on the line, and in steam days there were as many as 280 people living here, tending the locomotives. Steam is, of course, a means of rail traction which lends itself to efficient and useful operation only when three conditions are met—ample water, ample coal, and ample labour. The wastelands of Australia have none of these items, so dieselization was adopted very early on (in 1952) for the Commonwealth Line. Steam services are still found in Australia around Newcastle in New South Wales, where the right conditions (aided by rich local coal deposits) are encountered.

When morning tea came round to the cabins, not accompanied by a newspaper because none are published in the wilderness, it was light and the train was in different country, virtually desert, with low hills showing in all directions. At 7.23 a.m. a stop was made at Pimba, 939 miles from Kalgoorlie and 1,347 from Perth, where a South Australian Government fruit inspector joined the train to prevent the importation of West Australian (or Overseas) fruit—reminiscent of such action taken at the California border. Away to the North rocket launching pads could be seen, for Pimba is the station for Woomera, the Commonwealth rocket centre. A newly built branch line goes off from here to serve the growing desert community, five miles away. Britain's Blue Streak is tested here and the European nations combined space programme, which has not had a great deal of success, is carried out around Woomera.

Great dry saltpans came in view, the train running around their edges for great rains can come to the region about every five years and when they do these salt pans become water-filled oceans in the desert. Stark mountains were shaping up ahead, the outlines of the Flinders Range, and wild life was becoming more noticeable. During breakfast, a mob of kangaroos was sighted approaching the train with emus scattering in all directions. Sheep appeared and some permanently grassed slopes brought back memories of agriculture.

Eventually, and exactly on time, the train pulled in to Port Augusta, a community of nearly 3,000 people at the head of the Spencer Gulf 1,052 miles from Kalgoorlie and 1,460 from Perth. We were two thirds of the way across Australia, at 10.35 a.m. on the second day out. From here on, although the country is settled, the going was to be slower over new tracks and through junctions and hills. A fifteen-minute stop enabled newspapers to come aboard while passengers went for a 'walk-about', many admiring the plaque to Norris G. Bell, C.B.E., Engineer-in-Chief who built the Trans-Australia Railway in record time between Port Augusta and Kalgoorlie between 1914 and 1917, a feat unsung at the time because of the First World War in which Australia was deeply involved.

There remained a run through settled areas and wheat fields with the waters of the Spencer Gulf always in sight to Port Pirie Junction, fifty-six miles further on, reached at 12.25 p.m. At this important station, many things happen. There is a stop for nearly one and a half hours, and some passengers go on a taxi tour of the town, which boasts the largest zinc smelter in the world. It is one of the very few places in the world where three different rail gauges meet (the Commonwealth standard, South Australia's 5 feet 3 inches and 3 feet 6 inches). The Indian Pacific is thoroughly cleaned; its diesels are changed and others come on at the other end; a blue rake of coaches for Adelaide waiting on the adjacent platform accepts passengers for the South Australian capital. During all this, the third sitting of lunch continues aboard 'Indian Pacific', served by waiters who will leave the train afterwards.

At 1.50 p.m. the Trans-Continental leaves, heading North East, over an entirely new standard gauge line going towards Peterborough, rarely out of sight of the old and now abandoned 3 foot 6 inch tracks. Running is quite good over the new line, although one or two freight trains derailed on it at the beginning of operations early in 1970. Coming to a halt near the little station of Gladstone, South Australia, the express finds its opposite number from Sydney pulling into position alongside, and the South Australian crew, which has only been aboard for an hour, just over 30 miles, climbs out and into the westbound train. A New South Wales Government Railways crew, very smart and dressed in the traditions of that system (which is the biggest industrial enterprise in the Southern Hemisphere) replaces them for the run to Sydney. This change over happens on Tuesdays and Saturdays, at 2.50 p.m.

Running on to Peterborough, now an important centre with a clean new station and an electronic signal box, the 'Indian Pacific' halts to await the arrival of a three coach diesel unit from Adelaide called 'The Quail'. This will have left Adelaide at 11.15 a.m. and offers a quicker and more comfortable new route to Sydney than the old one going via Melbourne. The fifteen-minute stop is ample to take care of change-overs and to attach three South Australian coaches to the rear of the 'Indian Pacific' which spoils the look of the consist but is demanded by the South Australians as compensation for the loss of their own 3 foot 6 inch gauge line to Broken Hill. These accommodate sitting passengers making the relatively local trip.

Into the grassy hills of South Australia the train rolls, with fine glimpses of big red kangaroos and plenty of emus, for this is well watered if sparsely populated grazing country. Before darkness falls, the watchful passenger should have seen anything up to 200 big kangaroos, some of them sitting close to the tracks. These unique marsupials are being shot to destruction by unrestricted hunting, and are in need of protection, but they have learned there is no danger of death close to the railway. Darkness will have fallen long before Broken Hill is reached, and the sittings in the diner will have finished, enabling all passengers to go for a walk along the bright main street of the 'Silver City' during the thirty-minute stop. The new railway station is right in the heart of town, 1,763 miles from Perth and 699 from Sydney. The second and last time change occurs here, when the clocks are advanced half an hour on to New South Wales time. At 9.19 p.m. N.S.W. time, the 'Indian Pacific' continues its journey along tracks which have existed as standard gauge since 1927 but are now in need of more upgrading to meet the heavier traffic. The going becomes rough and stays that way until Parkes is reached the next morning. Work is going on to ballast them up to the standards required for fast traffic. This third night in the train was the only one when I, in company with most other passengers, was awakened from time to time due to severe lurching.

A grey cold morning broke to show views of undulating wheat and sheep country, which persisted until we reached the Central West Tablelands 'capital' of Parkes. We had ten minutes here just before breakfast, but it was too chilly to do more than merely put one's nose outside the doors. Climbing away from Parkes on to the Tablelands proper we soon reached Bumberry Dam at 2,034 feet above sea level, and the track, in position since about 1890, was giving much better riding. Rain which was falling suddenly turned to sleet and then to snow. West Australians aboard the 'Indian Pacific' were wildly excited, some of them not even knowing what the white stuff was that fell from the skies. Shortly before the train reached Orange at ten in the morning, with the snow falling heavily, I saw a remarkable sight—a small mob of kangaroos hurtling across whitening pastures with snow on their tails!

Orange is situated at 2,846 feet, but even so it was early in the Australian autumn for snow to be falling (not yet mid-May). The Royal Train carrying Queen Elizabeth and the Duke of Edinburgh had passed over these tracks between Sydney and Orange only a week before, and it had been commented on at the time how cold the weather was turning. Now it was real winter, by any standards. The railway descended a bit to Bathurst, where the snow was not lying but welcoming fires had been lit around the station yards for gangers to warm their hands. After a seven-minute stop the 'Indian Pacific' moved on, climbing again from the 2,150 foot mark to over 3,000 feet at Lithgow amid the Blue Mountains—only the western sides of these magnificent mountains were more white than blue! At Lithgow, 2,365 miles from Perth and a mere ninety-seven from journey's end at Sydney, the type of traction was changed for the first and only time as a powerful electric locomotive backed on to take over from our two New South Wales diesels. The railway is double and quadruple track from here to Sydney and has been under the wires for a number of years.

There was a short length of climbing to do before the summit at Mount Victoria, 3,424 feet, was reached, and here it was not snowing but instead was crisp, bright and windy. We rolled through the mountains, twisting and turning past Medlow Bath and Katoomba, places with pleasantly cool summer hotels and villas, outer suburbs of Sydney really, like the shoreline of Long Island Sound in relation to New York City and the Sussex Coast for Londoners. The dramatic view from the escarpment beyond Katoomba showed us the sunny Pacific from 3,300 feet up, and the sprawling mass of Sydney ranging for fifty miles alongside the ocean. In between were precipices and deep forests. . . .

The electrics coasted downgrade over the last leg, through Valley Heights to Penrith and then the true Sydney suburbs, the stations lined with school children waiting for local trains, all of them agog with admiration as the great glossy streamliner ran past. Through Parramatta (terminus of the first railway line built in New South Wales in 1860) and Strathfield into Sydney Central, rolling to a stop exactly on time at 3.50 p.m. with hundreds of people waiting to greet arrivals and to see over the shiny new train. Typical of the helpful, friendly service encountered on all Australian main line trains, the cabin attendants had taken the bags to the platform and were often reluctant to accept or surprised to be offered a tip. Never have I made a rail journey where a tip was so justified. . . .